Navigating the Sermon

Pentecost Season Edition for Cycle C
of the Revised Common Lectionary

A Compilation of "Charting the Course" Columns from
Emphasis: A Preaching Journal for the Parish Pastor
a Component of **SermonSuite.com**

CSS Publishing Company, Inc.
Lima, Ohio

NAVIGATING THE SERMON
PENTECOST EDITION, CYCLE C

FIRST EDITION
Copyright © 2013
by CSS Publishing Co., Inc.

For more information about CSS Publishing Company resources, visit our website at www.csspub.com, email us at csr@csspub.com, or call (800) 241-4056.

ISBN-13: 978-0-7880-2730-7
ISBN-10: 0-7880-2730-1

PRINTED IN USA

Table of Contents

Introduction

Over forty years ago, CSS Publishing Company was founded by two pastors and a Sunday school superintendent who had a vision to assist pastors "on the front lines" in their efforts to share the gospel of Jesus with people over the entire United States. The lectionary was taking hold over the country in an effort to bring a common message to people, no matter where they worshiped.

Over the years, CSS has published many different products. Of the more than 1,700 publications that have been produced in the history of the company, **Emphasis: A Lectionary Preaching Journal** has been one of the most popular. In its history, thousands of pastors and their congregations have benefited from the commentaries and insights found within its pages.

Navigating the Sermon is a collection of commentaries from "Charting the Course," which is at the core of what **Emphasis** is about. For each Sunday in the Cycle C lectionary, the writers who contributed to these columns have provided thematic guidance drawing together the lessons for each Sunday in the church year. Not only have they provided one idea for each Sunday, but most days have multiple themes from which to choose.

We are excited to offer this new resource to the readers of **Emphasis**, both old and new, and pray that this book will be a blessing to you and an invaluable aid to your preaching ministry.

The editors of CSS Publishing Company

Pentecost Sunday
Acts 2:1-21
Romans 8:14-17
John 14:8-17 (25-27)
David Kalas

The day the Spirit moved in

Things change in a house when someone new moves in. Whether it is the birth of a baby, the arrival of an exchange student, the advent of a foster child, or the coming of an elderly parent needing care, things change in the house when someone new moves in.

Some of the changes that come are anticipated and welcome. We look forward to the fun and lovely patterns of life that will come with the new arrival. Other changes, however, are not anticipated — perhaps not even expected — and consequently those changes may not be welcome.

It's no different when God moves in. Things change. We'd be doomed if they didn't! But while some of the changes that come with his arrival are anticipated and welcome, some others are not.

We might say that Pentecost was an occasion when God moved in in a new and special way. The coming of the Holy Spirit changed things demonstrably in the church, just as his arrival and presence changes things demonstrably in an individual life.

We may find that people's comfort level decreases as we talk through the Trinity. A generic reference to "God" is widely accepted and embraced. Many different people may mean many different things by "god," but the word and the concept are easily accessible. Once you start talking about Jesus, however, there's a considerable drop off. Jesus is a more polarizing figure. Not all the folks who feel comfortable with talk about God are ready to get on board with Jesus. When the conversation turns to the Holy Spirit, even a lot of the folks who are willing to talk about Jesus — perhaps even a lot of the folks in our churches — begin to clam up. The Holy Spirit seems more mysterious and more threatening. He is not as easily relegated to heaven as the Father and not as easily relegated to history as the Son. The Holy Spirit is God "moved in," and we may rejoice in the results or we may be uncomfortable with them. Either way, though, the Spirit is here.

Acts 2:1-21

"They were all together in one place." After this day, that could never be said again of Christ's church. Not, at least, until the fulfillment of all things. At the beginning of this day, they were all together — all the believers, the followers, the disciples — in one city, in one room. By the end of this day, the believers were possibly heading and spreading to almost every place, "from every nation under heaven," from Mesopotamia to Rome.

It has often been said that the Acts of the Apostles might better be called the Acts of the Holy Spirit, for surely the Spirit is the driving force. He is promised in chapter 1, he comes on the Day of Pentecost in chapter 2, and he is the one who guides and empowers the work of the apostles and the church from that day forward.

The account of Pentecost features a handful of different images commonly associated with the Holy Spirit. Those images are revelatory, and we might use them to help our people gain a greater comfort level with the subject of the Holy Spirit.

First, there is the "rush of a violent wind." In Greek, as in Hebrew, the words for "wind," "breath," and "spirit" are largely interchangeable. It's not merely a case of homonymity (as with "lead" in English, for example). Rather, it is an instance of a single concept with several layers. It adds insight and depth to the image of God breathing his breath into Adam (Genesis 2:7) and makes for an illustration of the Spirit in Jesus' encounter with Nicodemus (see John 3:8).

Next, there is fire. In this instance, a manifestation of the Spirit is tongues of fire, but throughout the pages of scripture the presence (Deuteronomy 5:4), guidance (Psalm 78:14), refining (Zechariah 13:9), character (Deuteronomy 4:24), and judgment (Isaiah 66:15) of God are represented by fire. In addition to the imagery found in scripture, we have also come to associate fire with the Spirit in our hymnody. Samuel Longfellow's hymn, "Holy Spirit, Truth Divine," prays, "Holy Spirit, love divine, glow within this heart of mine; kindle every high desire; perish self in thy pure fire." Likewise, Henry Tweedy sang, "O Spirit of the living God, thou light and fire divine...."

Perhaps the most amusing association with the Spirit on the Day of Pentecost was wine. The behavior of the Spirit-filled apostles led a few observers to think that they were drunk. While their conclusion was not correct, it was insightful. Paul himself implies some similarity between being filled with wine and being filled with the Spirit (Ephesians 5:18). The image is further reinforced in Peter's citing of Joel's prophecy that the Lord would "pour out" his Spirit (v. 18). The picturesque language suggests a kind of liquid abundance, as well as a new understanding of what it could mean to live "under the influence."

The two key validations of the Spirit's presence and work in his people are signs and scripture. "Signs" and "portents" (v. 19) are said to accompany the Spirit's work, which in this instance means the many tongues. And throughout the New Testament, signs and wonders give evidence of the Spirit's presence and power (Romans 15:19; Hebrews 2:4).

Signs, however, are not enough. They can be deceptive (see Matthew 24:24), and so the other validation is also required. Peter's reassurance to the marveling Pentecost crowd was that the signs taking place before their eyes had been foretold in scripture. Seeing the signs of God was not enough; they had to square with the word of God.

Romans 8:14-17

What line delineates between the people of God and the rest of the world? For some folks in ancient days, it was the line between circumcised and uncircumcised. For some folks today, perhaps it is baptism, church membership, or adherence to a certain doctrine or creed.

In the three lections for this week, the demarcation of the people of God seems to be the Spirit of God. The gift of the Spirit to the people of Cornelius' house became the persuasive proof for Peter and the early church (see Acts 11:15-18). Jesus said that his followers would receive the Spirit "whom the world cannot receive" (John 14:17). And here, in Paul's letter to the Romans, the apostle claims that "all who are led by the Spirit of God are children of God."

We may be uneasy with this delineation, for it seems a little out of our control. (We may have that in common with the Jewish Christians in the early church who were reluctant to welcome Gentiles.) Things like baptism, membership, and beliefs seem to be our choice. The Spirit, however, does not flow at our direction, but moves independently, like the wind (John 3:8).

The greater importance of what Paul says in our selected epistle lection for this week, however, is not how the Spirit delineates between different people, but rather how the Spirit delineates within an individual person. The delineation is between past and present, between old and new.

The apostle Paul presents us with a "before and after" portrait of ourselves. The "before" picture is that of a slave who cowers in fear. He is insecure in his role and in his relationship to his master. The slave is property, with a set (and limited) value. The "after" picture, by contrast, is that of a confident son. He is not property, but progeny. And while he, too, has been bought, his value is inestimable (see 1 Corinthians 6:19-20). He is utterly secure in his role and in his relationship with the God he knows as "Abba! Father!"

John 14:8-17 (25-27)

This selected passage might just as well be used on Trinity Sunday as Pentecost Sunday, for it presents us with much fodder for a study of the of the three persons of God. The Son is at the center of the episode, but the passage offers us great insight into the relationship among the members of the Trinity.

While the traditional Christology of the Nicene Creed affirms that Jesus is co-equal with the Father, his earthly posture is one of submission to the Father. Jesus' remarks here about the Father and the Spirit reveal a complex interrelationship and interdependence. The Son will ask the Father, and the Father will send the Spirit (v. 16), but the Father will send the Spirit in the Son's name, and the Spirit will remind them of what the Son said (v. 26).

Philip's request at the beginning of the passage is met by some disappointment from Jesus. "Have I been with you all this time, Philip, and you still do not know me?" Of course, we ought not judge Philip too harshly, for it's apparent in other passages that many or all of the disciples had been with Jesus for so long without knowing or understanding who he was (e.g., Matthew 28:17; Luke 24:25-27, 36-45).

The commendable thing about Philip, meanwhile, is that he has learned this much from Jesus: God is Father. Philip's expressed request was not to be shown "God," but specifically to be shown "the Father." So while Philip had not yet grasped the nature of the Trinity, he had begun at least to understand the nature of God.

Jesus' surprising answer, meanwhile, was that Philip had already seen the Father. Such is the inexplicable mystery of the Trinity: Jesus spoke of the Father in the third person and to the Father in the second person, yet still claimed that "whoever has seen me has seen the Father."

The beauty of the portrait of the Trinity here is that they do everything with and for one another: "I do not speak on my own"; "the Father may be glorified in the Son"; "I will ask the Father"; "he will give you another Advocate"; "the Father will send in my name"; and "the Holy Spirit... will... remind you of all that I have said to you." In total contrast to the self-seeking and self-serving that characterize the devil and fallen humanity, the persons of the Trinity are always serving and glorifying one another. That mysterious loving oneness is a model for marriage, as well as for the fellowship of believers, who are also meant to experience God's oneness (c.f., John 17:22-23).

Finally, the oneness of the Trinity is not a closed system. The three persons of God do not revolve around each other to the exclusion of everyone and everything else. Rather, we are the beneficiaries of God's readiness to share of himself (e.g., John 14:12-13, 16-17, 26), and we are graciously invited into that loving oneness of God (John 17:23).

Application

While Christmas and Easter enjoy almost unanimous celebration by Christians throughout our world, Pentecost receives a more uneven treatment. For some churches, they wouldn't know that Pentecost was a date on the church calendar if their pastor didn't tell them and many of their pastors don't tell them. Other congregations, by contrast, might be surprised — even offended — to discover that an observance of Pentecost was limited to just one single day in the year.

Different folks apply the story of Pentecost in different ways. For some, it is like the Crucifixion and Resurrection — a one-time event in history that has a once-and-for-all impact. For others, the event of Pentecost is viewed more like baptism — a one-time event in an individual's life, but not a once-and-for-all event in history. For others still, Pentecost is understood like other blessings from God (e.g., healing) — not merely limited to a single occasion but offered continually throughout a person's life.

Whatever your view or your congregation's understanding, we can take all three passages for this week together and agree at least on this: Whenever and wherever the Spirit moves in, things change.

The change manifested in the church in Acts 2 (and beyond) has several component parts.

First, the apostles come pouring out of the house where they were sitting and into the streets, proclaiming in every language the things of God. And that became the new posture of the church. No longer was it a "sit in one place all together" group. Now it had become a "pour out into the streets" group, proclaiming the good news throughout the world.

Second, we see a boldness in the apostolic church from this day forward. Peter, who just a few weeks before cowered at the suggestion that he might be associated with Jesus (e.g., Mark 14:66-72), now declared the name of Jesus in the streets. Two chapters later, he stood before the same group of leaders who had orchestrated Jesus' arrest and crucifixion, but he was unflinching and unwavering.

Finally, the Spirit's move into the church in Acts 2 was also manifested in signs and wonders. Page after page of the book of Acts reports the miracles and marvels that surrounded the work of the apostles.

Meanwhile, the Acts lection offers a glimpse into what happened to the church when the Spirit moved in, the John and Romans passages speak to us of what happens when the Spirit moves into an individual life. According to Christ's promise, the Spirit "will teach you everything" (John 14:26), as well as remind us of all that Jesus taught. According to Paul, it is this Spirit that confirms the change that has occurred in our relationship with God. Now that the Spirit has moved in, we have a new way of relating to God and a new understanding of ourselves, not as fearful slaves but as children who are joyfully confident in their Father's love.

Alternative Applications

Acts 2:1-21; John 14:8-17 (25-27). Pentecost is the holiday that comes after waiting. It is the celebration that comes only after some time passes.

Pentecost, as suggested even by the name (which refers to fifty days), required something of a countdown. The Old Testament law prescribed that the Israelites should "begin to count seven weeks from the time the sickle is first put to the standing grain" (Deuteronomy 16:9). Those seven sabbaths, plus the day after the seventh sabbath, represented the fifty days between the offering of first fruits, and this Pentecost (or Festival of Weeks) holiday. That was when the real harvest began.

The New Testament event we know as Pentecost was also a function of waiting. While Matthew's account of Jesus' ascension implies an immediate implementation of the Great Commission (Matthew 28:16-20), Luke's account features a specific instruction to wait (Acts 1:4-11). The global mission of Christ's followers remains in force, but Luke's record of Jesus' final instructions includes a prerequisite for that mission: to wait for the Holy Spirit and power (Acts 1:4-5, 8).

Jesus said that John baptized with water but that soon the disciples would be baptized with the Holy Spirit. So, it is that the first fruits are not the same thing as the full fruition. And Pentecost was the occasion when Christ's followers began the harvest in earnest.

Acts 2:1-21. When folks saw and heard the apostles on Pentecost, some assumed that the apostles must have been drunk. That was their limited way of explaining the apostles' appearance and behavior.

What do the folks who see and hear us assume? How do they explain our appearance and behavior?

It may be, of course, that there is nothing to explain. If we seem to be just essentially like everyone else, then that may be more an indictment of us than the Pentecost presumption that the apostles were drunk.

I wonder, too, if many of Christ's followers through the ages — perhaps including some of us — could never be mistaken for drunk simply because we seem irrepressibly sober.

I don't drink and so I am out of my league here, but I think I know what I would do if I wanted to keep a bit of a buzz on. I would start with a drink first thing in the morning. I would make sure always to have something with me — a bottle, a flask — so that I could imbibe continually throughout the day. A drink or two would accompany my lunch and my dinner. I would seek opportunities to get together with like-minded friends to get drunk together. And I would be sure to have a nightcap before bed.

That would be my approach if I wanted to live under the influence of alcohol. Perhaps it also serves as a model for how I might live under the influence of the Spirit. And then it might be my privilege, too, to be misunderstood by the people around me, just like those Spirit-filled forefathers in Jerusalem.

John 14:8-17 (25-27). I believe that Jesus' relationship with his twelve disciples serves as a model for his relationship with us. As we see him with them in the pages of scripture, we get a glimpse of how he deals with us — calling, correcting, teaching, reassuring, empowering, sending forth, and so on.

One of the components of Jesus' relationship with his original twelve disciples was the questions he would ask them. One penetrating question I believe he still asks many of us today is the one posed to Philip in this passage: "Have I been with you all this time and still you do not know me?"

The question has a thousand variations. Has this person been in church for so long without ever making a personal decision for Christ? Has this man believed for so long in the historical figure without knowing the living Lord? Has this woman cherished his teachings and example for so long without knowing his salvation? Has this preacher served him for so long without fully knowing his power or his presence?

Jesus seems surprised that Philip could have followed and seen and heard for those several years without coming to recognize fully who Jesus was. We might do well to ask ourselves and one another this Sunday if Jesus might be equally surprised and disappointed by us after "so long."

One God: Father, Son, and Holy Spirit

Christians are "stewards of the mysteries of God" (1 Corinthians 4:1). One of those mysteries is the self-revealed identity of God as Trinity. Christians themselves have had to struggle to understand what the Trinity means. The history of church theology is rife with heated conversations plumbing the depths of human insight on this subject. From Irenaeus in the second century to Augustine in the fifth century, the church forged basic formulas and commentaries that have since then shaped Christian thought on the matter. (It was in 381 at the council of Constantinople that the Trinitarian formula of the one God existing co-equally in three persons was first formally adopted. All three of the Ecumenical Creeds — Apostles', Nicene, and Athanasian — express this.) The Trinity has been a stumbling block for non-Christian faith systems to grasp what Christians in fact believe, let alone become convinced that Christianity contains the essential wisdom that perceives God's disclosure in the world.

The danger in the culture of the West, of which we are the heirs, is that there is an unholy trinity that strives to usurp the affections of the would-be faithful. Power, possession, and pleasure lure the hearts of all who search for God down deadly, blind alleys. Momentary satisfactions replace the deeper contentment in the truth. The eyes of our heart are not enlightened by an enduring relationship with the God who is; rather, the eyes of our heart are merely delighted by passing fancies that fail to fill the empty hole that is left by squandered efforts.

The texts assigned for this festival day celebrating the Trinity invite us to explore more deeply the nature of God's self-revelation, so that we may better understand the God who is and may better give an account of the gift of faith that is within us.

Proverbs 8:1-4, 22-31

Proverbs is typical of the wisdom genre that comprises a portion of the Old Testament literature. It does not rank equally with the law and the prophets or even the histories; but, it is valued nevertheless. It makes clear repeatedly that wisdom is to be found in the fear of the Lord. It describes the ways of the righteous and it gives practical insights on daily living and relationships. Truth be told, Proverbs 8:1-21 would have been a better pericope for this Sunday. But, since it has not been assigned as such, attention will be paid to those verses that have been assigned. Let the preacher be encouraged to explore verses 5-21 for added insights and images that can be used effectively in drawing out more fully the content of this discussion.

Just as Mexico markets itself in attractive ads in the first person ("I am ancient... I have many stories to tell"), the writer of Proverbs knows how to grab our attention, even when talking about something as ethereal as wisdom. Wisdom is personified as one standing by the gate, calling out to those who pass by, getting them to turn their heads and take heed to what is being said. Interestingly, wisdom, a word of the feminine gender, is described as being created by God (8:22), being brought forth (8:24) at the beginning of the generating acts of God. Wisdom is not God, but is beside God, like a *master workman or as a little child* (8:30). Wisdom neither stands as God nor in the place of God but *before him* (8:30), expressing mirth in the acts of God manifested throughout the creation (8:31). With this in mind, it makes no sense at all to elevate Wisdom (Sophia) to the role of recipient of our prayers or adoration, as some contemporary worship planners do.

Wisdom is part of the created order. Just like the sculpted body points to the heavenly sculptor and just like the painted sunset points to the heavenly artist, so too does wisdom point to the one who does all things well. The litany of creation is Wisdom's affirmation of the thoroughness of God's design (for example, 8:29) and a way to give glory to God, the originator of it all. This is part of Job's wisdom insight, that all things belong to God and are held in his hand (Job 1:21). Therefore, come what may, glory and honor are to be given to God. This is an expression of "the fear of the Lord" and finds its proper posture kneeling in ashes on a dung heap, repenting.

Since Wisdom is part of the established order, it is an immanent expression of God the Father, Creator of heaven and earth. Paul appeals to this aspect of God's self-disclosure in Romans 1:20-21 and again in Acts 17:22-28. So does Peter in Acts 10:34-35. What can be known of God is by necessity accessible to humanity in terms of awareness; the experience of God in the world makes sense to the other experiences of human existence. Proverbs 8:17 comments on this, giving positive encouragement to those who diligently seek the Lord: Lover and beloved will be united; seeker and the sought will be brought together.

This having been said, it must be admitted that sin clouds our understanding and even our ability to receive the truth; so, more of God's activity in self-disclosure needs to be forthcoming. It is not that there is something faulty with God's efforts to make himself known to us and beloved by us; it is that the fullness of God begs further expression and this, in fact, proves itself capable of penetrating the barriers that sin erects between us and God.

Romans 5:1-5

Don't miss the mighty "therefore" (5:1) that Paul uses to make a bridge between what he has already spelled out (especially in Romans 3:21—4:25) and what is to follow (especially Romans 5-8)! This is important because there is a decision that needs to be made in how one preaches this text. Is it proclamation or invitation? It all depends on what ancient manuscripts you accept as most authoritative. Arguments can be made on both sides in terms of the number of supporting manuscripts and in terms of the precedence of alternative traditions. However, when one looks at the context and the entire theology of Paul, the weight of the argument shifts to accepting in 5:1 (over the alternative reading), as presented in the Nestle-Aland and also Westcott-Hort text.

The key rests in the conjunction "therefore," as well as in the construction of (functioning like a gerund in English, "being justified"). Paul has made the case so far in his letter that justification is a gift of God's grace through the work of Jesus on the cross (Romans 3:21-26). *Therefore*, "we have peace with God" (5:1). This is declaratory; it is not an invitation into what might be. If Paul wrote this letter as email, he would have CAPITALIZED everything to emphasize his point! (Note: not in anger, but in joy, as he soon states!) Paul is proclaiming a new state of affairs, described in the present tense. It is a *fait accompli*, accented by his use of the perfect form of the verb "have" (5:2).

Paul acknowledges the work of Jesus as establishing the ground on which the believer can gracefully stand. He then applies the wisdom of faith to the hard realities of the believer's life, characterized by suffering. Suffering bears fruit: endurance, character, and hope (5:3-4). These are blessings from God (the Father), which reward the faithful witness who suffers for the name of Jesus. The practical result is a hope that does not disappoint, because it is confirmed by the Holy Spirit, which is present as a gift from God. This hope sets one's vision on the glory of God that is coming and will be shared with the believers in Jesus. It is not unlike the marathon runner who visualizes the tape at the finish line, an image that keeps drawing the runner step by step closer to the desired goal of finishing the race as the victor.

Using the Trinitarian formula, one could express the message of this passage in this way: The believer's relationship with God the heavenly Father is now one of peace because of the justifying work of Jesus on the cross, a work imparted by the Holy Spirit, giving one strength and confidence for all circumstances in life.

John 16:12-15

Nestled in the midst of Jesus' farewell to his disciples (John 16 and 17) after the Passover supper on Thursday night of Holy Week, Jesus speaks of the dynamic expression of God as Father, Son, and Holy Spirit. As the Son, he announces that he is heir to all that is the Father's. He also states that the Holy Spirit will take what is the Son's and declare it to the disciples. Through Jesus, the disciples will experience the fullness of God: himself as the Son, the Father who sent him, and the Holy Spirit who will be sent by him.

Jesus is the essential revelation of God, but he is not the complete revelation of God. Remember, he admitted that he did not know the hour of the day of the Lord (Mark 13:32); nor, was he able to impart to the disciples all that he wanted to. It would be necessary for the Holy Spirit to come and continue the self-revelation of God and lead those who believe into fuller communion with God, their creator and redeemer and sanctifier.

The Holy Spirit has a specific function in the divine economy. He is to apply the truth of Jesus to the lives of the disciples and all those who would come after them in faith. The Holy Spirit would specifically be about the business of giving witness to Jesus. "He will glorify me" (16:14). There certainly are many truths in the world worth knowing, just as there are many aspects of wisdom that the human mind is capable of grasping. But, the truth that the Holy Spirit is concerned with, just as the wisdom that biblical Wisdom is concerned with, is that which relates particularly to the Godhead and one's relationship to God in living faith.

These few verses in John's gospel are similar to other texts in the New Testament that are rendered with a Trinitarian formulation. Look, for example, at Matthew 28:19; John 16:1-11; Acts 1:1-5; Ephesians 1:3-14; Colossians 1:1-8; and 1 Thessalonians 1:1-10. The scripture writers knew that to speak about the fullness of God, they would need to speak of the Father, the Son, and the Holy Spirit. Anything short of that would diminish our experience and understanding of the one God, who reveals himself in these dynamic co-eternal and co-equal persons.

Application

Whether American politics can rise above its ground level of power, pragmatism remains to be seen. Perhaps it never can but hope rests eternal with every new election and the rising of a new generation into the fray. Of late, it cannot be said that we have leaders who exemplify wisdom and character in their statesmanship. Maybe such qualities are recognized only in retrospect and are granted only by a narrowed focus of memory. It remains true, however, that there is a general groundswell calling for rising above trivial pursuits of partisan politics and attaining to what would truly be advantageous for the common good of the many. For this to occur, wisdom will need to be sought after. It will be found ultimately and truly in God and it will be received by men and women only as a gift from God.

If Wisdom stands at the gate and calls out for adherents, then those who would be blessed by her instruction would best be found in petition on their knees. As Wisdom herself acknowledges the greatness of God and rejoices before God, then those who would be wise must learn the humility of receiving wisdom as a gift from God. To prepare with humility, one can engage the discipline of prayer and the focus on *the other* (as Dietrich Bonhoeffer taught us). For wisdom of which the Bible speaks does not serve self-aggrandizement but rather the lifting up and the building up of *the other*. Here the true intentionality of politics finds its expression. Here the Christian can heartily engage in the business of politics on every level — in the neighborhood, at school, within city management, for county and state and national government, and as an international advocate on issues that eventually affect all of us. In our ever-shrinking and more complex world, wisdom is a gift to be sought for the well-being of the community, more so than for individual decisions pertaining to one's own life exclusively (if even this were possible!). As one former president said, "Ask not what your country can do for you; ask what you can do for your country." As another president has said, "I ask you to seek a common good beyond your comfort."

God the Father, as creator, is the source of this wisdom and the one to whom such petitions are directed. When we pray in the Lord's Prayer to our heavenly Father, we ask that his will be done on earth as in heaven. This will of God is the wisdom for which we seek. To perceive God's will in any situation will give wisdom for one's response and consequential decisions and actions.

When Jesus was asked in John 6:28, "What must we do, to be doing the works of God?" he could just as easily have been asked about doing the will of God or living according to the wisdom of God. The response would have been the same at any rate: *believe in the Lord Jesus, whom the Father has sent into the world* (John 6:29). This is the central affirmation that has drawn Roman Catholics and Lutherans around the world together in new ways recently, manifested by the signing of the *Document on the Doctrine of Justification* (fall 1999) and celebrated together by Catholic and Lutheran siblings in Christ around the world.

How comforting a word to hear that peace is already the character of our relationship with God because of the work already accomplished by Jesus on the cross. It is "a done deal"! Now, we can simply rest in it and cease our striving to earn God's favor. We already *are* standing in the grace of God; *this* is the ground of our hope, our confidence about the future quality of our existence, whether delimited by time or by eternity.

This allows us, with Paul, to view the up-side of suffering. It becomes the opportunity to develop and manifest endurance and character and hope, giving glory to Jesus — the one who suffered the most for us. It would be helpful here to read the sequence of Paul's writing not in a linear fashion but in a circular one. There is a dynamic relationship between suffering, endurance, character, and hope. It is not so much that one leads reasonably and sequentially into the others. There is a creative tension between all of these qualities of Christian life that feed into and feed from the others. It has been said, "Sports does not build character; it reveals it." In one sense that is true; but in another sense it is true that sports builds the character it longs to show. So too, suffering can at times produce endurance, which in turn builds character, which is fertile ground for hope; but, it is also true that the confidence of hope generates and strengthens a new character that enables one to endure the harshest of realities. If one can picture such a "wheel of fortune," the cross of Christ would be its axle.

The Christian can have the confidence that God is faithful in the self-revelation of the divine economy. What is the Father's belongs to the Son, which in turn is passed on by the Holy Spirit to those who believe. Unlike the telephone relay game which ends up with a message that is totally foreign to the original, what the Holy Spirit imparts to longing hearts is the essential truth that arises from the very heart of the Father and is passed to the Son. This is why Jesus can refer to "the Spirit of truth" (16:13) and Paul can pray that the disciples receive "a spirit of wisdom and of revelation in the knowledge of him" (Ephesians 1:17).

Christians are encouraged to pray daily to be led by the Holy Spirit. Our confidence, based upon the promises of scripture, is that the Holy Spirit is working to bring us into the full knowledge of the truth (see Ephesians 1:17-18). This truth is more than wisdom; it is more than information about Jesus; it is more than the perception of where the Holy Spirit is indeed working. It is a truth that centers itself in a living, growing relationship between the believer and Jesus the Messiah. It is a truth that blossoms into "the fear of the Lord" (Proverbs 9:10), inspired by the work of the Holy Spirit who unwraps, like a gift, a fuller experience of God in the world, including one's own individual life.

The united colors of faith

The Italian-based clothing company Benetton Group has captured worldwide attention with its global ad campaigns simply titled "The United Colors of Benetton." Using gripping images and striking hues, the billboards portray people in real-life settings (rather than coiffed and posed models in a studio) wearing textiles produced under their brand. The implication is that no one size fits all, and that among the many varieties of cultures and experiences, Benetton engages and adapts.

This is a fitting analogy for the expressions of faith in today's lectionary passages. Elijah calls Israel to return to faith in Yahweh after the powerful showdown with the Baal minions of Ahab and Jezebel on Mount Carmel. Paul wrestles for the soul of the Galatian congregations who have quickly transformed saving faith into a Christianized version of works righteousness. And Jesus marvels at the trust of a man who commands others but now bows in submission. The many colors of faith, displayed in every congregation of God's people.

1 Kings 18:20-21 (22-29) 30-39

When the grand kingdom of David and Solomon became divided, its theological mission as witness to the nations was compromised. Yet the perspective of kings is that the northern tribes (now "Israel") and the southern portion (now "Judah") were never truly separated. Throughout the rest of these narratives the political fortunes of both territories were equally considered. Furthermore, the kings of both realms were similarly judged by the prophetic author as either following in the ways of David and Solomon (thus seeking to fulfill the destiny intended by Yahweh) or compounding the covenant-breaking of those who caused the nation to stray from its divine calling and mission. This is most obvious in the harsh assessments given at the time of the northern kingdom's destruction by the Assyrians (2 Kings 17).

In this connection it is interesting to note the emerging and changing role of the public "prophets." Moses and Joshua each had a unique and on-going relational interchange with Yahweh that made their leadership positions virtually unassailable (cf. Numbers 12, 16-17). After the nation was settled in Canaan, such clear, regular, and unequivocal communication with Yahweh appears to have been muted. During the times of Eli, we are told, "the word of the Lord was rare; there were not many visions" (1 Samuel 3:1). That is why, when Yahweh began speaking directly with Samuel, the Israelites were ready to follow him (1 Samuel 3:19-21). This seems to be the beginning of a national recognition of the status of prophets as part of the necessary social fabric.

When Samuel's leadership was challenged because the people wanted a king (1 Samuel 8), it caused the first subtle separation of church and state. Samuel was a priest by adoption and worked within the parameters of the cultic shrine. But the kings were clearly outside of the Levitical priesthood or its extended family. Prophets at first began to bridge the connection and then later sparred with the kings as the sovereignty role of Yahweh was increasingly forgotten.

This tension is clearly seen in the dominant stories of Elijah and Elisha who battled with the rulers of the northern kingdom in 1 Kings 17—2 Kings 8. Elijah was given the weapons of the curses of the Sinai covenant to bring Ahab and Jezebel to their knees (1 Kings 17:1). He wielded divine power in public displays of combat (1 Kings 18). He was authorized to determine and appoint the leaders of nations (1 Kings

19). When Ahab and Jezebel presumed that they could displace God-fearing Israelites from their divinely determined inheritance in the land (1 Kings 21), Elijah confronted the pair with stern prophecies that they instead would be removed.

Today's lectionary passage is at the heart of this conflict. The question of "who is the true king in Israel?" is tied to religious worship. Indeed, as David and Solomon knew, human regents can never usurp the divine right of Yahweh to claim Israel's royal allegiance. It is precisely because Ahab has become a charlatan intruder, multiplying his crimes against the true king of the nation by marrying Jezebel and allowing her to rewrite the religious agenda of the realm, that Elijah moves in to reassert the rights of Yahweh. The issue on Mount Carmel is not really about which God or gods can perform magic tricks on command, but who will own Israel's heart. Jezebel has coupled herself to Ahab and manipulates the religion of Baal to coerce their citizens into zombie-like subservience. Elijah wishes no one to worship him but seeks rather to break the spell of the wicked witch so Israel can return to its full human potential as the people of Yahweh. This is seen in the rousing final cry of those gathered: "Yahweh, he is God! Yahweh, he is God!"

While today's passage does not take into account the return of the rains after three years of drought, it would be good to mention this context for the Mount Carmel showdown. The Sinai covenant that shaped Israel's identity, bound her to Yahweh. It also included the "Blessings and Curses" section (Exodus 23:20-33, and expanded in Leviticus 26) that warned Israel about the consequences of turning away from Yahweh. Specifically identified among the curses was drought. When Israel, under the magnetic warping of Jezebel's weird ways, left Yahweh, it was not Elijah but Yahweh who brought the drought, hoping for Israel to remember and return. Now that Israel has resoundingly made again a declaration of faith in Yahweh, the rains will return.

Galatians 1:1-12

During a prayer meeting in the church of Antioch, probably in early 48 AD, the gathered group received a very strong divine message that their primary leadership team was supposed to be sent on a missionary journey (Acts 13:1-3). We do not have details about how the plans were laid, but it is reasonable to suppose that they arranged a trip into familiar territory. Cyprus was Barnabas' home turf, and it may well be that after they blitzed across that island they intended to travel back to Antioch along the Pamphylian coast, stopping briefly in Tarsus along the way.

Indeed, they traveled the length of Cyprus, preaching along the way and then boarded boats for the mainland. But at the seaport of Perga, John Mark left them and "returned to Jerusalem" (Acts 13:13). Also, it seems that Paul might have gotten sick at that point in their travels. What the illness was, is not certain, but when he later wrote to those he and Barnabas met in the highlands of central Asia Minor, he reminded them that "it was because of an illness that I first preached the gospel to you" (Galatians 4:13). A further clue to these events is found in Paul's later cryptic testimony that something was wrong with his eyes (Galatians 4:15). Since the Pamphylian coastline is marshy and mosquito-ridden, it might have been malaria that laid Paul low. That would explain why the team went immediately up into the highlands, rather than continuing along the shore.

In Pisidian Antioch Paul preached a historical review of God's work in the synagogue, leading finally to a message about Jesus being the messiah. A week later "almost the whole city" came out, for this new gospel was creating quite a stir. While many believed, jealous Jews incited a riot that forced Paul and Barnabas out of the synagogue. They spent the next days in the marketplace, speaking to Gentiles as well as Jews. But the animosity was building and soon the travelers were forced from the city (Acts 13:14-31).

Down the road, at a smaller town named Iconium, Paul and Barnabas again preached in the Jewish synagogue to good response. Like before, growing Jewish resentment caused them to turn to the Gentiles. Soon a plot against them was discovered, and they moved on again (Acts 14:1-7).

At Lystra the pair encountered a crippled man just outside of town. He was begging for alms, but Paul raised him up healed. This caused a serious commotion and the entire population turned out to worship Paul and Barnabas as Hermes and Zeus, key leaders among the Greek gods. When Paul convinced them that he and his companions were only human, worship turned to disgust, and enemies who had dogged their heels from Antioch turned the crowds against them. They were stoned and left for dead. Fortunately some sympathetic care providers nurtured back the almost extinguished sparks of life in them, and after a short while of secretive recovery, they moved on again (Acts 14:8-20).

Traveling briefly to nearby Derbe (Acts 14:21), the team preached about Jesus and then wended their way home. They stopped briefly in each highland community where they had recently spent a few days or weeks, appointing elders in the new Christian congregations (Acts 14: 22-25). Returning to Syrian Antioch, they brought a report of their mission journey to their home congregation (Acts 14:26-28).

That's when the trouble started (Acts 15; Galatians 2). Reports of Gentile converts to Christianity sizzled toward Jerusalem. Peter came up to Antioch to celebrate this exciting mission work, but others with less enthusiasm were soon sent by James (the brother of Jesus and leader of the Jerusalem congregation) to ensure that all was happening in an appropriate manner. These representatives announced that Gentiles had to become Jews in belief and practice before they could become part of the Christian church. After all, Jesus was Jewish, and was being acclaimed as the Messiah foretold by Israel's prophets.

These ambassadors of the Jerusalem church instituted separated meal and communion practices, making it clear that only those who were ceremonially pure could take positions of leadership in the community. Much to Paul's surprise, even Peter allied himself with those advocating these discriminating practices. Paul, of course, was anything but timid and accosted Peter publicly, creating even stronger polarization among the congregations on these matters.

The disease of Jewish superiority spread to the churches of Paul's and Barnabas' recent mission journey and threatened to split the infant Christian community before it had even an opportunity to get started. In response, Paul dashed off a letter to the churches of "Galatia," the Roman district through which they had traveled on their mission trek.

In the first part of this passionate letter (Galatians 1-2), Paul reviewed his personal journey to an understanding of freedom in Christ and lamented the recent developments that had seemingly stolen away this freedom from many of them. Next (Galatians 3-4) Paul went into a lengthy Jewish rabbinic argument about how Abraham was counted as "righteous" in his relationship with God already before he entered into the rituals of circumcision. Paul concluded that neither circumcision nor any other ceremonial expression was absolutely necessary for a meaningful relationship with God, and that Jesus' recent teachings, death, and resurrection only reaffirmed and expanded this truth. In fact, said Paul, the "law" (that is, the ceremonial dimensions of the Sinai covenant) was like a teacher who was no longer needed after a child became fully mature. Using a rabbinic allegory, Paul pointed Hagar and her son Ishmael as representations of Abraham's "slave" side of the family, regulated by the social codes from Mount Sinai. Sarah and her son Isaac, on the other hand, were symbols of Abraham's "free" side of the family and lived out of the delight that was expressed through ecstatic worship in Jerusalem. In the final portion of his letter (Galatians 5-6), Paul used very strong language to urge the expression of true freedom in Christ. This is found in neither the legalism of ritual religious regimens that bind and burden, nor in licentiousness that turns us evil and ugly. Rather, true Christian freedom is experienced when we no longer consider ourselves under external demands that have no important ends in themselves, but when we voluntarily give ourselves as slaves to God and others out of love. In this context there can be no division between "Jewish Christians" and "Gentile Christians," for the church of Jesus Christ has become the new "Israel of God" (Galatians 6:16).

It is in this context that today's harsh words from Paul emerge. They are aimed at recent converts who were already deeply religious when they came to trust in Jesus as Messiah and Savior. But in their passion to do the right things and be good for God, they began quickly to focus on what they could bring to the table and forgot the grace that saved them.

Luke 7:1-10

John Calvin said that there were two aspects to faith: *assentia* and *fiducia*. The first we often translate as "assent." It is in this dimension of faith that we acknowledge that something exists. *Assentia* is knowing something factually or knowing about someone only from a distance.

Calvin's second aspect of faith might well be termed "trust." It is a heart engagement, involving us personally in an emotional attachment with whatever we might have previously acknowledged only intellectually.

Take a chair, for instance. *Assentia* is our willingness to say that it could hold the person daring to sit on it. *Fiducia*, on the other hand, is the act of sitting on that chair ourselves, trusting its sturdiness to hold our bulk. Both are elements of faith. Both are important. But until the latter is added to the former, faith remains inert, distant, intellectual, impersonal.

The story in today's gospel reading offers strong incentive for us to get beyond talking about God and getting on with the business of engaging God as an active partner in our lives. Faith talk means little if we demand and coerce (like the good ruler knew he could do with his underlings) while never giving ourselves over to the necessary trust factor. This is the marvel that Jesus announces to others. Even God's historic people seem addicted to *assentia* without a lot of show of *fiducia*.

Dr. E. Stanley Jones told of an incident from his missionary days that illustrates James' point. A young girl was tired of things at home, said Jones. She longed for the freedom of the streets and the excitement of the nightlife. She ran away to a large city. It wasn't long before she fell under the spell of a pimp and was degraded into a prostitute.

The girl's mother was beside herself with anxiety. It was true that things hadn't been going right between them, but a mother's love is restless and protective, and she had to find her daughter again. She remembered the child who sat on her lap, and the daughter who whispered in her ear and needed somehow to renew their bond of trust.

Yet how should she begin the search? All she had heard were rumors about daughter, thirdhand reports that she was now wasting her body in the red-light district. The mother went to the city and simply began to walk, hoping to stumble across someone who might know her daughter. Up one street and down the next she trudged, talking to anyone who would listen, hoping for a clue to follow.

But to no avail. Her daughter didn't want to be found: shame, rebellion, spite. Who can say what reasons mingle in our deceptive minds?

Eventually the quest tired even the mother. But before she returned home, she did one more thing. She carried a photograph that had been taken several years before, a picture of the two of them, mother and daughter, at a happier moment in both their lives. She got the photograph enlarged and made dozens of copies. Then she scattered those pictures around the area, hoping that one would catch her daughter's eye.

On each photo she penned these five words: **Come home! I love you!**

One day the girl did see. She began to remember what love was all about. A holy restless gripped her soul, battering her resentment until she had to call her mother. The next day she was home.

Never once did the daughter stop *assenting* to the fact that she had a mother. But it wasn't until her mother's love called out the *trust* of her heart that she believed in all that "home" and "mother" and "love" could mean to her personally.

If Jesus were to take a picture of your faith today, like he did with the ruler in today's lectionary reading, how much depth would it show?

Application

Stories of conversion are not enough to sustain faith or to explore the wonder of life in the Promised Land of God's kingdom. Faith needs to grow. Horizons need to expand. Insights need to connect and skills of service need to be put to use. Most of all, dependence on God needs to multiply.

Growth in the Christian faith happens in several directions at once. As we move on from our first profession of faith we all need to increase our knowledge of the teachings of the Bible and the insights of the church's theology. Second, we need to develop our ability to understand our spiritual gifts and passions in order to take our place in the Christ-service of his body, the church. Third, we need to learn the vocabulary of faith so that we can communicate intelligently to others of the things God is doing inside of us and the vision he has for the world and eternity. Fourth, we need constantly to groom our understanding of the meaning and character of relationships so that we can live as supportive social beings. Fifth, we need to foster the intuitive dimension of our personalities in order to catch the wind of the Spirit and sail the seas of grace. Sixth, we need to strengthen our wills to be able to keep us compassionately strong through times of great stress and upheaval. Seventh, we need to deepen love as we practice care, living as God's signs of new life. These are among the many colors of faith.

The old hymn says, "Change and decay in all around I see." The changing face of life creates a kind of mist in which we can wander aimlessly or become silly in our self-importance. Yet there is also a lot of health in the changes that take place among people who are always growing. The only time we truly stop changing is when we die. More than that, the only time we truly grow well is when we grow in trust.

An Alternative Application

Luke 7:1-10. Even Charles Darwin was impressed by Christian faith that breathed through responsible Christian living, like that of the ruler in today's gospel reading. Darwin had disowned the Christianity of his childhood and was sailing for five years around South America in search of confirmation to his theories of natural selection and evolutionary development. When he stopped for a while at Tierra del Fuego he found a community that defied his prescriptions for normal human development. Under the teaching and ministry of a man named Thomas Bridges the whole society was being transformed into something better than it used to be.

The power in Thomas Bridges' leadership came from his own story. He was abandoned as a baby on the banks of the Thames in London, England. Passers-by heard his feeble cries and rescued him barely alive. It happened on St. Thomas' Day near several bridges over the river, so they called him Thomas Bridges. The family that raised him as their own gave him confidence in the love of Jesus. Though abandoned by his mother, he learned the power of faith that lives through deeds of those who care.

That is why he became a missionary of Jesus Christ and the reason his words, coupled with actions, rang with power. Even Charles Darwin, as he was becoming an atheist, supported Thomas Bridges financially for the rest of his life. Here was faith that made a difference and that was something the world needed more than another scientific theory.

Such faith is a marvel and a great example, as Jesus noted in response to the ruler's simple expressions. Assent wed to trust makes a profound declaration of faith, then *and* now.

Proper 5 / Pentecost 3 / Ordinary Time 10
1 Kings 17:8-16 (17-24)
Galatians 1:11-24
Luke 7:11-17
David Kalas

Distinguishing features

When our people hear these three passages read during our worship services this Sunday, they will see the immediate connection between the Old Testament and gospel readings. In both instances, a poor widow loses a son to death. And, in both instances, the man of God restores the young man to life.

The two stories are beautiful.

We begin by recognizing the unspeakable sadness of a parent losing a child. Certain kinds of grief and loss we expect in life, but not this. Even in our marriage vows we recognize the death that will part us. But no parent figures to outlive their child.

The sadness is doubled in the case of these women, for they are both widows. They have already experienced loss inasmuch as their husbands have died. This is grief upon grief for these poor women.

They are, almost certainly, poor women. The grief of death is further complicated by the economic reality for widows in that time and place. We will explore that issue in more detail below, but suffice it to say that these women shared the prospect of being destitute in the wake of losing their sons.

Finally, there is this tragic detail: The deceased sons are the only sons. One child surely does not replace another. Still, there is comfort for a grieving parent in the child or children that remain. But these two women have no such comfort.

Against that backdrop of tremendous sadness, God does his gracious and powerful work. This is the very recipe of the Bible's most beautiful stories: God's lovely work against the backdrop of human sadness. It is there in Israel's miraculous deliverance from slavery and in each of Jesus' healings. It is given voice in the comforting message of Isaiah 40 and seen in the gracious timing of Christ's saving death (Romans 5:8).

So, while we are presented this week with two conspicuously similar stories, those similarities are not the whole story. There is a larger pattern of God's work to be seen and to be celebrated.

1 Kings 17:8-16 (17-24)

Elijah arrives on the Bible's stage without introduction. He appears suddenly here in 1 Kings 17, with no reference to his calling as his prophet, his family background, or his personal biography. We are simply told that he is from Tishbe in Gilead. The exact identity and location of Tishbe is uncertain. Gilead, meanwhile, was the hilly, trans-Jordan region between the Sea of Galilee to the north and the Dead Sea in the south.

Next thing we know, this unidentified Tishbite has an audience with Ahab, the notorious king of Israel. His message is no-nonsense and bold: a chastening drought is on Israel's horizon, and Elijah controls the spigot.

It's an astonishing claim for some nobody from nowhere to make to a king. After all, in a world of thrones and monarchs, it is the king's word that holds sway. He is the one who speaks and makes things happen. Yet Ahab is powerless in this circumstance. His royal edicts make no difference to the sun and clouds. Instead, nature will respond only to Elijah's word.

In preparation for the drought, God makes provisions for his prophet. Specifically, we see two forms of providence: by natural means (the birds and the brook) and by human means (the poor widow). In either case, of course, Elijah's ultimate reliance was on God, yet it is always instructive for us to see the variety of ways by which God accomplishes his provident care and purpose. It is also noteworthy that Elijah's first source from God eventually dried up. The need exceeded that particular resource, though it did not exhaust the provider.

On the national stage, where the story began, we know that the drought eventually led to a confrontation with the king and a showdown with the doomed representatives of Baal on Mount Carmel. But our passage does not return to that broader, national focus. Instead, we move deeper into the personal story of the particular widow whom God used to provide for Elijah. (Or was it that God used Elijah to provide for the widow?)

That personal story turns tragic when the widow's son dies. The medical cause of death is vague, but "medical" isn't where the mother's mind turns anyway. Her response — "What have you against me, O man of God? You have come to me to bring my sin to remembrance, and to cause the death of my son!" — is poignantly true to life. Even in our sophisticated medical age, still our instinct in the face of tragic death is to seek spiritual answers or to assume spiritual causes. The doctor can explain that the child died of leukemia, but we still want the Omnipotent to answer for why the child contracted leukemia in the first place. And so we shake our fists at God for allowing — indeed, perhaps for causing — such calamity.

Interestingly, the prophet of God does not disabuse the woman of her paradigm. He does not take her aside and explain that what she's feeling is perfectly natural, while assuring her that God does not deliberately kill children. Instead, he echoed the very same complaint in prayer: "O Lord my God, have you brought calamity even upon the widow with whom I am staying, by killing her son?"

Scripture does not confirm Elijah's paradigm of cause-and-effect. On the contrary, it simply says that the son "became ill" and that "his illness was so severe that there was no breath left in him." Yet God does answer Elijah's request for the boy's life to be restored.

The miraculous resuscitation seems to be a combination of intercession and ancient CPR. In the end, the boy came back to life, and he is returned to his grieving mother. Interestingly, it is because of this event that she believes Elijah is a "man of God," though she had already witnessed miracles through Elijah (vv. 15-16) and had previously referred to him as a man of God (v. 18). Evidently whatever doubts had been raised by her son's death were put to rest when her son was raised.

Galatians 1:11-24

Unlike our lections from 1 Kings and Luke, this passage is not a story. Still, there is a story behind it. In order for our people to grasp the meaning of the passage, they will need to have an appreciation for the background story. That context has three elements: geographical, personal, and theological.

Geographically, we need simply to observe that Galatia was a region, not a city. While the epistles to the Romans, Corinthians, Philippians, and Thessalonians were all written to the believers in certain cities, Galatia was an entire province in Asia Minor (what we could call modern-day Turkey), where Paul spent many of his missionary miles.

That leads us to the personal context. The Christians in much of Galatia were personally known to Paul. He was the evangelist who had brought them the gospel of Jesus. He had led them to Christ, founded their churches, and maintained a personal sense of spiritual responsibility for them. The letter from which our selected lection comes, therefore, is personal correspondence.

Finally, the theological context is perhaps the most important layer of all. The Galatians have been infiltrated by a group sometimes referred to as "Judaizers." These Jewish Christians evidently taught that in order to be a Christian, a person must still observe certain requirements of the Old Testament law (e.g., circumcision of the males). This was not an entirely implausible argument within its original setting. Inasmuch as the Jews understood that the law was the full expression of the will of God, as well as the terms of his covenant with his people, it seemed to many earnest Jewish Christians to discount or cast aside any requirements of the law. Can we imagine some new wave of God's work that would nullify the Sermon on the Mount?

Some of the believers in Galatia apparently had acquiesced to the Judaizers' paradigm, and so the apostle Paul wrote to correct them. A reading of the larger letter reveals that his correction was candid (1:6; 3:1), impassioned (1:8-9), and sometimes even sarcastic (3:5; 5:11-12).

Because Paul perceived the Galatians as having turned to a different gospel (1:6), it was his endeavor to reassert the true gospel that he had previously proclaimed. To that end, he needed to establish two things: 1) the authority of that gospel; and 2) the credibility of its messenger.

As to the authority of the gospel, Paul's primary argument is that the gospel he had proclaimed was from God and not from human beings. We see here the recurring theme: "not of human origin," "I did not receive it from a human source, nor was I taught it," "I did not confer with any human being, nor did I go up to Jerusalem to those who were already apostles before me," "I did not see any other apostle except James the Lord's brother," and "I was still unknown by sight to the churches of Judea that are in Christ." Instead, he insists that he "received it through a revelation of Jesus Christ."

The distinction reminds us of Jesus' response to Peter's recognition that he was the Christ: "Flesh and blood has not revealed this to you, but my Father in heaven" (Matthew 16:17). It is an epistemological issue, and Paul is making the grand claim that his source of knowledge and truth was neither mortal nor traditional, but divine.

Meanwhile, this gospel of divine origin still had a human advocate, and so Paul felt the need also to establish his credibility as a messenger. Accordingly, he reminded the Galatians about his own history — his "earlier life in Judaism." We remember that his opponents in this controversy, the Judaizers, were perceived as zealous for God's law. And so Paul sought to establish the credentials of his own zeal, lest he be misunderstood as a rogue who was unserious about the law of God. His resume includes "advanc(ing) in Judaism beyond many," as well as being "far more zealous for the traditions of my ancestors." Also, the regrettable fact that he "violently persecute(ed) the church of God and was trying to destroy it" is considered a mark in his favor within this context.

The argument is reminiscent of portions of 2 Corinthians, in which Paul is similarly combating certain teachings and teachers in that church. In order to defeat the influence of the so-called "super-apostles" (2 Corinthians 11:5), Paul asserts his own spiritual credentials, even though he finds the exercise distasteful (2 Corinthians 11:21).

Having established the authority of the gospel he preached, as well as his credentials as the preacher, Paul is ready to proceed with the rest of his letter, correcting the Galatians and reminding them of the truth of the good news.

Luke 7:11-17

The town of Nain was another of the villages in the northern region of Galilee, the region where Jesus spent so much of his ministry. This episode is the only reference to Nain in all of scripture. Unlike some other Galilean sites — e.g., Capernaum, Nazareth, Bethsaida, Magdala — we don't have any other accounts of Jesus' activity in Nain and so this event is its sole claim to fame.

Luke reports that as Jesus was just arriving on the outskirts of Nain, he came upon a kind of funeral procession. We don't know any details about the deceased — name, age, cause of death — except his survivors. He was his mother's only son, and now she was a widow.

That brief detail is enough to tell us a great deal. It tells us that this woman had already known grief and loss in her life. It tells us that, within that ancient context, she was now in a desperate situation. The Bible's concern for widows (e.g., Deuteronomy 14:28-29, 26:13; James 1:27) and their frequent pairing with orphans (e.g., Deuteronomy 16:11; Job 22:9; Psalm 68:5; Lamentations 5:3) speak to the condition of a widow. She had no husband to support her. Absent an adult son; therefore, she was likely to become destitute (cf. Mark 12:41-44; 1 Timothy 5:3-4).

This weeping woman in the funeral process outside of Nain, therefore, was utterly bereft: emotionally crushed by the loss of loved ones, as well as financially in danger with a most uncertain future.

Luke reports that Jesus "had compassion" for the grieving widow is a significant statement. The underlying Greek word occurs just twelve times in the New Testament, and it is always accompanied by action. This is no empty sentiment, not pity that is all heart but no hands. This compassion results in practical assistance. Furthermore, we note that, in eight of those twelve occurrences, the word is applied to Jesus. In three of the remaining four instances, it is a word used by Jesus in order to describe a character in one of his parables — the forgiving master (Matthew 18:27), the good Samaritan (Luke 10:33), and the prodigal's father (Luke 15:20). The last remaining occurrence is when the father of a troubled son asks Jesus to have compassion on him (Mark 9:22), which he does.

After encouraging the poor woman not to weep (which we will discuss more below), Jesus stepped forward and touched the stand on which the coffin was evidently being carried. That stopped the procession, which suggests a terribly awkward moment.

In our day, we are accustomed to all traffic stopping for a funeral procession so that the sad parade can travel uninterrupted to the graveside. Can you imagine a car deliberately swerving in front of the hearse to bring the procession to a halt? Or as the pall bearers carry the coffin down the aisle of the church, can we imagine a person coming in and blocking their path?

Jesus stopped the funeral procession, which is its own sort of beautiful picture. Then he spoke to the corpse: "Young man, I say to you, rise!" It is a moment reminiscent of at least two other episodes in Jesus' ministry (Mark 5:41; John 11:43). And the scene brings to mind the truths elegantly expressed by Charles Wesley: "He speaks, and listening to his voice, new life the dead receive; the mournful, broken hearts rejoice, the humble poor believe."

The dead young man came back to life. The spectators, predictably, responded with mixed emotions. They were frightened and awed, and they were also filled with wonder and praise. And, as you might expect, the word about Jesus spread quickly.

Application

We have observed stories from two of our three lections that bear a striking resemblance to one another. The resuscitation of one young man by Elijah in 1 Kings and the raising of another young man by Jesus in Luke are closely connected in several obvious ways. But the important similarities go beyond the mere details of plot.

Perhaps you have known some individuals along the way who remind you very much of their parents. You know that the resemblance can take two forms. On the one hand, there is the simple matter of physical resemblance: same eyes or frame, same hair color or voice.

Beyond that superficial similarity, however, there are deeper matters: traits of style and personality that make others say, "You certainly are your father's son" or some such. It's one thing for a girl to have her mother's nose; it's quite another for her to have her mother's spirit.

Herein lays the real issue for the miracles that fill our three lections this week. The raising of two widows' sons is only the superficial resemblance. But see also the providential care of God for Elijah by way of the ravens and a brook. Then, when that provision seems to give way, it leads to the generosity of God sustaining three people — Elijah, the widow, and her son — instead of just the one. Finally, there is the testimony of the apostle Paul in the excerpt from Galatians: the story of the man who was completely turned around by Jesus Christ, transformed from persecutor of the church to its chief evangelist.

Beneath the surface, then, we see these two magnificent characteristics of God's work. First, he sees the needs of people and intervenes to bless. Second, he is capable of not just increasing what is good or decreasing what is bad; but, rather, he can completely turn around any circumstance, taking what is an extreme bad and turning it into an extreme good. From want to abundance, from persecutor to evangelist, from death to life: He is the God of total conversions. This is his distinguishing feature.

An Alternative Application

Luke 7:11-17. "Such a Thing to Say." Coming from anyone but Jesus, the words would seem embarrassingly inappropriate. Who says to a grieving woman, on the occasion of her son's funeral, "Do not weep"? On the contrary, we think ourselves good pastors and good friends when we give opportunity and permission for a mourning person to cry. Yet this is our Lord's unthinkable greeting to a bereaved mother: "Do not weep."

Of course, this is not the stunting and unhealthy command of an adult who is fed up with his child's tears. This is not an irritated, "Stop your crying!" But rather this is the comforting word from the one who knows that there will soon be no reason to cry.

Still, it's interesting that Jesus bothers to say it. After all, couldn't he simply have raised the young man to life while his mother wept? Surely she would have stopped weeping then!

Yet that's not the pattern. We recall that he told grieving Jairus not to fear (Luke 8:50) and the mourners outside Jairus' house not to weep (8:52) even before he had raised the little girl to life. We remember that the angels were surprised by Mary's weeping outside the empty tomb (John 20:13), even though she did not yet know that Jesus had been raised.

Coming from anyone but Jesus, the words would seem embarrassingly inappropriate. Of course, coming from anyone but Jesus, a lot of things he said would be an embarrassment of one sort or another. His audacity to forgive (Mark 2:1-7), his claim to fulfill prophecy (Luke 4:16-21), and his identification with God (John 14:6-9) are all startling examples. He presumed to speak authoritatively to demons (Luke 4:33-35) and to nature (Matthew 8:26), and he claimed for himself an apocalyptic exaltation and authority (Matthew 26:64; Mark 13:26; John 1:51).

In the end, you see, the final issue is not what is said, but who is saying it. Coming from anyone else, his words would be lunacy. Coming from him, they are truth, wisdom, beauty, and power. Our response, therefore, is not, "Such a thing to say!" but "Such a man who says it!" And so we don't resist but rejoice when we hear him tell us not to weep, not to worry, and not to fear.

Preaching to the choir

We preachers are sometimes confused about our audience.

Sometimes we preach like frustrated columnists, as though our high calling is to change public opinion about current events. Or we preach as though we had the president or governor or congress in our congregation, proclaiming what we believe they need to hear, even though they are not there.

One preacher may have such a heart for lost souls of Generation X that she preaches for them, forgetting that her actual congregation is made up mostly of members over fifty years old who have been in church their whole lives. While another preacher may be so recently steeped in the world of seminarians that he preaches to a congregation bewildered by his frequent and familiar references to the Deuteronomist, the Q document, Athanasius, and the eschaton.

The most famous example of a preacher being confused about his audience, of course, is the idiomatic practice of "preaching to the choir." This is an easy thing to do. We preach what the people who are not in attendance need to hear, leaving the faithful to sit and listen to what they already know and live.

But this Sunday may be just the occasion to preach to the choir. This week's lections may feature precisely the truths that the choir needs to hear.

1 Kings 21:1-10 (11-14) 15-21a

The conventional wisdom in real estate is that the three most important factors for any piece of property are location, location, and location. That old saw proves to be unhappily true for poor Naboth. The Old Testament writer introduces us to him with this concise summary: "Naboth the Jezreelite had a vineyard in Jezreel, beside the palace of King Ahab of Samaria."

Naboth's location is marked in terms of two coordinates: "in Jezreel" and "beside the palace of King Ahab." Since he is identified as a Jezreelite, the first coordinate seems appropriate. Naboth is where he belongs. He is at home. We discover later, his vineyard is family land — his "ancestral inheritance."

One might naturally suppose that living in the king's neighborhood would be advantageous. Is there any property in the land more valuable? More secure?

On the other hand, many of us have experienced to one degree or another, the pain and difficulty that comes from having a bad neighbor. And if the bad neighbor is also king, the pain and difficulty is magnified that much more!

Naboth's neighbor, King Ahab, wants to obtain Naboth's land. Apparently it was a nice piece of property, and being just outside Ahab's door and window, the king no doubt saw it every day.

It is the things right under our noses that we are most likely to covet. Not that I don't crave things that are far off; but the good things right next door are the ones I see constantly, and so they are most likely to become an obsession. Perhaps that's why the commandment specifies "anything that belongs to your neighbor" (Exodus 20:17).

Having been denied the opportunity to purchase Naboth's property, Ahab goes home unhappy. Jezebel detects that Ahab is glum, and she inquires about the cause. Being a no-nonsense person, Jezebel is not one to wallow. If something is not to her liking, she will take action to correct it, like here, in the case of Naboth's vineyard.

While Ahab had broken the tenth commandment by coveting what belonged to his neighbor, Jezebel climbed up the list a notch, arranging for false witnesses against that neighbor (see Exodus 20:16; also Proverbs 3:29). And, in almost no time, Jezebel has solved the problem — eliminated it, really — and Ahab is free to take possession of the vineyard.

That's where Elijah finds him.

It is a poignant business for the man of God to find you at the very scene of the crime. Nathan famously confronted David, but not as he was in bed with Bathsheba. This prophet-king confrontation is more reminiscent of the condemnation of Jeroboam at the site of his newly constructed altar (1 Kings 13:1-6).

At first blush, Ahab's greeting to Elijah sounds just like good banter. We discover that a constant tension exists between these two men, with their different allegiances, and so the angry salutation fits the hostile relationship.

This king-and-prophet combo reminds me a bit of Herod and John the Baptist in the New Testament. The king is mixed: equal parts disapproval of the prophet and fear of the prophet. He is antagonistic to the man and his message, and yet reluctant to exercise his sovereignty against the man of God. The wife of the king in each case, however, has no such compunctions.

The way that Ahab addresses Elijah is more than just repartee, however. It is symptomatic and revealing. For what terrible thing does it say about Ahab that he regards the prophet — the courier from God — as his enemy? Call him "my critic," "my challenger," or "my nagging conscience." But "my enemy"? What a terrible, tragic thing to conclude: that the one who bears no weapon other than God's word is your enemy.

Galatians 2:15-21

I live on the south side of a little town in Wisconsin called Whitewater. I have a number of friends who live on the north side of town. I suppose that it would be accurate for me to say to them, "I live closer to Miami than you," but somehow I don't think that they would envy me my shorter walk to the beach.

It is true that I am closer to Miami. It is also true, however, that my friends on the north side of town and I are both very far away. Indeed, in the big scheme of things, we are almost equally far away. None of us is going to put on our swimsuits and sandals and walk to the beach from here. Both of us — north side of town and south — will have to drive or fly in order to get there.

In a high school science class, I once learned about "significant numbers." A tenth of a mile is a significant number when measuring how far it is from my house to my church. But a tenth of a mile is no longer a significant number when measuring how far it is from the earth to the sun, or from one galaxy to another.

Technically, I am closer to Palm Beach than my friends on the north side of town. But I am not significantly closer.

So, too, with the Jews and the Gentiles in this matter of salvation.

As the chosen people of God — recipients of his law and his covenants — the Jews were arguably closer to God than the "Gentile sinners." And yet the advantage was not significant, for the Jews and the Gentiles alike need the same long-distance transport in order to be saved. The Jews' proximity is not such that they are somehow within "walking distance" from God. They must be "justified... through faith in Jesus Christ," just like the "Gentile sinners."

Meanwhile, the role of Christ's death in our salvation is at issue here in an interesting way.

Some Christians tend to ignore Christ's death altogether, thinking that any soteriology that requires his death is a bit primitive. They emphasize, instead, the example of his life. Others have sought to make Christ's death relevant for something other than salvation (an example of human injustice, of unjust suffering, of heroic martyrdom, and the like). Meanwhile, most Christians through the ages have understood that Christ's death was salvific, though the specific paradigms have been somewhat varied.

In this passage, meanwhile, Paul presents us with a truth about Christ's suffering and death that is seldom affirmed in American Christendom. Paul claims that he had been "crucified with Christ" (v. 19).

We are accustomed to the gospel that says he died for us. We may not be so conversant, however, in the gospel that says we died with him. My picture of the cross on Good Friday shows him, not me. But this passage from Galatians may make this Sunday a good opportunity to expand my picture — and my congregation's picture, as well.

The great resulting truth to affirm, of course, is that "it is no longer I who live, but it is Christ who lives in me" (v. 20). Here is a part of the gospel that seems to have been left out of the diet of so many of our churches. We are naturally I-centered, and we have let the gospel and the Christian life become I-centered as well. Perhaps a great many matters of morality, personal priorities, and sense of purpose would be clarified if we awakened to the notion that it is no longer I who live, but Christ who lives in me.

Finally, I am conscious that Paul's final line in this week's passage is a provocative one that so many church folks need to hear and understand.

In my years of local church ministry, I have so often encountered a "good Christian" mentality that, in its own subtle way, exalts the law over the grace of God. These are the folks (and I expect you've met them too) who earnestly believe that their eternal reward in heaven is secured by the good life they've lived. Or they make that same affirmation on behalf of a friend and loved one who has recently died. "Well, you know, Bill wasn't a very religious person, but he was about the nicest person you'd ever care to meet."

The mentality does not wrestle with the rigors and specifics of God's whole law. Rather, some homespun revision of the law has been developed to identify what is a "good person," and it is that goodness — rather than God's goodness — that guarantees one's salvation. It's a common heresy, and Paul follows it through to its logical and startling conclusion: "then Christ died for nothing."

Luke 7:36—8:3

One of the hallmarks of Luke's gospel is the prominence of women in the story. From Mary and Elizabeth at the beginning of the gospel to the women who first bear witness to the resurrection at the end, women play a large role in Luke's account of Jesus. And this week's gospel lection is yet another example of that pattern.

In the main story of the selected passage, it is a woman who emerges as the unexpected paragon. We'll return to her story in a moment. Then, as a bookend to the passage, we meet several other exemplary women. Luke mentions "the twelve" — a kind of impersonal reference to the disciples — and then he goes on to call by name some women who were also part of Jesus' faithful contingent. There is Mary Magdalene, whom we know well. There is also Joanna and Susanna, plus "many others." These women are not merely tagging along with the men. Decidedly not. Rather, these women, it seems, are the ones whose significant generosity and resources provide for the needs of the entire group.

The real star of this passage, however, is the anonymous woman who anointed Jesus while he was in the home of Simon the Pharisee.

While Luke does not tell us her name, he does tell us one significant thing about her: She "was a sinner." No details, just a label, and the rest is left to our imaginations.

In the context of that culture, this unnamed woman and the named Pharisee were at opposite ends of the spectrum. Sinner and Pharisee. Righteous and unrighteous, with Jesus in between. The tableau is a powerful image as the two opposite characters are, for a moment, on either side of the Lord. The woman is prostrate, weeping at Jesus' feet. Simon is likely more elevated, probably face-to-face with Jesus as they reclined to eat. Yet, as in Jesus' parable (Luke 18:9-14), it is the humble and undeserving character who is truly right with God in the end.

Simon assumes that Jesus' status as a true prophet is at stake in this episode. After all, if he truly were a prophet, Simon reasons, he would know the kind of person with whom he was dealing.

Of course, Jesus did know. He knew the kind of woman who was touching and anointing him, and he also knew the kind of man who was hosting him. The woman's life and heart were not the only ones transparent to Jesus there at that table.

Jesus turns the tables on the scene and on Simon. Simon thinks that the issue is who is more sinful and by that measure he comes out on top. But Jesus recasts the issue, asking who is more loving, and on that scale Simon is found wanting.

The paradigm shift is typical. It resonates with the God who "does not see as mortals see; they look on the outward appearance, but the Lord looks on the heart" (1 Samuel 16:7). It is reminiscent of the God who surprises the self-satisfied religious people of the eighth century BC (Isaiah 1:11-17; Amos 5:21-24). It is consistent with the teacher who exalted the Samaritan over the priest and the Levite (Luke 10:30-37), the tax collector over the Pharisee (Luke 18:9-14), and the one lost sheep above the 99 in the fold (Luke 15:4-7).

Simon reckoned that if Jesus knew who this woman was, he wouldn't let her touch him, but Simon had it backward. When Jesus is in our midst, the question is not whether he recognizes us; the real issue is whether we recognize him. That was a part of his point to the woman at the well (John 4:10), and that was certainly at the heart of the matter when he prayed for the forgiveness of his tormentors (Luke 23:34).

It is at this point that a surprising hero emerges from the scene. While conventional wisdom of that day would have put the white hat on the Pharisee and the black hat on the sinful woman, she is the one who comes out on top. For she seems really to recognize Jesus and to honor him appropriately, while Simon had missed it. The Lord himself was in Simon's home, but Simon's inadequate response shows that he didn't recognize the Lord.

Finally, it may be worth noting that the woman offers a picture of love that we may easily lose sight of. Because our conventional picture of Jesus is as the one who touches us, who heals us, who blesses us, we may have an underdeveloped picture of us touching him, of us blessing or caring for him. It is a picture implicit in Jesus' teaching about the sheep and the goats (Matthew 25:31-46). It is a picture tenderly portrayed in Mel Gibson's *The Passion of the Christ* in the characters of Mary, Simon, and Veronica along the Via Dolorosa. It is an image captured marvelously in Christina Rossetti's Christmas song, "In the Bleak Midwinter" — "Angels and archangels may have gathered there, / Cherubim and seraphim thronged the air; / But His mother only, in her maiden bliss, / Worshipped the beloved with a kiss." And it is a picture offered us by this woman who, by what she did for Jesus, "has shown great love."

Application

Let us say that "the choir" represents a certain sort of people. They are faithful and reliable. They attend and they assist. You can count on them to be there, doing their part, week in and week out. They are the quintessential good church folks.

So when you're preaching to the choir, what should you preach? What does the choir — the good church folks — need to hear? Well, for starters, it is worth pointing out that the choir probably needs to hear the same things as the preachers. When we talk to them, we are talking also to ourselves. They and we may need to hear two of the passages that we are assigned this week.

First, those of us who are so habitually and commendably law-abiding need to hear again that we are not justified by the law. In a manifestly bad world, it's easy to feel satisfied with our goodness. So we benefit from Paul's reminder that we are saved by God's goodness, not our own.

Then there is the other hazard of our human goodness. Not only that we may "nullify the grace of God" by some self-reliance, but also that we may be shallow in our love. This was the surprising fault of Simon.

Our natural ally in the gospel lection may be Simon the Pharisee. We are not much attracted to him, and we have inherited a very negative view of Pharisees. But the hard fact remains that he is the one most like "the choir." He is faithful, good, and religious. But he had not been forgiven much. Or at least he didn't recognize that he had. That is the natural plight of the good person, and so it may be our liability too.

Preaching to the choir, therefore, may include the sober reminder that "the one to whom little is forgiven, loves little."

An Alternative Application

Luke 7:36—8:3. "The Trouble with Jesus' Hosts." What an inconvenient place to have to find Jesus.

This woman, "who was a sinner," was apparently eager to find Jesus. She wanted, it seems, to express to him her love, her gratitude, perhaps even her worship. We don't know the details of her story leading up to this moment. Perhaps they would be unnecessarily salacious. It is sufficient to know that Luke the narrator and Simon the Pharisee readily identify her as "a sinner."

We gather from the assorted accounts found in the four gospels that multitudes of people sought out Jesus. We see crowds pressing in on him personally, crowding the house where he stays, chasing the boat that he rides. And so we imagine the excitement certain individuals must have felt when they learned that Jesus was nearby.

This woman was one of those individuals. She learned that Jesus was in the neighborhood. She wanted to go to him. But then came the unhappy specifics of the situation: She "learned that he was eating in the Pharisee's house."

What kind of courage did it take for her to go there? To presume into the private space of Simon's home? To pass through the door into a place where she was neither one of the family members who belonged there nor one of the guests invited to be there? To go in and be noticed — pointed at, whispered about? To go where she knew she would meet with disapproval, condemnation, and perhaps even outright rejection?

What kind of courage does it take for a sinner to find Jesus among the religious and righteous crowd? More courage, I suspect, than many other folks of that day had. More courage than many folks have today, as well: people who are understandably too afraid, too ashamed, and too guilty to come find Jesus in our churches. What an inconvenient place to have to find Jesus.

Searching for truth in all the wrong places

Gods and goddesses are plentiful these days, luring adherents into strange expressions of faith. Lam Sai-wing is a very up-scale jewelry salesman, who boasts the world's most expensive bathroom. It cost him $4.9 million to appoint his toilet facility with solid gold furnishings, jewels on the ceiling and two 24-carat commodes as the center of attraction. This extravagance is Lam's way of giving testimony to his fortune, which he claims hit the stratosphere after he worshiped the goddess of mercy, Kuan Yin, at one of her temples on the Kowloon Peninsula in China. Today, he has a pure gold, nine-foot statue of the goddess on his property. (By the way, patrons to Lam's store may use the luxurious facility, but only if they purchase at least $138 US of merchandise.)

Where in the world does one go to find truth? Can it be discovered just about anywhere? Are the rewards of truth finding worth the effort? Just what are those rewards? The Christian church throughout the centuries has charted a course for finding the truth and celebrating the reward, which is more than the pot of gold at the end of the rainbow. The course is mapped out in the Bible, especially the New Testament, where the Holy Spirit leads believers to find the treasure of life in relationship to Jesus. The journey is certainly an adventure, sometimes fraught with dangers, especially from those who value other objects they consider the real treasure. The journey requires faith as the passport to reach the destination of true life with the true God.

1 Kings 19:1-4 (5-7) 8-15a

It was a bad day for Baal. He not only lost the contest on Mount Carmel but also his priesthood (1 Kings 18:17-40). When Jezebel got word of this, she vowed to eliminate Elijah. Elijah fled, like so many of God's people do when their adversaries challenge them. Adam took off in the garden after having a fruit snack. Moses left Egypt after dispatching an Egyptian for beating up a Hebrew. David hid in the cave of Adullam when Saul was in a fury. Jonah headed west instead of traveling east to Nineveh as instructed. Peter went private instead of going public when it came to his faith in the temple courtyard.

Like all these flight-fancy followers of God, Elijah is found by the Hound of Heaven and strengthened for the task at hand. God does not give up on his people, especially when he has plans for them. It is most interesting to see how God manifests himself to Elijah. There is the display of wind, earthquake, and fire that accompanies the Holy One, the almighty of heaven and earth. Nature herself pays tribute to the Lord with awesome spectacles for an awe-inspiring God. Yet, notice that God is not pleased to disclose himself to Elijah in these phenomena. God could have, of course, but God had a higher purpose in mind than simply to stun Elijah with his magnificence. Because God wanted more than wonder and worship, God selected to wait until he could simply speak with Elijah. Communication in relationship is what God sought. For Elijah to understand what was on the mind of God, words were necessary, not just spectacular displays of power, however they might "blow you over," "shake you to the bone," or "bake your biscuit."

It is in "a still small voice" that God reveals his purpose for Elijah. It would be advisable to extend the pericope beyond verse 15a to verse 19a. The reason for this is fourfold. First, the authority of God over the political rulers is reaffirmed, because Elijah will be anointing the successors not only for Israel, but also for Syria. Second, God assures Elijah that his work will continue in his successor, Elisha, whom he is also to anoint. Third, God jolts Elijah out of his self-pity by informing him that he is not the only true believer left; there will be 7,000 other faithful followers of Yahweh! This is the powerful stuff of purpose and promise that catapults Elijah out of his cave of hiding to re-enter the dangers of real life where the likes of Jezebel await him. Verses 15b to 18 provide the meat upon which Elijah could chew to find strength and courage to get on with his duties as prophet of God. Fourth, Elijah demonstrates his faith in God's word by leaving the cave. "So he departed from there" (1 Kings 19:19a).

Galatians 3:23-29

Gentiles who are *in Christ* (3:26) are legitimate heirs of the promise given to Abraham and reaffirmed through his progeny (see Galatians 3:6-9). The Law, as custodian, was more than a code of conduct to identify God's people among the nations. The Law was *Torah*; it was life with wholeness, because it was lived *coram Deo*. The Law was given by God with love, so that the people would know how to express their thankfulness to God for their deliverance from Egypt. It points to God as the source of salvation, and so prefigures Christ, who would come to fulfill the Law (Matthew 5:17). He said of himself, "I am... the life" (John 11:25; also John 14:6). The gospel writer John affirms this in his opening sentences: "In him was life" (John 1:4). It is as if Jesus were saying, "Follow me and live *coram Deo*. Believe in me and live *coram Deo*, for you are seeing the Father in me. As I now live in you by faith, you will know life." The custodian, the law, now turns the keys of the kingdom over to the master of the house, Jesus.

Faith is referred to five times in these few verses of pericope. Another word for faith is trust. Paul is defining faith by its object, Jesus. Faith means to trust Jesus, to put one's entire stock in what he accomplished in his ministry and passion and resurrection for us. Elsewhere Paul explains that faith is a gift from God that receives the grace of God that saves the sinner (Ephesians 2:8-10). Just as Abraham believed God when he made promises — and this was reckoned to him as his righteousness — so too are Christians today like Abraham, as they put their trust in Jesus' accomplishments on their behalf.

Throughout the scripture, faith is understood as a dynamic relationship between God and man that has the qualities of assent, affection, and action. First, there are truths that can be attested to when one says, "I have faith in Jesus." For example, he is the Son of God, the promised Messiah, the crucified Savior of the world who rose from the dead. Doctrine explores these truths and seeks to express them coherently and consistently. The three ecumenical creeds summarize the body of truth to which Christians give their assent, in contrast to other faith systems such as Buddhism, Islam, Baha'i, Shintoism, and Taoism.

Second, the relationship between Jesus and the follower is to be a living one, filled with love. Jesus asked Peter, "Do you love me?" To confess belief in Jesus involves not only the mind, but also the heart. Our affection is directed to Jesus who, as the hymn describes, is the "lover of my soul." The mystics of the Christian tradition have expressed this dynamic throughout the centuries (for example, Catherine of Siena, Meister Eckhart, and John of the Cross).

Third, faith invites and demands action. The believer does not just think the truth, nor just feel a joyous bonding with the truth-giver; the believer also follows the way of the truth in a multitude of daily behaviors that give muscle to the confessions of one's mind and the affections of one's heart. There are disciplines that demonstrate one's allegiance; for example, tithing, prayer, fasting, chastity, and service.

Woven throughout these three aspects of faith is the Pauline thread that ties one to Jesus Christ as the only worthy object of faith. Jesus validates our faith as a saving grace and guarantees our inheritance of all the promises of God, which find their yes in him (2 Corinthians 1:20), promises such as the forgiveness of sins, deliverance from death and the devil, and life everlasting. How can gold compare with these treasures?

If you like bacon, you may not appreciate this pericope. But, if you were a faithful Jew, following the tradition of the elders and observing all the kosher regulations, you would be quite taken by the events that transpired on the far side of the Sea of Galilee, with the exception of some discomfort that Jesus was going out of his way to minister to Gentiles. Luke has no discomfort in placing this story in a section of his gospel account that emphasizes Jesus' ministry in Galilee and to the Jews. It complements his inclusion of the healing of the centurion's slave, together with it anticipating the gospel going out to all the world, especially through the ministry of Paul, who later traveled through this same area on his way to Arabia and back (Galatians 1:17).

Culturally for a Jew, there was no loss literally to demonize pigs and drive them into the sea. For any Jew this would make perfect sense. What would strike the Jew's attention, however, would be the compassion Jesus showed for the man possessed by a demon (demons, for his name was Legion). The Messiah was concerned with the welfare of all God's human creatures, Jew and *goyim* alike. Plus, the Gentile man, once released from the demon's grip, proclaimed the praise of Jesus "throughout the whole city" (8:39). This nameless man was the first Gentile evangelical, according to Luke. He responded to the magnanimous gift of release from bondage that Jesus had given him. He would put to shame Jesus' own countrymen, who should have been even more eager to proclaim that the Messiah had indeed come to God's people, but who instead called for his death.

Notice how the demon recognized Jesus and asked not to be tormented by him (8:28), for Jesus had commanded the demon to come out of the man. To come out of the shadows of the man's skin and broken psyche, the demon would have to stand (crawl, cower, kneel, slink) in the presence of Jesus, the Light of the world (to borrow from John 1:4 and 8:12). This would indeed be torment for a creature of the dark. This is reminiscent of C.S. Lewis' *The Great Divorce*, wherein the travelers from hell on excursion to heaven experience the pleasures of the redeemed as pain, e.g., the tender grass underfoot was hard as diamonds and felt like walking over "wrinkled rock"; space was enormous, "which made the solar system itself seem an indoor affair," and filled with a strange mixture of freedom and danger; the travelers upon disembarking the omnibus were revealed as phantoms: "Now that they were in the light, they were transparent... man-shaped stains on the brightness of that air" — "the light, like solid blocks... thundering upon [exposed heads]." It was a bad day for demons.

For a resident of Gergesa (modern Kursi, a village on the shore; or Gadara, six miles southeast of the lake; or Gerasa, located 33 miles southeast; there is some debate as to which area is being referred to), questions would be raised about the wholesale loss of an entire herd of pigs, which could feed the people for many months. Perhaps it would become like a Gentile parable, raising the question of treasure (Matthew 13:45-46) and where the heart is (Luke 12:32-34), what in the end is of more infinite worth (Matthew 6:33) and what one should really be concerned about (Luke 12:4-5). In other contexts, Jesus would talk about the worth of a sparrow and the lily of the field to lift up the value of an individual person. Could it be that Jesus would not even think twice about sacrificing an entire herd of pigs in order to save one soul? Again, we see what a high value God places on any human who is in need and who needs to experience the wonder of God's love through Jesus!

Still, the people rejected him out of fear and asked him to leave their country (8:34-39). The reception of the Son of God does not seem to go any better outside Jerusalem than inside, with those who should be glad to be included in the salvation of the world than with those who should have recognized the salvation of the world when it arrived!

Application

In our increasingly secularized world, many Christians will find it harder to witness of their faith. It will feel like foreign territory for them to "go public," let alone say something that challenges the status quo of cultural expectations or allowances. In most of our churches it is probably more true that we are not in flight for fear of our lives, like Elijah, as a consequence of our taking a prophetic stance on a public issue. We are just quiet, hoping no one will really take note of us, unless they want to "join the church," of course.

The *still small voice* speaks to us, "What on earth are you doing for heaven's sake?" What *are* we doing in all the locations where the people of God find themselves? We may be fearful to speak a countercultural word. We may be at a loss as what to say exactly. We may be embarrassed that we have remained in our caves for so long. And, so, the *still small voice* speaks to us also, and we need to hear its thunder!

Take heart. God has not given up on us. Just like he pursued Elijah, God will dog us faithfully until we become faithful to the mission that he has planned for us. Twice God graciously encouraged Elijah to eat what was set before him. What God provided was sufficient and also enduring. Elijah "went in the strength of that food forty days and forty nights" (19:8). So can we, when we feast upon the word of God (both in print and in the bread and wine). It will not be easy to speak and embody God's word in the world today, but we are called to do so nonetheless. Paul himself experienced this with his thorn in the flesh (2 Corinthians 12:7-10). With him, we too can realize the sufficiency of God's grace to bring us through any challenging opportunity to witness to Jesus and carry on the tradition of the early disciples from that Pentecost day.

There will be obstacles that would thwart us from doing this, contemporary expressions of the law (in the Pauline sense) that would bind us from being free in Christ. Consider the "unholy trinity" of our culture: individualism, relativism, and pluralism, to which growing allegiance is given from every quarter. Individualism tempts us to put our trust in self as the final arbiter of truth and what is right. Relativism tempts us to affirm everyone's right to view the world from their own particular perch, authenticity and justification to be found therein. Pluralism tempts us to acknowledge many forms of equally valid realities, which may be contradictory to one another, but nonetheless seem to have some foothold on the terrain of truth. All three — fool's gold at best!

When we are baptized into Christ, we surrender the claims of the self (the Old Adam and the Old Eve) to the claim of God on our lives. We are called to perceive the world through the given revelation from God as the absolute standard to which all truth is subject, "having the eyes of your hearts enlightened" (Ephesians 1:18) by the gospel of Jesus. He alone is "the way, the truth, and the life" (John 14:6), at whose name "every knee should bow, in heaven and on earth and under the earth, and every tongue confess that Jesus Christ is Lord" (Philippians 2:10). Here is the true treasure of the church, which it has to share with the world, even if it seems at times like casting pearls before swine.

What do we make of demon possession these days? Ironically, in our post-modern culture, the door of credulity is open to consider such a phenomena. Not too many year's ago psychiatrists would have treated the poor Gerasene as a nudist necrophiliac, prescribing a change of scenery and some behavior modification along with a line of credit at JCPenney. The populace, however, has become more willing to accept the strange and unexplainable in terms of "other-worldliness," as dramatized, for example, on *The X-Files*, *Dark Angel*, *The Sixth Sense*, or *End of Days*.

More tangible and to the point of our everyday life is the possession of the human spirit by the consumer demon. A brief drive through any new subdivision with homes sporting three-door garages will give ample evidence of its powerful presence. Houses, having the floor space of two to three times a more common dwelling and costing five to ten times the building price of a Habitat home, more than dot the landscape. The loss of a herd of pigs is a signal sent to all who put their pride in possessions, their security in what they own (or what owns them!). Jesus reminds us, "One thing is needful" (Luke 10:42). Similar words were spoken to the rich young ruler who sought advice on going to heaven (Matthew 19:16-22). Amidst all that seeks our attention, that competes for our passions, that desires to seize our souls, we need to hear the call of Jesus, "Follow me." He has the power to cast out the demon of self-centeredness, which is self-destruction, and cast a new light on the path of life that gives one a thrilling new future of self-sac-rificing service to the glory of God.

The Gerasene returned home, "proclaiming throughout the whole city how much Jesus had done for him" (8:39). What an apt description for the life of the Christian, for the witness of a congregation — to be at home in our homes (familial and spiritual) sharing our experiences of life with Christ. The season of Pentecost is an opportunity for Christians and their congregations to take stock as to how they are doing just that.

Proper 8 / Pentecost 6 / Ordinary Time 13
2 Kings 2:1-2, 6-14
Galatians 5:1, 13-25
Luke 9:51-62
Timothy Cargal

A share of the Spirit

"Be careful what you wish for, because you just might get it." Now there is a bit of sage advice that has a multitude of applications. I thought of it recently when I was watching the video of the film *Bruce Almighty*. I am generally not a big fan of "Divine comedies," even though I am certain God must have a sense of humor (the evidence is just too overwhelming). But this one struck me as far better than most and worthy of some serious reflection.

The story is about Bruce Nolan (played by Jim Carrey), a local news reporter for a station in Buffalo, New York. He is denied a promotion to anchor that he was certain he deserved and was going to get. He launches into a tirade against God for the lousy job God is doing of taking care of his life and expresses complete confidence that he himself could do God's job better. The next day, he has a meeting with God (played by Morgan Freeman), who bestows the full range of divine powers upon Bruce and then leaves on vacation.

Once Bruce realizes these powers are real, he immediately begins to use them for his personal enjoyment, enrichment, and even revenge. But as the prayer requests of even just the residents of Buffalo begin to pile up, God meets with Bruce once again to point out that doing God's job requires attending to far more than just one's personal desires. Being God comes with not only power but responsibilities.

The film raises a number of religious and theological issues in generally sensitive and constructive ways. (For instance, when Bruce asks God during one of their check-in sessions how he can make someone love him without violating their free will, God responds, "Welcome to my world; let me know when you figure that one out.") But within the context of the scripture lessons for Proper 8, it is the question of why anyone would desire godlike powers and what one would do with such powers if they were available that comes most to the fore.

2 Kings 2:1-2, 6-14

You have to wonder if Elijah didn't feel a bit like the God character in *Bruce Almighty* as he traveled with Elisha toward his rendezvous with that "chariot of fire" on the other side of the Jordan River. Having parted the waters of the river by striking it with his cloak, Elijah had then essentially asked Elisha what wish he could fulfill for him as a parting gesture. Elisha knew what he wanted; "Please let me inherit a double share of your spirit." Elijah was taken aback. "You have asked a hard thing," he responded, "yet if you see me as I am being taken from you, it will be granted to you."

Well, Elisha did see Elijah taken up into God's presence, and he picked up Elijah's mantle that had fallen to the ground. He returned to the banks of the Jordan, struck the waters with the mantle, and in a test of what he hoped were his new abilities demanded, "Where is the Lord, the God of Elijah?" (not unlike Bruce parting "the red soup" in a diner). The waters parted just as they had before, and as the other prophets saw Elisha approaching they declared, "The spirit of Elijah rests on Elisha." Difficult as it may have seemed, Elisha's wish had been fulfilled.

But wait a minute. That was just too easy. Elisha only had to watch something most of us would gladly pay good money to see and to pick up a cloth shawl to have his wish fulfilled. How come Elijah had insisted he had "asked a hard thing"? Was it really the difficulty of fulfilling the wish that Elijah had considered "hard," or was the "hard" part something else altogether?

Let's go back and look at the details of this story again. We need to start by making sure we understand who all the characters in this story are. This story is not just about Elijah and Elisha; it is also about "the company of the prophets." This "company" was a training guild, a kind of informal school where one could learn to be a prophet much like one could apprentice to become an artisan or to learn a building trade. The Hebrew expression would more literally be translated as "the sons of the prophets," and the recognized prophet to whom they discipled themselves — in this case, Elijah — was their "father." Thus, upon seeing the chariot of fire Elisha exclaimed, "Father, father! The chariots of Israel and its horsemen!" he was calling out to Elijah, the leader of the prophetic guild in which he was apprenticed.

Now this familial language of "fathers" and "sons" within these prophetic associations plays a key role in this story. Listen again to Elisha's wish: "Please let me inherit a double share of your spirit." The "father" of the guild is about to be taken away, and so Elisha is now concerned about how the inheritance is to be divvied up among the "sons." Thus, his request for a "double share" is not about having *twice* as much of the Spirit as Elijah. Rather, what he is asking for is the "birthright," the legal principle in that society that the firstborn son was to receive two of the equally divided shares of the father's property as compared to his younger brothers' single share each.

It is not quite the whole truth to then characterize his wish, as some commentators have, as requesting only a fraction rather than twice as much of the spirit that Elijah had. What is more important than the relative quantities of spirit divided among the members of the prophetic guild is that along with the "double share" of the birthright comes the authority of being the next "father" over the "sons of the prophets." The "hard thing" to which Elijah referred in responding to Elisha's wish was not the difficulty of fulfilling the wish, but the responsibility Elisha would need to live it out. Sometimes the very things we wish for are not the answer but rather the source of our difficulties and struggles.

Galatians 5:1, 13-25

What is one to make of Paul's seemingly self-contradictory statement that those who have been "called to freedom" must nevertheless "through love become slaves to one another" (v. 13)? Aren't "freedom" and "slavery" by their very definitions mutually exclusive categories?

Inherent in Paul's understanding is the conviction that there is no such thing as absolute freedom. We tend to think of freedom as a kind of right, or indeed a power, that enables us to act in accord with our own desires. It is hardly incidental in this regard that so much of our ethical and philosophical discussions of freedom deal with the issue of "free will." Freedom is the opposite of constraint; it is being released from the control of another's will or needs. We think of freedom primarily in terms of "freedom from" something.

Paul does not discount this "freedom from" dimension; that is why he can say, "Christ has set us free" (v. 1). But Paul would remind us that there is a second dimension or aspect of our freedom, what we might call "freedom to" and that Paul speaks about in terms of how we "use [our] freedom" (v. 13). He draws the distinction between the different uses of freedom as to whether they are characterized by "self-indulgence" or "love" expressed as obligation toward others. So strong should our sense of obligation nevertheless remain in our exercise of freedom that Paul can describe the freedom to act with love as "becom[ing] slaves to one another." Freedom does not equate with antinomianism, freedom from the very notion of an external law or constraint itself. Freedom contains within itself the "freedom to" fulfill the wisdom of God's gracious instruction to humanity ("the whole law," v. 14) about how to live in community.

It is indeed possible for these two dimensions of freedom — "freedom from" external obligation and "freedom to" act for not only ourselves but others — to fall into conflict with each other. Those who see freedom as only a means to self-indulgence have confused it with "the desires of the flesh" (v. 16). To give yourself over to such desires in fact is an abdication of freedom because "the desires of the flesh" will "prevent you from doing what you want" because you will be enslaved to the "law" of the flesh rather than bound by the "whole law" of God in which "you are led by the Spirit" (v. 18).

Paul would argue that seeing freedom only in terms of "freedom from" obligation to anything other than one's self results in self-indulgence and a long list of vices (vv. 19-21). These attitudes and actions not only devour others in their attempt to satisfy themselves, but ultimately consume those who engage in them as well (v. 15). But those who properly conceive of freedom as not only "from" but also "to" others produce the virtues of the "fruit of the Spirit" (vv. 22-23).

Luke 9:51-62

The exasperation Jesus seems to feel toward his disciples in the gospel lesson is almost palpable. Within the span of these twelve verses, the evangelist reports that Jesus "rebuked" his own disciples and rebuffed the responses of three different would-be disciples. What might be missed by reading this passage in the isolation of the lectionary is that the evangelist has carefully placed each of these vignettes at the outset of a major transition in the narrative structure of the gospel. The reason for Jesus' apparent exasperation is that the first phase of his ministry has drawn to a close and still neither his inner circle nor those who might yet be drawn in to join his ministry seem to be able to conceive its ultimate purposes and costs.

The evangelist's comment in verse 51 about the approach of time when Jesus would be "taken up" and his consequent determination "to go to Jerusalem" is not made in passing. It is in Jerusalem that Jesus' ministry will find its culmination in his passion, resurrection, and ascension. This journey to Jerusalem will provide the structure for Luke's account down through 19:27, where the final Passion Week will commence with Jesus' "Triumphal Entry" into the city (19:28-46). All along the way, Jesus will continue to instruct his disciples.

In the first of these vignettes, Jesus and his entourage are denied hospitality by a Samaritan village precisely because they are on their way to Jerusalem. Clearly the root of this snub is the centuries-old feud between the Samaritans and the Jews regarding the proper site for sacrificial worship of the God of Israel (cf. John 4:19-26). For James and John this slight should be punished by calling "fire to come down from heaven [to] consume them" (v. 54). No doubt they believed this was the purpose of Jesus' journey to Jerusalem itself, to bring down the fiery judgment of God upon all God's perceived enemies. Jesus' rebuke is aimed not just at an egregious overreaction to an ethnically motivated slight, but at the notion his ministry is in the first instance about destroying rather than redeeming those who alienate themselves from God.

Bringing reconciliation rather than destruction to those who oppose you is costly business, as Jesus' responses to the would-be disciples make clear. It can mean foregoing even one's own legitimate needs in order to commit one's self to ministry for others (vv. 57-58). It places demands on our lives that at times conflict with the normal obligations of society, even from within our own families (vv. 59-60). It requires that we commit ourselves completely to the cause of God's reign of justice without looking back to what we may have left behind (vv. 61-62). All of these things Jesus had done as "he set his face to go to Jerusalem," and those who would truly follow him must do the same.

Application

The transformative moment of the film *Bruce Almighty* comes when Bruce finally recognizes that the only proper use of those divine powers is to meet the genuine needs of others rather than his own or even their personal desires. Foremost among those needs is for one to know the love that God has for us, to have someone in our lives who, as Bruce expresses it to God, will love and see us through God's eyes.

It is a moment that Paul himself could have scripted, for no sooner had he announced to the Galatians that "Christ has set us free" from bondage to our sin than he immediately warned us all "not [to] use [our] freedom as an opportunity for self-indulgence." Could such "self-indulgence" have been what motivated Elisha to strike the Jordan and to demand, "Where is the Lord, the God of Elijah?" Had he wanted the "double share" of Elijah's spirit in order to assume the "birthright" of leadership over the prophetic band or to indulge his own sense of self-importance at being able to conjure such miracles as Elijah had performed? Was he driven by compassion and love for his fellow "sons of the prophets," not wanting them left wandering and hopeless without a "father" to lead and instruct them? Or was he driven by "enmity, strife, jealousy, anger, quarrels, dissensions, factions, envy," lest some other of his once colleagues should rise up to be the new leader over him. Why do we seek Christ's freedom and God's blessings — to use those freedoms and blessings to love our neighbors as ourselves or to satisfy our own desires even if at the expense of others? "If you bite and devour one another," Paul warns, "take care that you are not consumed by one another."

Perhaps had Elisha really understood the "hard thing" that he had asked of Elijah — had he recognized that the "double share" of Elijah's spirit was to enable him to serve the prophets and the people as a "slave" rather than to lord power over them — perhaps then he would not have sought miraculous power to keep his own feet dry as the first proof that his wish had been fulfilled. It is our sinful nature that seeks to put our own desires ahead of all else. Indeed, when the God character in *Bruce Almighty* asks Bruce why he has not been dealing with that backlog of prayers, he confesses that there were some perceived injustices in his own life that he wanted to redress first. "By contrast," as Paul wrote, "the fruit of the Spirit is love, joy, peace, patience, kindness, generosity, faithfulness, gentleness, and self-control" (Galatians 5:22). These qualities of life are directed toward the needs of others. These attributes are the proof that "the spirit of Elijah rests upon" us.

We don't really need the ability to invoke miraculous power to deal with the mundane details or common problems we face in our daily lives. What we really need, like Bruce Nolan and those young men in ancient Israel's prophetic guild, is to be in relationships that sustain and nurture us. What we really need is the freedom to find ourselves in service to others. The good news is that it is not a "hard thing" for God to fulfill our longing for a "double share" of the Spirit that can produce the fruit of love, joy, peace, patience, kindness, generosity, faithfulness, gentleness, and self-control that enable us to understand, serve, and be in relationship with one another.

It is not a "hard thing" for God to give us a "double share of the spirit," yet it is as Elijah knew, and Elisha and Bruce Nolan came to understand, an important responsibility for all those who receive this gift. God gives us the Spirit not for our own benefit, but in order that we might benefit others as agents of divine grace. A tremendous responsibility, yes, but never a drudgery. May we all fulfill Paul's challenge: "If we live by the Spirit, let us also be guided by the Spirit."

Alternative Applications
Galatians 5:1, 13-25. This lectionary reading invites us to explore the meanings of freedom at not only the personal level but at the level of societies and nations as well. What does it mean for the United States and other democracies to "promote freedom" around the world? Are we just promoting "freedom from" the tyrannies of dictators and a "freedom to" fulfill our personal desires, or do we make it clear that there is no absolute freedom apart from a continuing obligation for others? If other societies see our notion of freedom as promoting lawlessness, have we ourselves forgotten the necessary correlation between rights and responsibilities that are essential to genuine freedom?

2 Kings 2:1-2, 6-14; Luke 9:51-62. There are several parallels between the Elijah and Elisha stories and particular details in the gospel lesson. Maybe James and John saw themselves as being in the same league with Elijah in their ability to call fire down from heaven, and maybe a desire for such ability initially motivated Elisha's wish for a "double share" of Elijah's spirit. Elisha's own call to follow Elijah had involved plows and a reluctant severing of family ties (cf. 1 Kings 19:19-21). In the end, however, both Elisha and Jesus' disciples came to recognize the responsibility for others that lies at the heart of God's call on our lives. In what ways might our own failings to recognize the implications of God's call be exasperating to God? What can we learn from the purposes and costs of Jesus' ministry that can help us to live out our own calls?

Proper 9 / Pentecost 7 / Ordinary Time 14
2 Kings 5:1-14
Galatians 6:(1-6) 7-16
Luke 10:1-11, 16-20
David Kalas

What must I do?

The Philippian jailor does not appear in any of our selected readings for this Sunday, but his fundamental question reverberates through our texts. "What must I do to be saved?" he asked Paul and Silas (Acts 16:30). It is an elemental question and our selected passages can help us elucidate the answer.

What do I need to do? This is the pragmatic question of the would-be home buyer sitting with the loan officer in the bank. It is the poignant question of the husband who wants to make things right with his wife. It is the desperate question that the patient asks the doctor in the wake of some positive test result, some unfavorable diagnosis.

"What must I do?"

As soon as we understand the high stakes involved in a given situation, this is the question we ask. As long as we are happily ignorant, we may skate along without any sense of urgency or responsibility. But once we recognize the scope and the gravity of the situation — whether financial, academic, relational, or medical — we want to know what must be done. What we must do.

That was Naaman's circumstance. He had a severe medical need, and he wanted to know what, if anything, could be done. As an accomplished man, a man of action, he stood ready and willing to do whatever he needed to do in order to find a cure. Still, he was unprepared for the answer that came down.

For the Christians in Galatia, the circumstance was not a medical one, but a spiritual one. It was the jailor's question. It was the central issue of what we must do in order to be saved — in order to be justified, to be reconciled, to be made right with God. They had heard the answer to that question from Paul. Since he was last there, however, they had heard divergent answers from other preachers. Plausible answers, it seemed to them. Paul wrote to remind them of the right answer — God's answer — to the great question.

In the end, we discover that the answer — to Naaman, to the Galatians, and to the people in our pews — is fundamentally the same. And that is the good news we are privileged to proclaim this week.

2 Kings 5:1-14

In just one verse, the biblical author tells us all we need to know about Naaman. He was a "commander," "a great man," "in high favor" with the Aramean king, a "mighty warrior." And he was a leper. Up until that final detail, his portrait was unblemished. But that one detail clouds every other thing.

Our modern idiom says, "If you have your health, you have everything." Well, Naaman didn't have his health. He had everything else, it seems. He was accomplished, high-ranking, famous, honored, strong, brave, and probably rather wealthy.

For all of his other achievements, however, here was an enemy that Naaman could not defeat. His skill, his strength, his strategy, and his sword were all useless in this personal battle. He was a man accustomed to winning — if not, after all, he would likely be either demoted or dead — and yet he had no strategy for victory here, no plan of attack for beating leprosy.

Then there came a ray of hope from a surprising source. A servant girl in Naaman's house — human loot from one of his many military campaigns — knew of a way that he could be healed. There was a prophet in Samaria who could cure Naaman of his leprosy.

As a military man, Naaman was probably accustomed to using intelligence gained from indigenous sources. Perhaps this young girl was on to something. And so, with a rich reward and a letter from the Aramean king in hand, Naaman set off for neighboring Israel to find healing.

Like the Magi of the Christmas story, Naaman went at first to the wrong address. Like them, he went first to the local king: a testament to our human reflex toward worldly power, importance, and resources. But the Israelite king was as unable to cure Naaman's leprosy as the Aramean king was. He took offense at the provocative assignment, until Elisha, the prophet, sent word that the incurable patient could be referred to him.

Naaman's entourage was forwarded to the home of the man of God. We do not know Elisha's address or neighborhood, but we might reasonably assume that it was a humble abode. There is certainly nothing in Elisha's biography, or in what we know more broadly about the prophets, to suggest that he would have been well-to-do. So we are presented with a picture of contrasts when Naaman arrives at Elisha's door.

Naaman frequented the palace in Aram, yet now he knocked on the door of a commoner in Israel. Naaman knew what it was to lay siege to great walled cities, yet now he came as a petitioner to the door of a mud house. Naaman carried with him a reward whose sum likely exceeded the entire net worth of Elisha and his household.

A military man might look at life in terms of rank. He gives orders to those under him. He takes orders from those above him. In Naaman's case, virtually everyone was below him; it may be that he took orders only from the king himself. As he stood outside Elisha's door, he may have been pondering their relative rank.

What piece is worth more: a bishop or a rook? Who ranks higher: the commander of the Aramean army, or an anonymous prophet from Israel? In the worldly realm, there's no question that Naaman wielded more power and authority. Perhaps in some other realm, however, this reputed man of God held sway.

Perhaps Naaman reconciled himself to an exercise of mutual respect — peers who salute simultaneously. He would honor and reward the prophet, in keeping with the great favor that the prophet would do him. And the prophet, meanwhile, would make an appropriate fuss over the visiting dignitary, bowing appreciatively before both the rank and the reward.

Instead, however, the prophet's servant appeared at the door to pass along to the commander an instruction: "Go, wash in the Jordan seven times, and your flesh shall be restored and you shall be clean."

Naaman was indignant. This was not at all the sort of treatment to which he was accustomed. Forget the mutual respect: nothing around him was of comparable rank. The flea-bitten prophet and his servant were not worthy of him. The muddy Jordan was not worthy of him. The undignified assignment was not worthy of him. He turned on his heel to leave when one of his own servants stopped and exhorted him.

That servant's exhortation becomes the turning point in the story and in Naaman's life. The substance of that exhortation is what you and I get to preach, as we will explore.

Galatians 6:(1-6) 7-16

Circumcision is not easy pulpit material for most of our churches.

In my situation, I am very fortunate to have a director of Christian education and a director of music who work hard to create a service that has thematic integrity. So the children's sermon and the choir's anthem are designed and selected each Sunday to echo the theme of the sermon. I would hate to tell either of them that I will be preaching about circumcision this Sunday.

Still, circumcision is central to the larger context of Paul's letter to the Galatians, and it is operative in our selected text, as well. Indeed, the word for circumcision (in several forms) appears five different times in our lection.

The Galatians had fallen under the influence of the so-called Judaizers, who preached an amended gospel. Paul was profoundly disappointed by how easily swayed the Galatian Christians were by such heresy. So he wrote a letter that is, even at its trough, emphatic, and rises to sarcasm, harsh critique, impatience, and anger.

For the Judaizers, the central issues were likely God's law and his everlasting covenant with the Old Testament people of Israel. Paul saw their conclusions, however, to be at odds with what he understood about faith, salvation, and life in the Spirit.

In Galatians, as elsewhere, we see that Paul operates with a spirit-versus-flesh paradigm. Now when a modern reader thinks about the works and the desires of the flesh, the associations are with standard fare physical appetites. But for Paul, even a dependence upon the circumcision of the old covenant is a way of catering to the flesh. And he believes that "what the flesh desires is opposed to the Spirit, and what the Spirit desires is opposed to the flesh; for these are opposed to each other" (Galatians 5:17).

Paul uses an agricultural metaphor to illustrate the choice we face as human beings. We may "sow to [our] own flesh" or "sow to the Spirit." As in the case of ordinary sowing, there is a predictable harvest. A farmer knows going in that by sowing corn he will harvest corn in the end. Likewise, we should be as matter-of-fact about our sowing in life. Sowing to the flesh, according to Paul, reaps corruption, while sowing to the Spirit reaps eternal life.

Paul's presentation is a refreshing one to folks who are weary of notions that eternal life is being tied to human merit or a capricious god. Paul offers an orderly picture: simple cause-and-effect.

The apostle also uses the natural image of sowing and reaping to offer an encouraging word. "Let us not grow weary in doing what is right," he writes, "for we will reap at harvest time, if we do not give up."

How often have I seen in my pastoral work — and how often have you seen in yours — people who have needed to hear precisely this word? I have sat with profoundly disappointed spouses, discouraged parents, sick patients, and from time to time I have looked in the mirror at a disheartened pastor and preacher. These folks are all weary in their own ways, and they are on the verge of giving up. But Paul says, "no" — an encouraging "no."

I have counseled people who have said that they could endure almost anything — for a time. And they could keep on going in their present circumstance if only they had some assurance of a light at the end of the tunnel.

Well, Paul offers just such an assurance: We reap what we sow. There is a natural order, and God is faithful. In the face of all the disappointment and despair, therefore, we cling to the predictability of the harvest — "if we do not give up."

Luke 10:1-11, 16-20

Ask your people this question: "Who are the people who are not in church?"

Some of them may think immediately of individual names. They think of regular attenders who happen to be out of town, or certain folks they haven't seen in a while, or perhaps some close friends or family members who simply won't come to church.

Other people in your congregation will not think of specific individuals, but rather entire groups: inactive members, high school kids, young adults, or perhaps the great general category of "the unchurched."

After you have given your people a moment to cogitate on the question for themselves, you can suggest what might be Jesus' answer: workers.

At first blush, it will seem to be a great insult, of course, to suggest that your church lacks workers. You and I know very well how hard working some of those folks in our pews are. And not just hard working in the other areas of their lives, but hard working in the church, as well, faithful, loyal, tireless workers.

Still, I think that is the gist of how Jesus would answer the question.

For the uncommitted, inactive, and unchurched not to be in church is no great surprise. They are simply playing their part. They are the harvest, and they are precisely where they ought to be: out in the mission field! And those folks are not lacking, according to Jesus. It's the workers. That's who is missing. Those are the people who aren't in church.

Or perhaps they are in church, but where they should be is out in the fields.

Jesus sends out his disciples to be workers in that field. And he doesn't airbrush, for them, the picture of their assignment: "I am sending you out like lambs into the midst of wolves."

In one moment, we are workers going into the fields. In the next moment, though, we are helpless lambs walking into a lair. What gives? Why the sudden — and significant — change in imagery? Because workers-in-the-harvest describes our mission. But lambs-among-wolves describes our experience.

That's an important distinction to make. For we are not called to victimhood; martyrdom is not our mission. Our purpose is not to risk our lives, but rather our purpose is to bring in the harvest. That mission may meet with hostility, and Jesus prepares his followers for that contingency.

Jesus' matter-of-fact instructions to his disciples are refreshing reading in our day. Culturally, we are so afraid of offending anyone that we think their offense is an indictment of our message. Not so. It is the foreseeable response of a certain percentage of the hearers. Remarkably, Jesus does not seem to fret overly much about those who reject the word. No apologies necessary; just shake off the dust against them.

When the disciples returned from their short-term mission, they were giddy with excitement. But their excitement may have been misplaced. It was not the salvation of souls that had them so thrilled; rather, it was the submissiveness of demons.

So it goes. So often there is a discrepancy between the objects of human fascination and the things that are truly important. The disciples had misunderstood what was truly exciting, truly thrilling. They were more taken by their relationship to the enemy than they were with their relationship with the Lord; more fascinated by power than by love and grace.

That preoccupation did not die with Peter, et al. In every generation, and still today, it is easy for the followers of Jesus to become distracted by the peripheral. But Jesus calls our attention back to this central-ity: "Rejoice that your names are written in heaven."

Application

"What must I do?"

Naaman must have asked that of the doctors back in Aram. And that question must have been near the forefront of his mind as he and his entourage traveled down to Samaria and to Elisha's house.

Naaman's servant knew the import of the question, for he appealed to its possible answers. "If the prophet had commanded you to do something difficult, would you not have done it?"

We know the answer. If the prophet had required of Naaman some great, heroic feat in order to achieve his own healing, this proud and accomplished man would have set right to work. We are reminded of Saul's sinister requirement that David present him with the foreskins of a hundred Philistines as the bride price to marry Saul's daughter. The ambitious David both achieved and doubled the requirement. Surely Naaman would have done the same.

Similarly, if the prophet had made Naaman's healing an expensive affair, wouldn't the commander have willingly paid the price? After all, his life was at stake. What wouldn't he have done? What wouldn't he have spent?

When the word came back, however, that what he had to do was a simple and humble thing, Naaman balked. There was no personal achievement involved in this business of bathing in the Jordan. No purchase. No pride.

The Galatians, too, were caught up in an exaggerated notion that they had to do something to earn their salvation by legalistic works. But Paul reminded them that there was no boasting in the flesh involved in salvation. No, only the simplicity and humility of the cross of Christ.

Still today, there are folks in our midst who, like Naaman and the Galatians, would find God's good news far more palatable if it involved some room for personal achievement. Perhaps they are proud, and so they want salvation to be a product of their own righteousness. Perhaps they are guilty, so they feel they need to earn it. Perhaps they are legalists, and they feel compelled to comply. Perhaps they are pragmatists, and they find a free gift incomprehensible.

Whatever the case, some servant or apostle or preacher needs, again and again, to come along and say, "If you had to do a difficult thing to be saved, you would do it. So why not a simple and humble thing? Believe on the Lord Jesus, and you will be saved."

An Alternative Application
2 Kings 5:1-14. "Out of the Mouths of Servants." It's hard to read the story of Naaman without being struck by the contrasts between the human beings involved. Three particular characters sit in positions of importance and power by human standards: the king of Aram, the king of Israel, and, to a slightly lesser degree, Naaman himself. Two monarchs and a high-ranking military commander represent considerable earthly power.

In the face of Naaman's physical malady, however, these three men are powerless. Naaman clearly needs to go to someone for help. The best that his lord can provide is a letter of introduction, and Israel's king is dumbfounded by the whole affair.

Meanwhile, we meet three other players — people who can't compare to the rank and influence of the first three. There is the little servant girl in Naaman's household. She is young, helpless, and something of a victim. Yet she — unlike the previous three characters — knows where to turn in the time of need.

Shortly after, we meet the Israelite prophet. He has no crown on his head or stripes on his sleeve. Yet he is clearly in touch with a power that dwarfs all of the kings' and commander's resources.

Then there is the unnamed servant of Naaman: The one who talks him out of his rage and into the river. He sees and reasons clearly when Naaman does not.

The two sovereigns and the soldier are basically powerless in this story. Instead, it is the three other individuals, comparatively insignificant by worldly standards, who are the agents of power. We are reminded by Paul that "God chose what is foolish in the world to shame the wise; God chose what is weak in the world to shame the strong; God chose what is low and despised in the world, things that are not, to reduce to nothing things that are, so that no one might boast in the presence of God" (1 Corinthians 1:27-29).

Living forward in the present

"I felt almost guilty thinking too much of heaven." That is what David Burton, a Southern Baptist turned Catholic told a writer for *Time* in 1997. Burton, brought up to think of eternal life as the ultimate reward for living a Christian life, was surprised to encounter some religious leaders in his new church who didn't want to talk about heaven. Believing that most of us just don't have the knack of living righteously without the "carrot" of eternal life dangled in front of us, Burton found himself saying about good works: "Let's do this so we can go to heaven." Almost at once, someone in his new surroundings would say, "No, no, no. Let's do it because we *should* do good."

Burton found himself thinking that heaven was "too much like an ace in the hole, that it was sort of like cheating" he said, to hold eternal life out as a motivator for holy living (*Time*, March 24, 1997, p. 72).

Odd as it may seem to us religious types, a lot of people today aren't much moved one way or the other by talk of an afterlife, no matter whether it's for judgment or reward. But we cannot go far, especially in the New Testament, without considering the power of eternal life in calling believers to righteous living in their present, earthbound circumstances.

The three pericopes for today offer a fine opportunity to talk with your people about eternal matters. Amos, though living in a time that had no firm concept of afterlife, nonetheless spoke words of damning judgment with final consequences. Paul, writing to the Colossians, praised them "for the hope laid up for [them] in heaven" (Colossians 1:5). And Jesus, with his story of the good Samaritan, provided a memorable answer to the question, "What must I do to inherit eternal life?" (Luke 10:25).

Amos 7:7-17

It is unfortunate that Amos is among those who are referred to as "minor" prophets in the Old Testament. Of course, they are "minor" only because their writings are shorter; not that their message is any less important. Amos, as his name suggests, bears the burden of God's people in his heart and proclaims on his lips God's word to them. It is a word of judgment that "all the sinners of my people shall die by the sword" (Amos 9:10). There is only a brief glimpse of restoration given at the very end of his prophecy. Although, it only takes a little light to dispel darkness, in Amos' world there is a lot of darkness to dispel.

Called from his peasant upbringing as a herdsman and dresser of sycamore trees, Amos takes on the powers of the nations and the king of Israel. Coming from Tekoa, six miles southeast of Bethlehem, Amos locates his pulpit in Bethel, the religious center of the northern kingdom. The time is mid-eighth century BC during the reign of Jeroboam II (c. 786-746), a generation before Isaiah arises as prophet in the southern kingdom. Amos utters God's judgment against the surrounding nations (chs. 1-2) and then specifically against Israel (chs. 3-6). He rails against apostasy, greed, immorality, and oppression. His herald cry is: "Let justice roll down like waters, and righteousness like an ever-flowing stream" (Amos 5:24).

The plumb line vision (7:7-17) is third among five visions that conclude his written record. Although the judgment described in two visions is mercifully set aside (the plague of locust and the devouring fire; Amos 7:1-6), the plumb line remains in the midst of the people. There will be no averting this word from the Lord. Destruction will come. The religious places will "be made desolate... be laid waste" (7:9). The political fortunes of Jeroboam will go by way of the sword. What an ironic use of the plumb line! It is intended to aid in building straight and true. It's message here is that the judgment is true and will come straight upon the nation with God's exacting precision.

Amaziah, seeking to protect his turf at Bethel, rebuts with the same kind of wide-eyed optimism that Jeremiah had to face 150 years later (Jeremiah 7:4). Amos is not deterred. He is not a professional prophet with transferable credentials. He must obey the direction of God and simply do what God put in his hands to do where God instructed him to do it. The plumb line therefore also falls on Amaziah with a personal word of judgment (7:17).

Colossians 1:1-14

Even though writing from prison (Colossians 4:3, 18), Paul sets a positive tone for this letter. He is gratified to see that the gospel is "bearing fruit and growing" not only in Colossae but also in the whole world (1:6; granted, "the whole world" was a tad bit smaller to Paul than it is to us). Epaphras was the sower of the gospel among the Colossians. Paul may never have visited this congregation in person, though he passed through the area on his third missionary journey. He is content to let this letter and the prayer with which it is sent connect him to the Christian fellowship growing there.

Paul gives thanks for the cruciform life of the Colossians. They believe in Jesus as the Messiah, which can be represented by the vertical beam of the cross, signifying the relationship between the human and the divine. They also have love for all the saints, which can be represented by the horizontal beam of the cross, signifying our human relationship with one another. Paul's own suffering counts as nothing compared to the life of faith and love growing in Colossae. The gospel is pre-eminent.

Paul's prayer (1:9-10) is a great blueprint for the prayers of pastors for their flock, parents for their children, and Christians for their friends. First, he prays that the Colossians will know God's will. This involves more than just mental cognition of what God's will is. In his *Small Catechism*, Martin Luther spells this out in commentary on the Third Petition of the Lord's Prayer: "God's good and gracious will comes about without our prayer, but we ask in this prayer that it may also come about in and among us."

This brings Paul to the second prayer request, that the Colossians "lead a life worthy of the Lord" (1:10). This will certainly be done, when God's will is worked out in daily life — the decisions made, the actions performed, and the words used.

As this becomes the character of life, Paul's third request will be fulfilled that the Colossians will increase in the knowledge of the Lord. This growth, like bearing fruit from a mature plant, will manifest the very intent of the will of God, namely, to be active existentially in the life of the believer, bringing about the desired responses in word and deed. Thus, it becomes ethical knowledge, not esoteric knowledge, and abounds more and more in the life of the believer, like a light on a rheostat switch being turned on brighter and brighter (see 2 Corinthians 3:18).

And thus there is "the hope laid up in heaven" for the Christian from Colossae (Colossians 1:5).

Luke 10:25-37

The good Samaritan story is such common knowledge that President Bush could allude to it in his inaugural address and expect to be understood: "When we see that wounded traveler on the road to Jericho, we will not pass to the other side," the new chief executive said. What is not so well remembered is the question that brought about the story. The question is not so much the one about the neighbor, though that is the immediate question. Rather the question to which the story and Jesus' other words respond, is the one about inheriting eternal life. Jesus pushes the impertinent lawyer to answer the question himself. It is written in the law that one should love God (Deuteronomy 6:4-5) and love their neighbor (Leviticus 19:18). The lawyer, as well as any good Jew of the day, would know that.

"What must I do to demonstrate that I have the quality of life that is valued by God?" This recasts the focus of the question toward the here and now of life. It would be easy to talk about eternal life as a kind of "never-never land," off in the sky somewhere, at which one will arrive after this life has run its course. But Jesus keeps the focus on this gritty earth, telling a story that enables one to conclude that the love of God and the love of neighbor are characteristic of the eternal life that one hopes to gain. When we behave as the Samaritan demonstrates, we have some grounds for saying we have inherited eternal life. It surely comes to us as a gift (Romans 6:23b), and that gift finds expression in how we actually love in our daily life. That's why it's important to ask, "Who is my neighbor?"

The neighbor is the one in need; the neighborly one is whoever provides for the need.

Mercy is characteristic of neighborly love. Notice how the Samaritan went out of his way *to* the wounded man, rather than out of his way to pass by *on the other side*, as the priest and Levite did. This is not just a physical matter but also a cultural one. For Jews and Samaritans did not have much to do with one another, due to a long-standing history of animosity fueled by jealousy and judgmentalism (see John 4:1-42). It is a quality of mercy to set aside preconceived notions, however justified one may feel about them, to enable one to respond to another's need. Notice also how the Samaritan was generous and self-sacrificing, offering two-day's wage initially to care for the man at an inn, based on need and not on the deservedness of the individual. Again, a quality of mercy.

Application

Our era had been tagged as the Communication Age. The church has a communication to give to our nation and to the world, just as Amos had for his day. It is an echo of the judgment that Amos rendered audible and visible through the words and images with which he communicated "the word of the Lord" (7:16). In our age, of course, there are enough problems — wrongdoings, hatreds, broken promises — to keep a regiment of Amoses busy issuing divine judgment. Thus, the church today sometimes needs to bring out the plumb line and raise a prophetic voice — locally, nationally, and globally.

Because of the revelation of Jesus Christ, Paul remained hopeful, even under the hand of persecution and rejection, of the hope laid up for eternal life that would be manifest in his present age as well, with Christ being all and in all (Colossians 3:11). Therefore, his prayer for the Colossians can become our prayer for one another today. This prayer will help us focus on what is truly important in life — the rule of God in our hearts and in the cosmos. To increase in the knowledge of God means the transformation of the self away from this age only, but to color this age with the hues of eternity.

This is the way to live, "because of the hope laid up for you in heaven" (Colossians 1:5). To live in the present in a way that anticipates the future reality of God's rule over all affirms the importance of the present, however fleeting and however partial. "Already now we can live in the power of the future; already now we can shape our lives in accordance with God and his future kingdom," is the way Eberhard Arnold expressed it in a 1923 lecture. His contribution to the welfare of Christian community was to stress that Jesus was serious in his call to radical discipleship. "This is why the church exists: to dare to start *now* with this future, perfect world of God's kingdom." (See *Salt and Light*, a collection of writings and talks by Eberhard Arnold.)

This last comment was made to his brothers and sisters in Christ of the Rhon Bruderhof facing oppressive measures from the Nazi regime (1933). Soon this community of radical Christian idealists would be raided by the Gestapo. They would have to whisk their children off to Switzerland for safety. In the face of this, they felt compelled, in the words of Emmy Arnold, "to continue to live for the witness entrusted to us and to speak out... and so we continued to build" (*A Joyful Pilgrimage*).

What a benediction verse 11 contains for those who are sick, struggling, dying, doubtful, fearful, or tired. Because Christians are the heirs of grace, we can thank God at all times, for God will strengthen us with the gifts necessary for daily life. Paul learned this through all his trials and was able to report God's salutary word to him, "My grace is sufficient for you" (2 Corinthians 12:9). These similar words to the Colossians are very encouraging to Christians today. They point them forward through trials because God's strength for endurance will be present. They can proceed with confidence, for joy will be their reward as they exercise patience, knowing they can thank God in all things (see also Romans 8:28-30 and Philippians 4:4-7).

The hope laid up for us in heaven, as Paul writes, has the power to shape our lives on earth in the here and now. The good Samaritan is to be every Christian, not striving to "inherit eternal life" through works of righteousness; but, rather, manifesting the already-inherited gift of eternal life through righteous acts of mercy in the name of Jesus, who commands his followers "Go and do likewise" (Luke 10:37). He commands us already as disciples. We are heirs of grace and now called upon, in Paul's words, to "work out your own salvation in fear and trembling; for God is at work in you, both to will and to work for his good pleasure" (Philippians 2:12-13).

Proper 11 / Pentecost 9 / Ordinary Time 16
Amos 8:1-12
Colossians 1:15-28
Luke 10:38-42
Mark Molldrem

After the handshake and the hug

The master brought his disciples into a darkened room with one instruction: "Find the truth." One disciple came upon a table and declared that the truth is flat and square. Another touched the wall and said, "The truth is hard and wide." A third disciple stumbled upon a ball and concluded that the truth was round and bounces. The fourth disciple simply stood in the middle of the room, not impressed with the other statements. He thought and thought, until finally concluding, "The truth is empty." Finally, the master lit a candle, visually revealing the objects and space that gave rise to the various comments and announced, "The truth is that you have all been in the dark."

Amos, Paul, and Jesus each have something to say about perceiving the essential nature of their given situations. As we listen to them, it will be like a candle lit in a dark room, illuminating our reality for clarity in thought and action.

Amos 8:1-12

With another text from Amos this week, we return to the eighth century BC. If God is going to "never again pass by" (8:2), it would be well and good to understand why. Perhaps in that knowledge there may be found courage for endurance unto the other side of silence.

In his fourth vision, Amos sees a basket of summer fruit. It is one basket representing one fate for the nation. This is in contrast to Jeremiah's two baskets (Jeremiah 24:1-10), one that represents the future of the exiled remnant and the other that represents the lack of future for those who will perish in Jerusalem and Egypt. Israel, i.e., the northern kingdom, has reached the end of its story. Assyria will write the final chapter. The summer fruit has been picked. It is rotting now under the hot sun, never to see autumn.

Judgment will come upon the people because of their oppression of the poor (8:4), their cheating, and their greed (8:5). There is more interest for the sabbath to be over for the sake of gain, than for the sabbath to come and linger for the sake of rest and refreshment. God will not overlook any of this impertinent behavior, just like one cannot help but notice the floodwaters of the Nile. As the waters outside the banks devastate the land, so shall devastation result from the flood of disobedience, drowning the people in their sin. Instead of songs of victory, praise, and thanksgiving in the temple, there shall be lamentation.

Amos visualizes the people in sackcloth and baldness as signs of their wretchedness before the Lord. Whereas Pharaoh mourned for his firstborn son on the day of deliverance generations ago, this generation will enter into mourning as "for an only son" (8:10). When the hearts of God's people are hardened, they too shall know "a bitter day" (8:10).

More penetrating than these images of judgment, is the absence of God that Amos declares (8:11-12). How dreadful for a people who have been blessed by the word of the Lord from their founding days (whether one marks that in Ur or at the foot of Sinai)! The promise will not be repeated; the Torah will not awaken any ear or stir any heart. The people will be left in silence, because they will not be able to find the word of the Lord, as during a famine when no grain can be harvested (8:11). Here is God's wrath at its most horrible expression, for it means that those left in silence will perish! If it is true that mortals do not live by bread alone, but by every word that proceeds from the mouth of God (Deuteronomy 8:3), what else but death could result from the silence of God?

This death is applied to the up-and-coming generation, those "fair virgins" and "young men" who will, in fact, "faint for thirst... fall, and never rise again" (8:13-14). The gods they sought out in their darkness, whether in the shrines of Samaria (see 2 Kings 17:30) or in the calf idol at Dan (1 Kings 12:28-29) or the powers that be in Beer-sheba, will prove impotent. The one, true God will stand by in silence and grieve the people of his making, who now reply to him with mocking, substituting hands-on deities for the inscrutable deity of cosmos and history.

Colossians 1:15-28

When Paul was in Athens (Acts 17:16-34), he found himself in an idol-laden city among philosophers of several stripes who loved to chat about anything new in the world of ideas. When pressed by these talking-heads, Paul seized the opportunity to present the gospel of Jesus in the Areopagus, a public setting where kings had once been advised by councils. Paul connected with his audience in a most unusual way. He did not address them on what they thought they knew, whether they were Epicurean or Stoic philosophers or religious believers. He started with what they did not know, drawing attention to the altar "to an unknown god."

In Colossians, Paul fleshes out the Christology upon which his very knowledge of God (the unknown, unless God chooses to reveal himself to the world, 1:25-27) is based and upon which his confidence in the resurrection rests. These descriptors of Christ can be better understood against the background of gnostic thought that pervaded so much thinking at the time. Although there are always variations from person to person and between schools of thought within a general outlook, basically, the Gnostics relied on "insight" rather than "revelation." Knowledge of God was attained by taking one's self as the starting point.

Typical of gnostic cosmology is a multi-storied universe, filled with emanations upon emanations from God, proceeding from pure spirituality to more material substance. Tertullian (160-220 AD) in *Adversus Valentinianos 7*, characterized the gnostic universe as an apartment building, "with room piled on room, and assigned to each god by just as many stairways as there were heresies: the universe has been turned into rooms for rent!" Though gnosticism surely had pre-Christian roots, it infected Christian tradition with heretical notions that reduced the status of Christ in salvation history and spiritualized the resurrection. (For a more complete understanding of gnosticism and the role it played in the formation of early church doctrine and structure, see Elaine Pagels' *The Gnostic Gospels*.)

Paul claims that Christ is the very image of the invisible God, not a distant emanation from God. Christ is the firstborn of all creation (1:15). This is not meant in terms of a temporal sequence. It emphasizes that Christ stands above and beyond creation in an essential way, such that he is superior to it. This term refers not so much to his relationship to creation, as it does to his relationship to God. For Paul goes on to describe how all things were created "in him... through him and for him" (1:16). All things hold together in Christ, who is "before all things" (1:17). All these prepositions work together to elevate Christ above the creation, as God the creator is above the creation. Jesus Christ is neither a *lesser god*, nor is he *mere mortal*; he is the fullness of God (1:19; see also John 1:14).

His work is "to reconcile... all things" to God by means of his sacrificial death, "making peace by the blood of his cross" (1:20). This is a work external to humanity and becomes a revelation to humanity for the sake of salvation. It is a work done by God through Jesus Christ. One cannot attain to it through mere insight. It is a gift from the very Son of God (see Colossians 1:3), the mystery of God's heart unwrapped for the whole world to see.

This is the very reason that Jesus Christ is also the head of the church. This is not just a titular distinction, but one in fact, dynamically lived out in time because he is firstborn from the dead (1:18). His pre-eminence is established by the singular event of the resurrection.

This is the faith in which Paul urges the Colossians to remain "stable and steadfast" (1:23; see also Ephesians 4:14; Galatians 1:6-7; Revelation 2:10). He offers his own sufferings as a sign for the Colossians to take him seriously, an authentic witness to the gospel of Jesus, into whom all disciples are to grow in maturity.

Luke 10:38-42

It is true that in John 11—12:11 we learn of a more intimate relationship between Jesus and the Mary-Martha-Lazarus family. Yet, in Luke we are treated to a scene in which Mary teaches us a very important lesson in life: *one thing is needful* and that is to listen to Jesus (10:39, 42).

The same family word is used regarding Martha receiving Jesus into her house and regarding the reception of the seventy in the outlying villages (Luke 10:8 and Luke 10:38). In this receiving there is implied an openness to hear the message of Jesus. Mary embodies what this means when she literally sits at Jesus' feet to listen to him.

Jesus sees in Mary a person who has chosen the one thing needful. This is highlighted by Martha's busyness in serving daily bread in contrast to Mary's choice to receive the Bread of Life. This is "the good portion" that will endure beyond the mold of daily bread. The preposition under or beneath attached to the verb "to receive" not only prefigures Mary's posture with Jesus, but also the depth of her devotion. Unfortunately, Martha "was distracted with much serving" (10:40) and gained only anxiety for her efforts, rather than "the good portion."

Jesus can look on an entire crowd and have compassion on them all (Matthew 9:36); yet, for Martha, he can dismiss her anxiety and not lift a hand to help her, but rather lift up Mary as an example to redirect her attentions. That would necessitate a choice for Martha. If John 12:1-11 is a different perspective on the same scene, we still have Jesus lifting up the importance of attention and devotion around him. A choice still has to be made, whether between the poor and an extravagant offering to Jesus, or between feeding others and being fed by the supplier of all.

Application

Imagine Amos' prophecy applying to us today. It is really not too hard to imagine. There is a growing disparity between the rich and the poor in America, with some suggesting that the middle class is becoming smaller and smaller. (Compound this with the dramatic difference between quality of life in first-world nations and third-world nations.) One out of five children in America, the wealthiest and most powerful nation on earth, live in poverty. Every day in most every newspaper there are reports of greed and graft from armed robbery to embezzlement to stock fraud. Court TV shows are filled with claims of deceit, broken promises, and meanness — and we find this entertaining!

Further imagine what it would mean to have the judgment of God fall upon us now. What would we grieve? The loss of our pensions? Our church buildings? Our national identity under the perception of manifest destiny? Would it ever dawn on any one of us to reel at the loss of our salvation? Does anyone dread the silence of God, or do we think that with the radio, television, and internet so available that we are bound to hear something important along the way? Or even more scary: Do we think that as long as our churches are paid for and the appointments kept clean and in place that we are guaranteed God will remain in our midst?

Look carefully at Amos 8:13-14, although they are not part of the assigned lectionary. They should be. It is very unpleasant to hear these words that cast the future into severe doubt. Dare we consider that the next generation may not rise up, but rather fall? *En mass* they have already fallen for just about anything and everything that is not holy. Granted they are on a spiritual quest, but they have ventured into the fields of pluralism and relativism so as to avoid having to be decisive. They only have to select one among many possibilities, any of which could suit their purpose. They do not perceive the choice as singular and a matter of life or death. The only thing that will be sacrificed on the altars of our own making will be ourselves. Such a sacrifice is not strong enough to bond us to God.

The "shifting from the hope of the gospel" that Paul fears may have already taken place today. So much of the language of Christians today has lost it Christo-centric heart. From self-professing Christians when talking about other faith systems, one hears such expressions as: "We all believe the same thing; we are all going to the same place; there's only one God." This seems to be the core of the faith of so many these days, especially in an effort to be conciliatory and inclusive. The result for Christians is a watered-down religiosity that does not shape one's life distinctively but more-or-less sets a mood of spirituality. This mood links one's daily endeavors to factors other than one's specific relationship with the living God or his mediator, Jesus Christ.

John Dart, once news editor of the *Christian Century*, wrote an article for the January-February 2001 issue of *Sojourners* magazine in which he observed that, whereas in the past, religious coverage was conducted on a denomination vs. denomination model, in the future it will pit believer (whether Christian, Muslim, Jew, Mormon, New Age, Hindu, and so on) vs. non-believer (atheist, agnostic, secularist, areligious). He also projects that "if religious literacy continues to slide [in the media]... religious nuances might seem irrelevant when all one needs to know is if a group's members are believers or non-believers."

The "divine office" (Colossians 1:25) from which pastors work is a gift, through which the pastor makes the word known so that the believer can be presented mature in Christ (Colossians 1:28). This is the goal of Christian ministry. Parishioners must, therefore, hear over and over again that Christ is pre-eminent by virtue of his work and his relationship to the Father. Paul writes of a veil that is over our eyes preventing us from seeing God clearly, a veil that can only be lifted through Christ (2 Corinthians 3:14). In worship, the veil is lifted through liturgy, word, and sacrament.

A question every congregation should ask itself is whether it is so focused on people and programs that it neglects the person of Christ. We say we do these things in the name of Christ (hospitality and focus groups and fellowship events, and so on); yet, how easy it is to engage in these activities and not mention the name of Christ. We become a distracted Martha, rather than a needful Mary. We must never forget that the purpose for ourselves and those we would evangelize is to sit at the feet of Jesus, to choose the good portion, which cannot be taken away from us when the handshake and hug are over, the discussion ended or the program folded.

Fullness by any other name...

"The whole experience was dirty, draining, and depressing." That's how George Stephanopoulos, in his book *All Too Human*, described one period in the run for the Clinton presidency. In the book, Stephanopoulos tells the story of his political education, which, to a point, was also a spiritual education. With ambition and vanity, George quickly rose in the ranks of those who served President Clinton. He became the president's senior advisor and basked in the fame and the fury of that position. Then he discovered that this lifestyle did not provide him with the fullness of life that he wanted. He admits in this painfully honest and revealing book that he failed to heed the advice of his father, who, after reminding him of the myth of Icarus, said to him upon Clinton's election to the White House, "Be careful. Keep your balance."

How do we keep balance in our furious world? How do we maintain an even keel amid siren sounds promising fulfillment and satisfaction in this pursuit or that acquisition? Let's listen to what Hosea and Paul have to tell us from what they witness in the course of human events. They will direct our attention to how God is acting in the world, an attention that will ultimately be focused on the cross of Christ. From Christ Jesus we will hear today some important words about prayer, which is God's gift to keep us in the balance between heaven and earth, God's rule and our temptations.

By the way, I am using the word "fullness" a good bit in this discussion. Admittedly, it's one of those churchy words that people don't use often in everyday speech. (If you doubt that, just go to an internet search engine, type in "fullness" and see how many religious and how few secular sites come up!) But if you look up "full" in a dictionary, there are plenty of connections to life. If you choose to speak about fullness using that term, you might want to remind your hearers of some of those associations.

Hosea 1:2-10

The prophecy of Hosea, along with that of his contemporary Amos, sealed the fate of the northern kingdom. "The days of Jeroboam" (Hosea 1:1) would be among the last days of Israel. God, through the hands of the Assyrians, would see to that. Before the close of the eighth century BC, Hosea's harsh words against the house of Jehu would be fulfilled: not pitied and not my people will be the name by which Israel will be remembered. There was a dreadful price to be paid for the religious apostasy that characterized the nation. Rather than relying on God as their fortress and their might, the leadership crafted political alliances with the Assyrians and the Egyptians. They permitted and even promoted Baal worship in concession to local culture. Immorality was rampant, as the priests filled their personal coffers with gain.

Onto this scene strides Hosea (whose name means "salvation," related to the root word for Joshua) with a word of judgment. In contrast to Amos' visions (for example, the plumb line and the basket of fruit), Hosea lives out a personal parable through which he speaks volumes to the nation. Hosea is instructed by the Lord to take a wife — and not just any wife, but Gomer, a woman unfaithful in relationships. In his marriage, Hosea would be mirroring God's relationship to his people. Just as Gomer practiced harlotry, so too had the people of Israel practiced harlotry, even though they had been married to the Lord (1:2). Gomer's three children by Hosea are named prophetically as types of the people of Israel.

First born is Jezreel, named to recall the sins of Ahab and Jezebel (2 Kings 9:7-10), the latter whose flesh would be eaten by the dogs of Jezreel. What is sobering about this judgment is that God judges the very ones whom he had used for his judgment earlier (see 2 Kings 9:30—10:36). No one escapes the wrath of God, not even those whom he raises up to execute his wrath. The house of Jehu will be brought down, just like the house of Ahab was brought down, by the hand of the Lord in judgment for its sins.

Second born is Not Pitied. God will no longer offer his mercy to the people who have proven so rebellious. Judah, however, will still be favored to carry out God's purposes. Instead, through Judah, the promises made to God's people will be fulfilled. They shall inherit the moniker "Sons of the living God" (1:10).

Third born is Not My People. Not only will God remove his favor from the people, but also his identity. They will no longer be known as the people of God, for they will be no more. When God removes his presence from the people (symbolized by his removing his name from them), their presence on the landscape of time disappears. After the Assyrian rampage through the countryside under Sargon II, the rod of God's anger (Isaiah 10:5), was completed in 721 BC, that is exactly what happened.

Colossians 2:6-15 (16-19)

Apparently, Paul has not visited this congregation (Colossians 2:1-5). Epaphras was the seed-planter of faith and Paul is confident in and appreciative of the work that he did (Colossians 1:7-8). Paul does, however, want to affirm and encourage the Colossians in their faith (Colossians 2:2, 5).

In these few verses of our pericope, Paul provides a synopsis of the faith in terms of the incarnation, crucifixion, and resurrection of Jesus the Christ. To say that "the whole fullness of deity dwells bodily" in him (2:9) is to strike down the gnostic notion that Christ is a demigod, a distant emanation from the one, true God. Placing the prepositional phrase "in him" at the beginning of the sentence is Paul's way of emphasizing that precisely in Jesus God has incarnated his presence and love for humanity (see also John 1:14). We get the real McCoy in Jesus, not a hand-me-down! This underscores the sufficiency and the superiority of Jesus when it comes to the knowledge of God amid competing truth claims of various philosophies and human traditions, which Paul decries as "empty enticements" (2:8). The writer to the Hebrews argues this same point, only within the context of the sacrifice system of the first covenant (Hebrews 8-10 especially).

Verses 13-14 make wonderful declarations about our sins and the cross of Christ. It is similar to what Paul writes in Romans 5:6-11. Our sins are our death. God takes the initiative to cancel "the bond which stood against us with its legal demands" (2:14; see also Romans 3:26 and 6:23a). The indictment is nailed to the cross with our sins in the body of Jesus, so that we may be free of their curse. This is what forgiveness means, what grace is all about (2:13).

Just as Christians are buried with Christ into death in baptism, so too in that same baptism are they raised to new life, fullness of life in him (2:10). Because Jesus is raised from the dead, he is the head of all rule and authority and can provide us with that which we could not attain to ourselves, namely a growth that is from God (2:19). Paul goes on to describe this growth later in his letter (Colossians 3:12f), as he applies the grace of God to the various situations and conditions of human life together.

As Christians are rooted in what Christ has done, making them alive to God, they can be built up into a fullness of life that also comes from God. This fullness of life is not necessarily manifest in ascetic disciplines or ritual practices (2:16-18), but in a growth into Christ-likeness, represented by Paul's expression to hold fast to the head (2:19). In the second half of this letter, Paul details what this means in terms of the character of daily Christian life.

Luke 11:1-13

One cannot read the gospels without noticing that Jesus was often in prayer. Whether that be in a lonely place apart, in the upper room, in Gethsemane, or on the cross, Jesus was certainly a man of prayer. It is not strange, then, that the disciples would approach him and ask him to teach them to pray. It was common custom for a rabbi to give a special prayer to his disciples, so that they too could use prayer to voice their heart to God. The disciples saw John the Baptist giving his disciples such a prayer, and this band of devotees wanted one from Jesus, their rabbi.

In response, Jesus encouraged them not only to pray, but he also gave them precious words to use in their prayers. Whether they used their Lord's prayer before or after their individual prayers, or in place of them all together, they would be praying for the essentials of the godly life. First, their petitions would honor God and seek God's rule in their lives and on earth above all else. Second, their petitions would focus on essential human needs for life — namely, personal well-being, well-being in human relationships, and well-being in relationship with God.

One of the interesting words used in Luke's version of the Lord's Prayer is the conjunction which, in this instance means, "for, the ground or reason being...." The petition to forgive us our sins is offered, strangely enough, grounded on the observation that Christians in fact forgive those who are in some way indebted to them (11:4). The way this should be understood is not as an argument with God based on works righteousness: "God, you must forgive our sins, based on the fact that we ourselves have already forgiven others." That would go against the basic understanding throughout the New Testament that forgiveness is a free, unmerited gift from God. Instead, think of it as a human touch-point that provides assurance that God is indeed a forgiving God; for, if we can be forgiving, then certainly God, who is above and beyond us, can be forgiving. We are, after all, created in God's image.

It is interesting that Matthew's version of the Lord's Prayer uses the adverb in this petition to express the relative manner in which God should forgive our sins — as we forgive those who sin against us. Jesus' explanation in Matthew 6:14-15 (see also Matthew 18:21-35) confirms this nuance of meaning. In contrast, Luke's recording of Jesus' reflections on a father's treatment of a son's request (Luke 11:11-13) validates the intentional use of the word meaning "for, the ground or reason being" is an expression of the reasoning by which we may approach God expectantly with our requests.

This is further drawn out in Luke by Jesus' little story of importunity (11:5-8). It's odd, don't you think, that friendship is not the basis for response to a request; rather, audacity and obtrusiveness is (11:8). Jesus again lifts up this angle on prayer in Luke 18:1-8. The point is simply not to lose heart; be persistent and keep knocking on heaven's door. That is the privilege of prayer. God invites us to come before him like an insistent child will approach daddy ("abba" — the Aramaic expression for the Greek Pater, which lacks the formalism of the traditional and liturgically oriented formulation found in Matthew's version of the Lord's Prayer as "Our Father in heaven ...").

Application

How many Jews going through the Holocaust and those living in its aftermath have considered themselves Not Pitied and Not My People? Berish, the innkeeper in Elie Wiesel's *The Trial of God*, declares, "God is merciless, don't you know that?" He states, what the people of the northern kingdom in the eighth century BC could have uttered anachronistically, "Purim is over. For good." (Purim is the feast celebrating the deliverance of the Hebrew people from the plotting of Haman, recorded in the book of Esther, possibly written in the fourth or fifth century BC.)

Yet, there is a promise in God's word of judgment: "In the place where it was said to them, 'You are not my people,' it shall be said to them, 'Sons of the living God' " (Hosea 1:10). Though six million indeed perished in the Holocaust, yet as a people the Jews survived. Again, from *The Trial of God*, in a terse exchange Sam, a stranger, says, "Blessed be the Lord for his miracles." To which Mendel, the eldest and wisest of the ensemble, replies, "A whole community was massacred, and you talk of miracles?" Sam rebuts, "A Jew survived, and you ignore them?"

How can we speak of fullness of life in the midst of such tragedy? It certainly is not easy and only comes after much struggle; but it is possible, because God's promises persist. Just as God provided a promise in the midst of his judgment upon Israel, so too there are promises in any and every situation where we may find ourselves. Fullness of life, after all, is not found in our own satisfaction, but in satisfying God's will in our lives. Note how survivors of cancer, whether patients or bereaved loved ones, grow beyond their grief when they become involved in advocating education or funding research in the field. Note how some prisoners, upon release from incarceration, join the battle for prison reform. The faithful not only look for practical responses like these to hard-knock situations; they also search for a deeper understanding of the mysteries of God and how to communicate them to a world that puts God on trial. The faithful will still find fullness of life in the midst of tragedies, as they continue to praise God and love God — in spite of themselves and for the sake of the neighbor who is struggling to find God's true nature.

In his book *Why Christian?* which he describes as "for people on the edges," Douglas John Hall strives to provide a convincing, Christian response for people who are looking for resolution to their spiritual longings, whether they are on the edges of faith or on the edges of the Christian tradition or on the edges of the church. This apologetic work attempts to make clear connections between Christian belief and the human situation.

This is so needful in our day and age when spiritual energy is strong, but, more times than not, misdirected. The Zeitgeist has endorsed the spiritual journey and consecrated by the powers of individualism, relativism, and pluralism, it is considered to be self-defined and self-directed. Paul, in Colossians, helps guide the quest to find its fullness "in him," that is, in Jesus Christ. Over and over again, the reader of this letter is directed to Jesus in order to find the fullness of life (in him) that is the longing of every human heart.

There may be some discussion just how to translate the last prepositional phrase in verse 15, whether it should read "in him" or "in it" (that is, the cross). This simply points to the obvious, so that to find Jesus one must look to the cross. To look to the cross is to see just where Jesus does his work on our behalf. To see the cross is to see how God shows his love for us and to what extent God will go to claim us as his forgiven and accepted beloved. It is as the beloved that the believer grows into the fullness of life that God intends.

What better way to grow into the fullness of life that God intends for his beloved than to pray? Today, what we learn about prayer from Jesus is that prayer is offered to God's glory; it is asking for needs, not wants; it is concerned about right relationship with God as well as one's neighbor. Ultimately, prayer is communication with God that there be communion with God (Luke 11:13) — that we have God, like a log absorbs fire into its very being until it changes its wood fiber composition into heat and light. In this way the log becomes more than itself; transformed into fullness of life. In the same way, Christians become more than themselves as they let God's Holy Spirit burn within them to will and to work his good pleasure.

Proper 13 / Pentecost 11 / Ordinary Time 18
Hosea 11:1-11
Colossians 3:1-11
Luke 12:13-21
Mark Molldrem

"Up" is not the only heavenly direction

Annual meetings, whether for a business corporation, a nonprofit agency, or a local congregation, usually yield official resolutions. These documents outline a concern that is then addressed with a "Therefore, be it resolved...." The resolution calls for a course of action to respond appropriately to the situation. Some of these actions involve signing up, turning on, moving out, focusing in, rising above, getting beneath, hunkering down, pushing through, facing off, aiming toward and away from — potentially heavenly directions all.

The Bible is God's record of resolutions in dealing with humanity. Although there are many different instances throughout the Bible when God expressed his resolve regarding a specific situation, the essential resolve of God is to love his entire creation, reaching out and drawing in. God's resolve to love shapes our resolve to love not only God, but also one another.

Hosea 11:1-11

One of the most beloved images of God in the Bible is that of a parent. Jesus prays to his heavenly Father. Paul often refers to God as Father (for example, Colossians 1:3 and 1 Thessalonians 3:11-13). Deuteronomy compares God to a mother eagle hovering over her young (Deuteronomy 32:11). And Hosea speaks God's word to the people in terms of the parent-child relationship: "When Israel was a child, I loved him, and out of Egypt I called my son" (11:1).

Despite this love, the family relationship was strained, like all earthly families are, with rebellion. Just as teenage youth tune out their parents, the people of Israel would not listen to the voice of God. They went after what intrigued them at the time (11:2). There is a line in the hymn "Borning Cry" by John Ylvisaker, which expresses this well: "in a blaze of light you wandered off to find where demons dwell."

Just like children can take their parents' care for granted, not even noticing all that is being done for them out of love, so too the people of God in Hosea's time were oblivious to the many ways God provided for them. Being taught to walk righteously, being healed, supported and fed, the people had every reason to be grateful to God but they were not. Instead, they "wandered off." They listened to the siren sounds of other gods, distracted by subtle, sweet lies.

For this there would be discipline, a hard love resolved to purge the sin, yet save the sinners (11:8-9). Verse 8 alludes to the war of kings (Genesis 14:1-12) as an example of what God does not want to have happen. Just as Abram provided deliverance then, God would restore his children to their family inheritance after the discipline. It is true that the northern kingdom, as such, was obliterated, never to resurface on the map of history. However, Judah was the salvaged remnant. Of course, the Gentile Christians were later grafted onto the tree of God's pleasant planting, as the New Israel, the church, inheriting the promises of God through the Messiah who had come and in whom they believed (Romans 11:17-24).

Note the anguish of God in being true to his holiness as well as his compassion. His holiness calls for judgment, such as that regarding his rebellious people: "They are appointed to the yoke, and none shall remove it" (11:7). The Assyrian conquest was decisive, as the archaeological and historical records reveal. Still, God's compassion calls for a word of hope (11:11), which was indeed extended to Judah (Assyria's intrusions were thwarted short of the total devastation that the northern kingdom was subject to) and by further extension, to the New Israel, the church.

God's resolve to love even his rebellious children would bring him to express his righteousness through Jesus the Christ, who would endure the wrath of sin for our sake and release his compassion of forgiveness, which would open the way for life abundant and life eternal.

Colossians 3:1-11

One of the ways we structure our language is through directional metaphors. "Wake *up*." "He *sank* into a coma." Spatial orientations such as up, above, and over carry with them a more positive, desirable connotation than down, under, and low. It is better to have one's health at its *peak*, than to *drop* dead. It is better to *come in* than to *wander off*, as the people of Hosea's day did. So, it is no accident that Paul would use such an expression as "seek the things that are *above*" (3:1). He, then, goes on to use a different image of clothing — "put off... put on" — to talk about the character of the Christian life (the quality of which Hosea would have loved to see in his day and for his people!).

The resurrection of Jesus and our participation in it introduces us into the superior life, the stronger life, the godly life. Paul describes the character of that life in 3:12f. In our text for today, he identifies those things that are antithetical to such a life. It reads like a dirty laundry list: fornication, covetousness, malice, slander, foul talk — to mention just a few. The list is suggestive, not exclusive. Such clothing is not becoming for a Christian. It is to be *put off*, not in the sense of a time-delay ("Don't put off till tomorrow what you can do today"), but in the spatial sense of putting away from one that which should not be near, neither to the body nor to the soul.

Paul's premise is that Jesus has been raised from the dead and that *that* resurrection has the power to change the life of the believer. "If then you have been raised with Christ" is not a quandary; it is an appeal to reason. Paul takes believers in Christ Jesus and walks them into the next step with Jesus. The life that was lived *for us* will now shape the life that will be lived *for him*.

One can imagine Paul leading a tour through the Christian home, as it were. He has already shown us the washroom (Colossians 2:12; baptism). Now, he is showing us the laundry room where our Christian apparel is made presentable. In this matter of dress, we are all subject to the same standards, for Christ is "all and in all" (3:11). By the power of his new resurrected nature, he gives believers a new nature that is continually being shaped in his likeness (3:10).

Luke 12:13-21

Jesus talks a lot about money and its relationship to spirituality. He takes a coin and distinguishes what belongs to Caesar and what belongs to God. A widow's mite impresses him more than the apparent generosity of the wealthy. A field with buried treasure gives him occasion to talk about the value of the kingdom of God. When profit motivates the provisions for offerings in the temple, he gets quite physical in his outrage. It should come as no surprise that someone would ask him to settle a matter of inheritance. Jesus knew the tradition of Deborah (Judges 4:4-5) and Solomon (1 Kings 3:16-28) and might have been tempted to take pride that he should be considered worthy of judging a matter of such importance. This was not a trick question, like so many of those by the Pharisees and scribes. This was a genuine request to arbitrate a very sticky issue.

Jesus goes to the heart of the matter: covetousness. To what extent will one go to get what one considers a right belonging? That one would come to the Lord to resolve the matter is a good first step. But one must be ready to take the step in the direction Jesus indicates. Despite Jesus' protests to the contrary, he *is* the appointed judge in all matters of sin. Covetousness is a sin that strikes at the heart of commandments nine and ten. Covetousness will easily come between the bonds of family, certainly between friends, and without mercy between strangers. Jesus answers the request with a parable that points the hearer to seek the things that are above. That means, one will only discover true wealth and the inheritance that endures when one becomes rich toward God.

To be rich toward God ultimately leads one into a lifestyle of generosity. The wisdom imparted to those who value "things above" is that this is the only way to find peace, satisfaction, and contentment among things down below.

Application

There is a weakness in every human-divine analogy. It can never be a 100% correlation. The analogy of parenting is no exception. We would be sorely mistaken if we thought that God must act like the best concept of parenthood we have.

In teaching positive discipline these days, it is common to hear about "lap talks" for toddlers, "time-outs" for preschoolers, and "revoked privileges" for grade-schoolers. There is a progression of dealing with errant children in order to redirect them to the proper behavior. Of course, it gets more difficult the older and the bigger the children get. Ask the parent of any teenager or young adult who still lives at home. It is understood that there is a limit to the extent to which parents can go in disciplining their children. Spanking has become a "no-no" in our abuse-sensitive age. And grosser forms of restraint, severe corporal chastisement, and even threat of death are outright illegal — for human parents.

We would be remiss if we subjected God to such standards from below. God, from above, is free to exercise his divine right to deal with his creation in any manner so chosen, for God is God. Jesus warned his disciples to fear him who could (not necessarily *would*, but could!) not only kill the body but also cast it into hell (Luke 12:4-7). He was not talking about the devil here. God is not subject to our human standards or expectations. From the beginning God was entirely and eternally free to do what God chooses to do! The wonder of God's self-revelation through Jesus is that God has clearly chosen the sovereignty of compassion over the sovereignty of holiness as the essential core of divine being. God's holiness is still present and will also find expression; yet, when we look at the larger picture of unfolding history, we see the unmistakable stamp of compassion upon his creation and upon his people.

When we hear such words as Hosea's today, we should frame them in a personal, existential context so that they address us now. Otherwise it is too easy to take an objective and distant view that focuses on a historical, political, and social analysis of God's word and misses the dynamic, ever-present urgency for every new day. When we examine our own lives in light of God's word (even as addressed to his people in the eighth century BC), where do we experience ourselves educated, healed, loved, supported, fed — touched by the compassion of God? Where do we experience ourselves yoked and chastised, judged by the holiness of God?

Not only our personal lives, but also our collective cultural life, need to be attentive to God's word. As a dramatic comparison regarding the changing standards of our society, compare the early television sitcoms of the '50s, when spouses could not sleep in the same bed, to the sitcoms of today when couples on first dates are going to bed together... when Elvis' hips could not be shown on the screen to when sexual intercourse is displayed. In this and many other ways, it could be said that behavioral expectations are much lower. Some may talk about how good it is that there is a growing tolerance for what is acceptable behavior, given the variety of human predilections. Others would say that we have become a more crass, rude, and value-vacant society.

Christians need to ask constantly the question, "What do I wear today?" The answer has public consequences. The "clothes" that we put on will reveal to the world how Christ is "all and in all" in us. What behavior, what personal expressions will embody the new nature that is consistent with Christ-likeness?

How can we best love our community, our culture, our nation? Christian congregations around the country can be like a public address system, interlinked and blaring out for all to hear: There is a better way to live, and together we must set our minds on things that are far *above* our current standards of morality. Imagine what it would be like if the church actually spoke forth the character of the redeemed life and embodied it not just as a congregation of people but also as individuals scattered throughout the community.

The Christian call (see Philippians 3:14) is to rise above what may pass as acceptable human standards and live by virtue of the standards that Christ sets for us and commands us to imitate, as he does in John 15:12f. Ethics is not an optional addendum to the Christian faith, but a critical and necessary expression of it. How Christians live their lives is an expression of Christ in them. When Paul says, "Christ is all and in all," he is expressing the power of the risen Christ to change the believer inside and out. He himself experienced this and reflected upon it over and over (Acts 26:4-13; Romans 7:7-25; Galatians 1:11-17; Philippians 3:4-11).

Many wealthy Christians are involved in a group called Responsible Wealth. Its purpose is to advocate tax fairness, a living wage, and also initiate responsibility-oriented shareholder resolutions. Made up of people who are in the top 5% of income earners in America, Responsible Wealth is resolved to love the society into a more equitable system that will benefit others, even at the expense of some of their own advantages. (See *Sojourners* magazine, January-February 2001, "What's Right With This Picture?") These folks take seriously Jesus' words that warn against covetousness.

In our consumer culture with its aptitude for acquisition, it is necessary to discover how to value earning power in a free market economy and how to discern the godly purpose for which it is to be used — which is not the self, but to meet the needs of others and thereby serve and glorify God. One's true treasure does not become the abundance of possessions or the ability to acquire them, but the kingdom of God, the rule of God in all aspects of one's life (Matthew 6:33, 13:44-46; Luke 10:25-37).

In this way, one becomes rich *toward* God, the most heaven-bound of directions.

Proper 14 / Pentecost 12 / Ordinary Time 19
Isaiah 1:1, 10-20
Hebrews 11:1-3, 8-16
Luke 12:32-40
Mark Molldrem

The goodness that roared

In the study of the martial arts, the student learns the difference between the good, the higher good, and the superior good. If one seeks to do something that will benefit another and that very act will also reap a reward for the doer of the deed, then that person is said to perform the good (even though there may be an ulterior motive attached to it). If, however, one desires to assist another person without any personal regard to whether or not such an act will be of personal advantage, then that person is said to perform the higher good.

It is when one can act unconsciously in a way that simply benefits another person, because that is the way one is, it can be said the individual has performed the superior good. Sang Kee Paik, a master student of the San-Sang system of oriental martial art, writes, "A black belt always carries with him his power capability. He must always carry with him his ethic of superior good... He must develop his ethic so that his ethic perseveres over any and all circumstances, no matter how difficult his situation may be."

Today, the scriptures exhort us to learn to do good, whether during a time of judgment, persecution, or simply waiting for the Lord's return. Beyond even the superior good, one might think of it as the heavenly good, for it is done out of obedience to the command of God and to God's glory.

Isaiah 1:1, 10-20

Not a whole lot was going right for God's people in the eighth century BC. By the last quarter of the century, the northern kingdom was absorbed into the Assyrian Empire. The southern kingdom, Judah, with its capital at Jerusalem was under siege. At first, Israel and Syria where nipping at the borders; then, Assyria assumed the rod of God's wrath against a rebellious and ungrateful people (Isaiah 1:2-9). This century was a watershed in the history of God's people in the north and in the south. It marked the beginning of the end of their identities as autonomous states (until the period of the Maccabbees, 165 BC until the Roman conquest). The north disappeared altogether; the remnant of the south continued to be just that, only a remnant, never to attain again to the ideal of the davidic kingdom, an ideal fulfilled in the coming of the Messiah, Jesus of Nazareth.

Throughout the history of God's people there has been a dual call to worship God rightly and to serve his purposes faithfully. When the worship life of the people became tainted with syncretism from indigenous cults, the prophets rose up to sound the alarm, not just because idolatry had infiltrated the true worship of Yahweh (Isaiah's name means "Yahweh is salvation"), but also because the people had lost sight of the connection between worship of Yahweh and serving his purposes in daily life.

Hence, the definition of what is good, not in terms of proper worship practices, but in terms of proper habits in daily life. To be the people of God is not just to use the correct name of God. It is not simply to worship in the prescribed manner handed down from the time of Moses, and do so only in the places that are dedicated solely to God without any piggybacking from local deities. To be the people of God means to behave according to the will of God in relationship to one's neighbor: "seek justice, correct oppression; defend the fatherless, plead for the widow" (1:17). In short, to learn to do good. Not so much sacrifice as sacrificial living is what God desires. Micah, a contemporary of Isaiah, understood this also (Micah 6:8).

Concomitant with this call to more heavenly good is the offer of forgiveness for those who will repent and obey the word of the Lord (1:18-19). Like a spectrum analysis, Isaiah describes how completely God will forgive — as complete as changing the color chart. (Micah 7:18-19 and Psalm 103:11-12 use a dizzying spatial distinction to express the extent of God's forgiveness.)

In addition to forgiveness, when there is compliance to God's will, there are attendant rewards for the righteous. "You shall eat the good of the land" (1:19). These are bold words to speak in the midst of the civil chaos that was occurring at the time. No wonder the writer to the Hebrews lifts the prophets up as worthy examples of faith, trusting in the promises of God even when events unfolding would decry them (Hebrews 11:32-38).

Hebrews 11:1-3, 8-16

A church under fire needs encouragement. This is what the letter of Hebrews is all about. It was written to a church during a time of persecution. It was not a persecution to the death (Hebrews 12:4), yet it was severe enough (Hebrews 10:32-34) to warrant concern about the strength of faith to endure. To address this, the writer of this missive takes on the task of apologetics. He claims the all-sufficiency of Christ as superior to (fulfillment of) the Old Covenant (Hebrews 8:1—10:18). Based on this affirmation, the Christian community hears an encouraging word — to persevere (Hebrews 2:1-4).

In Hebrews 11, the writer provides example after example of those who lived by faith, not seeing the promise fulfilled in their day, but still holding on to the hope that it instilled in their hearts. So, the Christian community can hold on through the time of trial, even when they do not hold the fulfillment of the promise in their hands. In the next chapter, the letter develops the example of Jesus, who endured so much suffering and leads the believer forward through it. Then, comes a wonderful exhortation to "buck up" and let the world see just what Christians are capable of doing when hard pressed: "Therefore lift your drooping hands and strengthen your weak knees" (Hebrews 12:12).

Our pericope, focused on the example of Abraham and Sarah, defines the nature of faith. It is an assurance and a conviction (11:1).

The conviction is that the eyes of faith perceive a reality that is beyond the reason of mind or the immediacy of experience. This is the basis of Paul's comments in Romans 8:18-25, where he is convinced that there is a future glory that contextualizes all current suffering. It is this conviction that gives one wholeness (salvation) in the very midst of brokenness (see Romans 5:3-5 and 1 Corinthians 4:7-10).

The assurance is that what is perceived is indeed real (beyond what reason and experience can attest to with logical or scientific proofs) and can be trusted. The object of faith is foundational for taking any action. Thus, Abram was assured of his inheritance and acted upon that assurance by leaving his home and embarking to a new land — sight unseen. Though he in fact did see the land eventually, the true fulfillment of the promise was yet beyond him, embodied in the holy city, Jerusalem, in one respect and in Jesus Christ in another.

Luke 12:32-40

Little flock, indeed! What significance in number was the small Christian sect compared to the numerous adherents of Judaism? What insignificance in number were the followers of the way compared to the population of the Roman Empire! "Little flock" is an appropriate salutation. Because it is a collective noun, the imperative mood of the noun is in the second person singular, giving the reading as if addressed to each individual, thus personalizing the entreaty (12:32). Since the verb is in the middle voice, it emphasizes the subject's participation in the outcome of the action indicated.

"Be not afraid," Jesus says, to each lamb of the flock. The reason is that God's pleasure is to rule in us and over us. We will share the rule of God that ultimately takes in everything. How we can participate in that rule now and live in a state of not being afraid is to "sell your possessions, and give alms" (12:33).

Such actions are not only good for the recipient of the kindness; they are also salutary for the doer of the good. The entreaty invites participation in the very goal sought by acting in a way that manifests confidence rather than fear.

As Jesus goes on to talk about servants waiting for the master, he describes those who live in the present anticipating the future, which shapes their behavior of readiness. So too, living with the confidence of the coming rule of God disarms fear in the present, regardless of how formidable the challenges or crosses appear. Those who do this become the "blessed, happy ones" of God.

The image of girded loins and burning lamps (12:35) is one of preparedness. The servants are to be dressed for work, not donned in leisure clothing, casually waiting for the master to return. The follow-up parable/explanation (Luke 12:41-48) makes this clear. The flame from the lamps will provide the light to see what needs to be done. It just may be that there is plenty of time to tend to the tasks at hand, because the master may not return until the second or third watch. Since not even Jesus knew when he would return (Mark 13:32), how could the servants expect to know? Therefore, constant vigilance is necessary.

Application

There is such a mix of public people in the world's spotlight. There are religious celebrities with feet of clay, strong moralists with no religious leanings, amoral individuals who push the envelope of our culture and justice system, immoral people who wink at God, and non-Christian religious folks with profound ethics. Amidst all of these, the average person on the street is looking for a word to guide the community into a better world. Isaiah's call to "cease to do evil, learn to do good" (1:16-17) will resonate with many and can be the basis of a conversation that will focus individuals on the importance of their particular life's opportunities and responsibilities.

Christians can ask of themselves how their personal piety is connected to the practices of daily life. What measure of consistency is there between the hearts and the habits of those who profess allegiance to God? As James reminds us, there is no good worship without good works. It is sobering for anyone at the altar or in the pew to hear these words: "When you spread forth your hands, I will hide my eyes from you" (Isaiah 1:15).

In what ways are our hands "full of blood" (1:15)? In what ways do our lives bear the stains that God decries? If the prayers of the righteous have great power in their effect (James 5:16), what happens to the prayers of those whose lives are flagrantly out of sync with God's purposes? How much more learning do we need before we can recognize any heavenly good shaping our lives with God-pleasing consistency?

George Forell's timeless little book, *Faith Active in Love*, makes the necessary connection between a heart that is alive to God in faith and the hands that are then active in loving deeds for God in the world. We could apply the nature of faith in another way today, if one's audience would warrant attention to this direction. In the ongoing debate between creation and evolution, rather than polarizing positions with either/or rhetoric, it would be helpful to acknowledge the different modes of perception with which faith and science operate. These do not need to be exclusive, but rather complementary. This could avoid the errors of religious scientism on the one hand and the errors of scientific religionism on the other hand.

In yet another direction for faith to be explicated in relationship to the necessity of learning to do good, one could delineate how an envisioned future is both gift from God and something that one must work toward. When churches (or communities) go through a revisioning process to discern the preferred future into which God is calling them, they need to understand that this is first and foremost a gift from God. This is not something that can be earned by merit of the congregation. The future is in God's hands and God will give it to his people when they are ready to receive it. Faith waits expectantly for the future to come, as in the closing remarks of the book of Revelation: "Amen. Come, Lord Jesus!" (Revelation 22:29).

Still, faith is not inert. It does not simply sit around like Estragon and Vladimir waiting for Godot (Samuel Beckett's 1952 tragicomedy *Waiting for Godot*). It is more like Martin Luther, when asked what he would do if he learned that Jesus would be coming tomorrow. His reply, "I would plant a tree in my garden today." Faith calls forth effort that strives toward what the promise holds forth. Abraham necessarily had to leave Ur and travel beyond the horizon, an effort of no small means. He did not earn what was beyond the horizon in the Promised Land. His faith, however, the assurance and the conviction of it, led him to act upon it.

Jurgen Moltmann in *Theology of Hope* makes a similar connection between the promises of God and the commandments of God. The promise points to the goal; the commandments point to the way. He writes, "The promise of the covenant and the injunctions of the covenant have an abiding and guiding significance until the fulfillment... The commandments of the covenant, which point our hopes in the promise to the path of physical obedience, are nothing else but the ethical reverse of the promise itself." One does not earn the promise by observing the law; but, one does observe the law as a way of living in the promise of what is coming. The law, or the learning to do good, is the proleptic embodiment of the future into which God is calling us. The future shapes us in the present through the effort that we put into living in the promise.

There is a definite countercultural current in the Christian lifestyle. In today's consumer ethos, where possession and accumulation are measures of wealth and power, Christians are guided by the words of Jesus to "sell... and give" (Luke 12:33). Because the Christian's true treasure is in the heavenly good, priority consideration is given to what one can live without in order to provide for another's needs. Here is a measure of true wealth that stems from having the right values (see Matthew 6:33 and 13:44-45). Since behavior will follow what is valued (Luke 12:34), it is vital to have right values.

When one's treasure is correct, namely the rule of God in one's life, then there is no fear of loss nor fear of purposelessness nor fear of worthlessness, for the treasures in heaven do not fail.

Proper 15 / Pentecost 13 / Ordinary Time 20
Isaiah 5:1-7
Hebrews 11:29—12:2
Luke 12:49-56
David Kalas

Hall of fame game

Every major professional sport has a hall of fame. So do a lot of more obscure sports. Many college sports boast a hall of fame of their own. Both the rock music industry and the country music industry enshrine their best and brightest stars in halls of fame. Inventors, cowgirls, and robots all have halls of fame, as well.

Being "in" a hall of fame, of course, can mean one of two things. If I say that I am in the such-and-such hall of fame, it can mean that I have been elected to membership in the hall, which is a great honor in that particular field. Or if I say that I am in that hall of fame, I might simply be saying that I am presently walking through the museum-like building that is identified as the hall.

The two meanings are entirely separate, of course. For the accomplished people who are "in" the hall in the first sense are probably very seldom "in" the hall in the second sense. Busts, pictures, jerseys, and memorabilia of the famous members are what I would find in each hall that I visited; I would not find the members themselves.

Let us imagine for a moment that the members were there and that such halls were not merely repositories of mementos and tributes, but that the actual people themselves were there. Then a visit to such a hall would be a heady experience, indeed.

Each summer the National Football League signals the beginning of the preseason with its hall of fame game. It is played in Canton, Ohio, at the site of the Pro Football Hall of Fame. On that weekend, the newly elected class of hall of fame members are honored and installed, and two current NFL teams play one another in an exhibition game as part of the festivities.

Mostly, the stadium in Canton is filled with ordinary fans that day. But suppose it was the members of the hall who were in attendance. What would it be like for a current player or team to play in front of the legends?

Imagine being a player on the field. You look up in the stands and see Johnny Unitas, Jim Brown, and Jim Thorpe — watching you play. Nearby are Sid Luckman, Walter Peyton, and Don Hutson. Face after legendary face: Raymond Berry, Dick Butkus, Chuck Bednarik, and Ray Nitchkie. And, in a special box overlooking the field, you see the imposing figures of George Halas, Tom Landry, Bill Walsh, Paul Brown, and Vince Lombardi.

These are the men to whom the game belonged before you took the field. Indeed, in many cases, before you were born. These are the players and coaches who set records and won championships. Trophies and awards are named after these guys — and now they're watching you play their game.

And so, "since we are surrounded by so great a cloud of witnesses," says the writer of Hebrews, let's play our best and play to win!

Isaiah 5:1-7

In the midst of the most unsavory episode from King David's life and reign, the prophet Nathan comes to him with a story. It is all innocently told in the third person until, at the end, the prophet reveals that

David himself has a role in the story. Here, in the book of the prophet Isaiah, we encounter a story with a similar dramatic shift.

In the first two verses, the audience is introduced to the owner of a vineyard, and they are told his brief story. It is, initially, a scene full of beauty and promise, but it ends with disappointment. Then comes the shift. What seemed to be a detached, third-person account suddenly becomes quite personal. The storyteller-prophet is displaced by the Lord himself. And the fruitless vineyard of the story, the audience discovers, represents them.

For some years now, it has been the popular practice among many preachers to distribute sermon note-taking sheets to their congregations. The sheets offer an outline of the sermon, often including sentences with blanks left to be filled in by the listener. But long before such sheets became fashionable in North American pulpits, the Old Testament prophets employed a variation with dramatic effect.

What Nathan did with David and what Isaiah did with the inhabitants of Jerusalem was to leave a blank on the sermon sheet, only to invite the audience members to fill in their own names on that blank. "Now, friends, do you see that blank line next to 'the vineyard'? Go ahead and write 'Jerusalem' there. Jot down 'Judah.' Or you may simply write, 'Us.' "

We may have a preconceived notion about the typical judgment-prophet's message. We recognize that the bulk of his material is divided under two broad headings: 1) the people's chronic sinfulness; and 2) the coming judgment of God. Both of these subjects are covered and cataloged in some detail.

This Isaiah passage, however, offers a somewhat different take on the people's sinfulness. For the prophet does not itemize their faults. He does not catalog here the details of their injustice, idolatry, greed, and hypocrisy. Instead, in the brief story of the vineyard, the people's failure is not cast in terms of what they were, but rather what they were not. We will explore further this poignant truth below, under the heading "What Might Have Been."

What began as a promise turned into disappointment. And what was disappointing, according to the prophet, would soon be destroyed. "I will tell you what I will do to my vineyard," the Lord says, ominously.

In broad strokes, the pattern of this Old Testament passage may remind us of several New Testament passages. Just as the fruitless vineyard can expect to be ruined, so John the Baptist warned that the fruit-less trees will be cut down (Matthew 3:10). Similarly, when Jesus was disappointed by a fig tree that had nothing to offer (probably symbolic of Jerusalem in the larger context), he cursed it, and it withered (Mark 11:12-21). Jesus also told an open-ended parable about a landowner who, upon discovering that a particular tree was not producing as it should, instructed that it be cut down (Luke 13:6-9). So we see this consistent theme of pragmatic judgment: doing away with the worthless tree or vine that is not functioning as it ought.

In the case of the Isaiah prophecy, the proposed judgment has a distinctively painful element. We sense that God does not need to do the vineyard harm directly; he needs only to remove his blessings from it (the wall, the care, the rain), and it will be devastated. We are reminded of David's wisdom, who, upon facing a choice of punishments, reasoned, "Let us fall into the hand of the Lord, for his mercy is great; but let me not fall into human hands" (2 Samuel 24:14). Forebodingly, it seems that the vineyard of Isaiah's day would no longer be in the hand of the Lord and that is perhaps the worst fate of all.

Hebrews 11:29—12:2

By the time we meet up with the author of this famous "faith chapter," he is already 28 verses into his marvelous litany. Having begun with a definition of faith, he has since been inspired to offer examples of it. Indeed, many examples of it! He begins in humanity's second generation, with the exemplary Abel, and works his way forward through the many early heroes of faith.

When we join his survey in verse 29, we discover that he has only made it to the book of Exodus. Even after accelerating a bit, he was only in Joshua by the end of verse 31. It's understandable, therefore, when he stops short of the judges, saying, "Time would fail me to tell of Gideon, Barak, Samson, Jephthah...." The author moves from individual examples to broad categories: men and women who, by faith, "conquered kingdoms, administered justice, obtained promises, shut the mouths of lions, quenched raging fire, escaped the edge of the sword," and on and on.

If I were still working with youth groups, I would present verses 33-35a as a sort of quiz, inviting the kids to give one specific example from scripture of each of the categories identified by the writer. My experience is that adults are not so receptive to such quizzes. Still, it would be a good exercise — for individuals or for small groups — to put names on these descriptions.

Meanwhile, in the midst of verse 35, there is a sudden and unanticipated polar shift. Having heaped up a great pile of blessings and victories, climaxing with a reference to people coming back from the dead, the writer abruptly turns 180-degrees, saying, "Others were tortured... suffered mocking and flogging... stoned to death, sawn in two, killed by the sword... destitute, persecuted, tormented." If reading were driving, we would have suffered whiplash from such a sudden and dramatic turn.

How can the writer move so seamlessly from victories to defeats? How can he shift, without warning or explanation, from tales of success to such images of failure? A quotation of verses 35b-39 should appear in the dictionary under "non-sequitur."

The author does not treat the accounts of destitution and death as being inconsistent with the early accounts of marvels and miracles. He sees a great continuity where we are inclined to see a great diversion. He recognizes a continuous flow where we perceive a watershed.

The linguistic link between the two sections is the word "resurrection." The word represents the climax of what we might call the victory section: "Women received their dead by resurrection." In the very next phrase, the writer repeats the word, but with a very different flavor: "Others were tortured, refusing to accept release, in order to obtain a better resurrection." And so begins the series of grim descriptions that we might call the defeat section.

But the writer of Hebrews would not call it that. He does not regard the accounts of torture, persecution, imprisonment, and martyrdom as defeats. For him, the escalator just keeps going up. There is, you see, "a better resurrection." By extension, there is a better life and reward than what the first group of heroes could experience here in this world. This world, after all, is not worthy of them. And so it is that, one way or another, faith always gains its reward.

Still, when the writer comes to the end of the chapter, we discover that the escalator has yet another floor to go. For all of these heroes of faith, saints and martyrs still "did not receive what was promised." There still remained "something better." And that something better, he suggests, came with the present generation, "so that they would not, apart from us, be made perfect."

Thus the author makes one more effortless, seamless shift. All of the preceding generations of the faithful, having been introduced in a line, are now collapsed into a single unit. They are all together now as an audience. And now it is our time — and our turn — to be faithful.

Luke 12:49-56

You probably receive, as I do, the religious catalogs featuring various bulletin covers and artwork that we can purchase for our churches. When significant holy days and seasons come round, there is a superabundant offering of options, including matching stationery and offering envelopes.

Perhaps the greatest supply of such resources is found during the Advent and Christmas seasons. One of the great recurring themes of the artwork and texts is "peace." The images are peaceful. The angels proclaim, "Peace on earth." One candle in the Advent wreath is designated as "peace," and the baby is heralded as "the prince of peace."

It seems, however, that Jesus did not get the memo.

"Do you think that I have come to bring peace to the earth?" he asks his followers. And with earnestness, hopefulness, and a bit of sentimentality, we eagerly answer, "Yes! That's exactly what we think!"

"No," he answers, "but rather division."

What follows may be a bit surprising for some in our congregations. Perhaps not having read much of the Bible for themselves, they are left with only what they have heard and what they have been told through the years. What they have been told, in so many cases, is that Jesus brings peace.

To address the discrepancy, we might do well to define just what we mean — or what scripture means — by "peace." The predicted "prince of peace" (Isaiah 9:6), on the one hand, may anticipate an eschatological messianic achievement of global peace among peoples and nations. The "peace I give to you" (John 14:27), on the other hand, may refer to a personal experience, an inner peace that is quite independent of the larger context.

In our gospel lection, meanwhile, it seems that Jesus is speaking of neither global peace nor inner peace. Instead, he goes on to reference interpersonal relationships: fathers and son, mothers and daughters, and in-laws.

The divisions that Jesus anticipates — indeed, causes — will not cut along the traditional lines of nations, ethnic groups, or social classes. Rather, the divisions will be close to home and very personal. The "us" and "them" are completely redefined, for "they" are not on the other side of the tracks, or a different color, or across the ocean. No, "they" are at the supper table with "us." It's an astonishing proposition.

I endorse the mostly unquestioned assumption that God would have us be good family members — that Christian husbands and wives, fathers and mothers, and children all bear a certain responsibility before God to play our parts well. That theme can be traced from the Old Testament law through the Proverbs and into the writings of Peter and Paul.

At the same time, however, this passage reminds us of the subordination and redefining of family that we find in Jesus' teachings. He insists that we love him more than the nearest and most natural of our love relationships (Matthew 10:37). He seems to take for granted that discipleship may require the certain abandoning of those relationships (Matthew 19:29). And he reformulates the boundaries and membership of family (Luke 8:19-21).

Application

You and I are called to be faithful, and we call our brothers and sisters, the friends and members of our congregations, to be faithful too.

And what does that faithfulness look like?

It doesn't look like Judah and Jerusalem of Isaiah's day. That generation of God's people had not lived in proper response to God's guidance and care. Their lives were not marked by justice and righteousness. They had not born fruit pleasing to God. Rather, they were a disappointment to him.

So what does faithfulness look like? The writer of Hebrews knows, and he shows us.

In his marvelous chapter on faith, the writer walks us through the snapshots and memorabilia of the faith hall of fame. There we see the inspiring busts of Abel and Abraham. We remember the stories of Moses and Joshua. We see old footage from the era of the judges. And we are reminded of the noble martyrs all along the way, suffering unjustly but staying faithful, even through pain and death.

Perhaps those great heroes of faith come to mind, too, when we read Jesus' teaching. He depicts faithful discipleship as a fierce personal allegiance that has priority over every other love, affection, and ambition. Personal faithfulness to him may create tension and divisions between us and other people, and it may cost us some relationships.

Now we know what faithfulness looks like. And to challenge us on to brave and no-nonsense faithfulness where we are, the writer of Hebrews shows us the stadium. All of those marvelous saints from days gone by — the legendary men and women of faith through the ages — they are "so great a cloud of witnesses." We run the race in front of that audience. When we get winded or wounded; when we are inclined toward discouragement or despair; we look up in the stands, and we remember what faithfulness looks like. Best of all, we look to Jesus and we remember what faithfulness looks like; then we "run with perseverance the race that is set before us."

An Alternative Application

Isaiah 5:1-7. "What Might Have Been." I don't remember many occasions during my growing up years when my parents scolded me. They were low-key parents, and I was a pretty good child. I do remember one occasion, when I was about sixteen years old, I was caught in the midst of a rather significant deception. There was no big scene at the time. And the next time I was in the same room as my mom, it was awkwardly silent. After several tense minutes, she finally was the one to break the silence. She turned to look at me, and she said, without raising her voice, "I'm so disappointed."

So many years later, I still feel the pain of that moment. I don't think she could have said anything more effective or more penetrating to me.

That is the thrust of God's message through Isaiah to the people of Judah and Jerusalem. He was disappointed — so profoundly disappointed. There was such hope and promise at the beginning. He had invested such effort and care, but the people did not produce accordingly.

We see hints of this divine disappointment from the very beginning. In the opening chapters of Genesis, we are introduced to a universe and a garden that are created to be so very good. The man and woman — they were created even better, for they were made in the image of God: "ordained to be transcripts of the Trinity," as Charles Wesley wrote, "creatures capable of God" in his hymn, "Sinners, Turn: Why Will You Die." Yet just a few chapters later, God looks at what has become of his good creation and creatures; he "saw that the wickedness of humankind was great in the earth, and that every inclination of the thoughts of their hearts was only evil continually. And the Lord was sorry that he had made humankind on the earth, and it grieved him to his heart" (Genesis 6:5-6).

The great tragedy of the vineyard — of God's people — is not merely how bad they were, but how good they ought to have been. When a C student brings home a D, the disappointment is not so great because the expectation was not so great. But when a straight-A student brings home a D, it's a stunning disappointment. We expected so much better from him or her.

God expected so much better from his vineyard. And he still does.

Mixed reactions

The promos for a new movie feature all sorts of glowing quotes from an assortment of reviews. The ads for a political candidate boast the support of important newspapers and individuals. And the over-the-counter product reports the endorsement of "four out of five doctors surveyed."

In fact, of course, not every review of the movie was favorable, not every significant paper and individual backs the candidate in question, and we never get to hear what that fifth doctor thinks.

The point is that very few things enjoy unanimous approval. Most things meet with mixed reactions.

That's fine, of course, for as long as we're dealing with matters of opinion, taste, or preference. The film embraced by one as "deeply moving" is dismissed by another as a "chick flick." One person's music is another one's noise. And what was just right for Papa Bear was too hot for Goldilocks.

When we move out of the realm of opinion and taste, however, mixed reactions can mean trouble. The doctor does not expect a wide variety of responses to the rubber mallet reflex test. The colonel does not permit a wide variety of responses when he gives an order. And the elementary school math teacher does not welcome a variety of responses to the equation "two-plus-two-equals...."

In some arenas of life, mixed reactions are natural and inevitable. In other areas, mixed reactions are surprising and troubling.

Remarkably, God gets mixed reactions.

Ever since Adam and Eve's misadventure in Eden, God has been getting mixed reviews from the human beings he loves so much. His miracles have yielded both converts and skeptics. His commands have prompted both devotion and resistance. His teachings have inspired both adherents and critics. From the assorted soils in Jesus' parable (Matthew 13:18-23) to the Jerusalem crowds of Holy Week (cf. Mark 11:8-10; 15:11-15), the Lord has suffered mixed reactions from the very ones created in his image.

The passages for this Sunday portray a wide range of reactions to God, his word, and his work.

Jeremiah 1:4-10

Here is the call of Jeremiah. It is personal and unique to Jeremiah, on the one hand, and it is absolutely typical of God's call, on the other.

The personal elements of the passage are lovely affirmations of the individualized nature of God's work in our lives. We are not mere numbers or replaceable cogs. Rather, the Lord affirms that he personally formed, knew, consecrated, and appointed Jeremiah. The prophet was not just one in a million called up in a draft. No, his creation and his call were the product of personal one-on-one involvement by God.

That personal quality is characteristic of how God works all through scripture. Though there is the larger theme (and unit) of a covenant people, still God deals with folks individually. We read the accounts of his individual calls in the lives of Noah, Abram, Moses, Gideon, David, Isaiah, Jonah, and on and on. Likewise, in the New Testament, Jesus does not broadcast an invitation to discipleship; he calls the disciples personally. The gospel of John features chapter after chapter of one-on-one encounters between individuals and Jesus. Later, God also calls the apostle Paul in such a personal and individual way that we might even say he was targeted.

God's call on Jeremiah's life was not well received at first. Jeremiah felt quite unqualified for the task he was being given (cf., Moses in Exodus 4:10 and Gideon in Judges 6:14-15), and he may have been right. But our human qualifications are not finally the point when it comes to the work of God. More specifically, *we* are not the point when it comes to the work of God.

God made that fact clear to Jeremiah. The real issue is not Jeremiah but God. See how many first-person, singular verbs God uses in this passage. First, there is the account of all that God has already done (I formed, I knew, I consecrated, I appointed). Then comes the list of what God is presently doing (I send, I command, I am with, I have put my words, I appoint).

Jeremiah has some first-person singular things to say too. Specifically, he says, "I do not know" and "I am only." Give him credit for his humility and perspective, for we do God's work no great favor when we rely too heavily on what we do know and what we are. Jeremiah was not mistaken in what he said about himself. His mistake was in thinking that he was the issue in the first place.

Hebrews 12:18-29

A familiar assignment to high school English students is the compare-and-contrast essay. The approach is also familiar to the reader of Hebrews, for compare-and-contrast is the name of the game in this epistle.

The author and audience of this epistle are less certain than with many of the other New Testament letters — more fodder for the scholars. This much seems evident, at least: the author and the audience were Jewish and intimately familiar with the Hebrew scriptures. Furthermore, the author reveals a strong Greek influence in his heritage or education, for his method of interpreting the scriptures reflects a distinctively Greek perspective.

Beyond those basic assumptions, the rest is guesswork. For myself, I think of the letter to the Hebrews as serving the same function as a French-to-English dictionary might for an American tourist in Paris. The writer of Hebrews takes what is new and unfamiliar — the gospel of Jesus Christ — and translates it in the terms of what is old and native — the Old Testament law and prophets.

The analogy is imperfect, of course, since there is a more derivative and deliberate relationship between the Old and New Testaments than between French and English. Nevertheless, the purpose remains the same: to help people understand what is new and foreign in the light of what is old and native.

The letter to the Hebrews is not useful in this function for most of the people in our pews, however. It is the symbols, stories, and rituals of the Old Testament that are foreign to so many American churchgoers, and so the law and the prophets do not make a helpful point of reference in explaining and understanding the gospel. If anything, we may find ourselves using the letter to the Hebrews in reverse — that is, using the gospel message to help our people gain an understanding and appreciation of the Old Testament.

In our particular passage, the compare-and-contrast approach focuses on the two covenants — the old covenant represented by Mount Sinai and the new covenant represented by Mount Zion. The writer offers dramatic side-by-side pictures. The former comes mostly from Israel's experience at Sinai in Exodus, and it demonstrates the awesome and terrifying context of the old covenant. The latter picture, meanwhile, is not the product of some particular event in scripture but is rather a more fanciful compendium of images designed to illustrate the glory and beauty of the new covenant.

The images associated with the new covenant — what we "come to" — are no less dramatic and awesome than those associated with the old covenant. Both elicit reverence and awe. But the new covenant imagery has a quality of approachability, welcome, and celebration that are plainly absent in the Mount Sinai scene.

The writer of Hebrews is eager to illustrate how superior the new covenant is. The invitation and opportunity are so much better than ancient Israel's relationship with God was or could have been. At the same time, however, the greater intimacy does not mean greater informality. The invitation is to be closer, not less careful.

The subject of a kingdom who stands outside the palace and the one who stands inside the throne room are suitably impressed by the majesty of the place. The latter has the greater privilege, of course, to enjoy a personal audience with the king. At the same time, while there is less distance, there is perhaps greater fear.

The fear should not be mistaken for the uncertainty that comes from serving a capricious God. Quite the contrary: We enjoy a stability ("a kingdom that cannot be shaken") and security ("the sprinkled blood that speaks a better word than the blood of Abel") that bear witness to the steadfast love of God. And so our fear is not insecurity, but "reverence and awe."

Luke 13:10-17

There are two different plot lines at work in this episode. The one is the plot line to which Luke is paying the most attention: Jesus' ministry and the growing antagonism of his opponents. The other plot line is the one that may be most important to the people in our pews: The life story of the woman who was healed.

We don't know anything about the woman except that she had been in her hunched over condition for eighteen years. What is the hope quotient after eighteen years? What level of expectation do we have that some circumstance or condition will get better after living with a thing for so long? While our sense of hopefulness naturally diminishes over time, the plot of this woman's story reminds us that Jesus can step in *at any time* with healing and deliverance.

The narrator attributes the woman's condition to "a spirit." That seems somewhat primitive to the modern mind, but we are willing to overlook it coming from Luke. It is harder to overlook, however, when the same kind of diagnosis comes from Jesus himself ("a daughter of Abraham whom Satan bound for eighteen long years").

We see in the story of the man born blind in John 9 (see vv. 1-3) that Jesus does not automatically concede the contemporary theological interpretations of illness or handicap (or even of tragedy, as in Luke 13:1-5). Yet here in this passage, Jesus affirms that the woman's condition is Satan's doing, she is in bondage, and she ought to be set free. It seems, in our day, like an impolitic way to talk about a handicapping condition. Perhaps we have largely abandoned our heritage of providing healing in favor of providing acceptance and accessibility.

The other plot line is the ongoing story of Jesus' ministry and the evolving resistance to him. This is the fourth episode in Luke's gospel (along with 4:16-30; 4:33-36; and 6:6-11) when Jesus appears in a synagogue, and the third occasion when what he says or does in the synagogue spurs anger and opposition. The controversy here (as in ch. 6) centers around Jesus healing on the sabbath. The uncertain matter is whether the sabbath was really the issue, or whether Jesus was really the issue.

If we are predisposed to be antagonistic toward someone, then we will find fault with almost anything that person does. Perhaps that's why Jesus' opponents here locked themselves into such an untenable position.

On the other hand, if we are slavishly devoted to some principle, our legalism may blind us to a greater good. Perhaps that sabbath-protectionism led to the myopia of Jesus' opponents here and in chapter 6.

We see in verse 15 a distinctive characteristic of Luke's gospel. While all four gospels include people calling Jesus "Lord," Luke is the only one of the synoptics that includes pre-resurrection references to Jesus as "the Lord" in the narration. Even in John's gospel, those narrative references are few before the resurrection (John 6:23; 11:2), while in Luke they are quite common (e.g., Luke 7:13; 10:41; 11:39; 12:42; 17:6; 18:6; 22:61).

Finally, we are presented with a striking contrast between the healed woman and the opponents of Jesus. At the end of the episode, she is erect and praising God. Jesus' opponents, however, are "put to shame." Her condition had changed that day, but theirs had not. Is it possible that it is easier to be set free from Satan's bondage than from that of legalism?

Application

The printed invitation includes these initials at the bottom: R.S.V.P. *Please respond.*

From cover to cover, scripture is full of invitations: invitations from God to humankind. And from the God who calls the hiding couple in Eden, to the good shepherd who calls the lost lamb in the wild, the underlying tone of the invitation is always the same: *Please respond.*

Some folks, like the first of the four soils in Jesus' parable (see Matthew 13:1-9, 18-23), are completely unresponsive. If the parable is to be taken literally, they are a minority. Among the majority who do respond to God, meanwhile, the responses vary widely.

The three selected passages for this Sunday are a study in those varied human responses to God.

The Jeremiah lection features the explicit response of Jeremiah to God's call, as well as an implication about the response of the people to whom Jeremiah is sent ("do not be afraid of them").

The Hebrews passage recalls the wilting, fearful response of Moses and the people at Sinai, as well as that earlier generation's failure to respond obediently to God's human spokesman — "the one who warned them on earth." Meanwhile, the writer of Hebrews exhorts his audience to an appropriate response: "Do not refuse to respond to the one who is speaking" and "Offer to God an acceptable worship with reverence and awe."

Finally, the gospel lection depicts the mixed reactions of the synagogue crowd. Jesus' opponents were "indignant" about his work, while others were "rejoicing at all the wonderful things that he was doing."

An honest and sympathetic look at the people involved in these stories will result in some conclusions that hit pretty close to home.

Many of us understand Jeremiah's resistance to take on some task for God, not because of any disrespect for him and his work, but rather because of our great respect. God and his work deserve better, more qualified servants. Instead of actually responding to God, we inadvertently respond instead to something about ourselves.

The congregation around Sinai, meanwhile, was not the last to stay at a distance from God, fearful and uncertain. Like the recipients of the epistle, many of us may need to be reminded of the profound and awesome invitation of the new covenant, lest we treat it casually or lightly, lest reverence is replaced by nonchalance.

A careful look at the folks gathered in the synagogue may also feel like a look in the mirror. They are, after all, an earnest, religious lot. It was not some obvious vice or wickedness that made them unreceptive to the Lord's work. Rather it was their own well-meaning devotion to their understanding of what it means to obey God.

If we review the record of our own individual lives, we will find that we have given God mixed reactions over the years. And if we review the record of scripture, perhaps it will help us see more clearly how we are responding to him now.

Alternative Applications

Jeremiah 1:4-10. We mentioned earlier the first-person, singular verbs that appear in the Jeremiah passage. One set of verbs identifies what God had already done in Jeremiah's life, and the other set what God was presently doing in Jeremiah's life. Either set would be a useful basis for an expository sermon exploring God's work in our lives.

The first set of verbs affirms the work and purpose of God in our lives from the very start. His work in us and his will for us did not begin just when we started paying attention to him. The newborn does not know or love the parent, and certainly the baby has no plans. But the parent knows and loves the baby, and the parent has so many plans, and so many preparations already in place. So it is with God and us: long before we know or love him, he already knows and loves us, and he has plans for us well before we are interested in knowing what they are.

The second set of verbs affirms the basic paradigm of God's call. The components in verses 7-10 are reminiscent of Jesus' Great Commission to his disciples (Matthew 28:16-20). Many of those elements are also seen in Moses' call experience at the burning bush (Exodus 3:1—4:23). We might explore and understand God's call in our own lives by examining the second set of verbs in this story of Jeremiah's call.

Luke 13:10-17. The wise man said, "Hope deferred makes the heart sick" (Proverbs 13:12a). How sick, then, must this hunched over woman's heart have been?

When it comes to hope, most of us prefer to make a low-risk investment. Not getting our hopes up is both a personal policy and our prudent advice to those dearest to us.

On the other hand, few postures could be so patently unChristian as despair. The man or woman of God should never be without hope.

Perhaps the story of the woman who, after a hopelessly long time, met with healing and deliverance should be a challenge and encouragement to us and our congregations. Perhaps we ought to reacquaint ourselves with the God for whom it's never too late (cf., Luke 8:40-55; John 5:1-9). Perhaps we ought to run the risk of hoping that the situation we had given up for lost can still be touched and restored to wholeness by the Lord.

Proper 17 / Pentecost 15 / Ordinary Time 22
Jeremiah 2:4-13
Hebrews 13:1-8, 15-16
Luke 14:1, 7-14
Timothy Cargal

Etiquette for God's realm

It has happened to me often enough in my ministry that I must conclude that it is a common experience among pastors. You have performed the marriage ceremony and have accepted the family's (usually insistent) invitation to attend the wedding reception, not infrequently because they would like you to say the prayer before the meal or attend to some other formality of the occasion. But formality not being what it used to be, you arrive at the banquet hall to find that not all of the seating has been pre-assigned with place cards. Most of the tables have what might be called "open seating," but the head table and perhaps a few close by do have designated seating for what must be presumed to be honored guests.

No host is directing the wedding guests, so what do you do? Do you assume that since you performed the ceremony and will soon be giving the invocation that there must be a place card somewhere with your name on it, and if not at the head table then certainly one of those nearby? But it would be embarrassing to nonchalantly make your way past each setting only to find that none of the settings had been set aside specifically for you. Besides, the evening would be passed much more pleasantly seated with folks you know from your congregation than with distant relatives who have come for the festivities from equally distant cities. So do you simply head for some much less prominent seating?

Being the pastor, you will immediately recall that Jesus told a parable relating to this very situation. You head for one of those undesignated tables. Better to be asked to join the prime seating than to be perceived as presumptuous (Luke 14:8-10). Proud of both your biblical literacy and your exemplary humility you find a seat on the fringes of the room. Yet as you sit there, you begin to wonder: Was Jesus really saying nothing more in this parable than the advice one might have just as easily found in the manners books by Emily Post or Amy Vanderbilt?

Jeremiah 2:4-13

The lectionary reading from Jeremiah is the second segment of a five-part oracle that spans all of chapter 2. The oracle begins by recalling the covenant fidelity of the Israelites to God using the imagery of a young bride and groom on what might be called their honeymoon (2:1-3). The remaining sections consist of alternating indictments of Israel and Judah's religious (2:4-13, 20-28) and political disloyalty (first with the Assyrians, 2:14-19, and later with the Egyptians, 2:29-37). The overarching structure of the oracle is provided by the use of the *riv* form, a type of "lawsuit" in which God substantiates charges against the people by calling witnesses, cites proof of God's own fidelity to the covenant, challenges the people to defend themselves against the charges, and finally pronounces the verdict and punishment.

Following a summons to hear these charges (2:4), the reading begins with a rhetorical question put to the people as defendants by God as the prosecutor. God asks what it was that the divine had done to provoke their ancestors to reject the covenant with God and to seek "worthless things, and became worthless themselves" (2:5). This charge plays on two meanings of the Hebrew word *hebel*; it is used to mean "idols" (see Jeremiah 8:19) and "something that is worthless" (most famously the "vanity" that is cited some 36 times in Ecclesiastes). Thus by turning away from the worship of God to instead make a covenant with "empty" idols, the people had become worthless themselves. Another wordplay is used when the specific god of these idols, Baal, is identified at 2:8. Baal is the name of a god in the Canaanite pantheon and the common Hebrew word for "husband." The people have left their marriage covenant with God, despite the blessings God had given them in the Exodus from Egypt and settlement in the bountiful land promised to Abraham, and taken on a new husband in Baal even though that meant going "after things that do not profit" (2:6-8).

God has been left literally dumbfounded by this rejection. Even those peoples throughout the Mediterranean basin who worshiped gods that in actuality were non-existent ("even though they are no gods") have nevertheless remained faithful in their loyalty to them (2:10-11). From this action God distills two charges against the people of Judah: "They have forsaken me," a real source of provision for the "living water" on which their lives themselves depend; and they have mistakenly concluded that they could provide for themselves when they "dug out... cracked cisterns that can hold no water" (2:13).

Hebrews 13:1-8, 15-16

The book of Hebrews closes with a number of briefly stated admonitions. The topics to which they refer are wide-ranging and switch rapidly. To the degree that the author makes any attempt to relate them to a common theme, that theme is expressed in the final verses of the lectionary reading. Doing good by sharing of one's self and one's possessions are "sacrifices" that are "pleasing to God," and the offering of such sacrifices is a continual responsibility.

The first set of admonitions (13:1-5) can be construed as specific examples of ways that one can fulfill the opening command to maintain "mutual love." Recognizing a mutuality between persons calls forth "hospitality to strangers" because there will be occasions in which we will all find ourselves to be the stranger. It reminds us that the inhuman conditions in which some people are imprisoned and even tortured is dehumanizing to us all. The mutuality of love within marriage, extending even to sexual relationships (a truly radical notion in the social context originally addressed by this author), must be honored not only between the partners but also by society itself.

Attitudes toward money and possessions are to be established by the recognition that God is the source of all that we have (13:5-6). God's provision is both secure and sufficient. Any affection relative to the material goods necessary for this life is properly directed to the one who supplies them rather than to the goods themselves or the money that is exchanged for them.

The specific "leaders" referred to in 13:7 would appear to be the elders within the religious community (cf. 13:17). They are the ones who "spoke the word of God to you" both by formal instruction and by the conduct of their lives, setting an example of faith for others to imitate. The foremost such leader is, of course, Jesus Christ, whose consistency of example is emphasized by the declaration that he "is the same yesterday and today and forever."

The lectionary skips over the material in 13:9-14. There would appear to be two reasons for this decision. First, this material at a minimum tends toward a "supercessionist" position of followers of Christ as compared to those who have remained within the traditional covenantal relationship of Judaism. It presents the kosher dietary practice as of no benefit, and exalts the "altar" at which this community worships as one at which the Jewish priests "have no right to eat." The irony is that these arguments follow very traditional forms of rabbinic disputation melded with specific Neo-Platonic philosophical speculation. Thus, the second reason for passing over these verses is that a proper understanding of the details in this argument (the significance of being "outside the camp," of "having no lasting city, but looking for the city that is to come," and so on) requires extensive explanation. If the religious and philosophical aspects of this argument are correctly understood, then it can be properly seen as a debate *within* a religious tradition rather than one religion superseding another. Unless the topic of the sermon was itself the relationship between Judaism and Christianity, the intricacies of explanation called for go far beyond what can be developed homiletically as background.

Luke 14:1, 7-14

The gospel lesson recounts two of a series of three parables (14:7-11, 12-14, 15-24) constructed around the behavior of hosts and guests at dinner parties. The evangelist has placed all of these parables in the narrative context of a sabbath meal to which Jesus had been invited (14:1). Whether the occasion prompted the series of parables in the manner that the evangelist presents them, or alternatively the evangelist gathered them together at this point in his narrative because they share a common setting, is of course now impossible to determine (cf. the cluster of parables about lost sheep, coins, and sons in Luke 15). It is also somewhat beside the point. One of the characteristic features of Jesus' parables, as with most successful parables, is that they draw on a common experience of life to explain the uncommon or unknown. Thus, these parables are not ultimately about table manners but about proper decorum for those "who will eat bread in the kingdom of God" (14:15).

The first of the parables is related from the vantage point of the invited guest. Elaborating on what was already well-established advice (cf. Proverbs 25:6-7), Jesus directs guests not to presume that they are among the most prominent persons invited to the meal. It is better to be brought up to a higher station among those who have gathered than to embarrass yourself and your host by being asked to make a place for others who are more honored. One could, of course, employ this bit of conventional wisdom as a way to game the system and seek to draw attention and honor to one's self. Deliberately and publicly taking a place associated with low honor, one could make a most public show of false modesty while being escorted by the host to a more honored position in the sight of the assembled guests. To cut off such Machiavellian schemes, Jesus underscores the moral of the story: "For all who exalt themselves will be humbled, and those who humble themselves will be exalted" (14:11).

The point of the parable is hardly about place settings at dinner parties. It is about the core value of humility within the realm of God. The evangelist has highlighted this purpose by identifying the story as a "parable," and phrasing the moral in the passive voice also subtly reinforces it. This verb form was commonly used to indicate divine agency without explicitly naming God as the one who acts. Thus, to say that some "will be humbled" while others "will be exalted" is to say that God will bring down those who exalt themselves and will honor those who are genuinely humble in deferring to the honor of others.

The second parable takes up the point of view of the host rather than the guests and is thoroughly rooted in the patronage systems of Greco-Roman society. Within those cultures people were able to place others within their debt by feting them as honored guests at public gatherings. If prominent members of the community accepted your invitation, you not only assured yourself a reciprocal invitation from them but also immediately raised your own social standing by their willingness to incur this social debt. Hosting one's peers or social superiors was a means of maintaining or advancing one's own social position.

Jesus advises people to instead host "the poor, the crippled, the lame, and the blind" at their banquets. Since such people in that culture were socially despised and economically disadvantaged and so unable to repay the social debt themselves (14:14b), it is possible to hear in this advice a reversal of the usual customs. But it may be the parable is less about overturning the patronage system than about recognizing the ultimate patron. Since God is the patron of the physically, socially, and economically disadvantaged who are invited as guests in the divine kingdom (as in the third parable of this sequence, 14:21b), then receiving them likewise earns God's favor. Once more the use of the passive voice ("will be blessed," "will be repaid") implies that God does for them what the disadvantaged cannot.

Application

When we are trying to teach the rules of social etiquette and decorum to our children, one of the tried and true principles is to point out patterns that make sense of what can otherwise be a hopelessly confusing hodge-podge of apparently *ad hoc* rules. Thus while we may hope that they will one day be able to immediately discern the difference between a salad fork and a dinner fork, between a soup spoon and a dessert spoon, between a butter knife and a steak knife, we usually begin by pointing out that the proper eating utensils for each course of the meal can be identified simply by working from the outside-in of a correctly arranged place setting. Obviously if they don't eventually learn the distinguishing characteristics of each utensil they will never be able to correctly set the table themselves, but familiarity with the patterns will itself help with learning the particularities.

So it is as well for learning the etiquette of God's realm. There are *similarities* between the world in which we live and the realm perfectly ordered according to God's will, and that is why Jesus was able to use parables as a means of relating our common experience to the all too uncommon expectations of divine justice. There are fundamental principles at work in God's wisdom that provide the basis for all the specific types of behavior that are expected of those "who eat bread in the kingdom of God."

The New Testament lessons for this week help us to identify those principles and patterns. One is the need for mutual love. When we recognize the interdependence we all share with each other, we will recognize our need to deal with others in the ways we would consider just for ourselves. Another is our ultimate dependence upon God. When we have the faith to see God as not only the source of what we have gained in the past but also a sure help for what we will need in the future, we will be able to keep our affections directed at the one with whom we are in relationship rather than on the things that arise from that relationship. Yet another is genuine humility. When we come to understand that the most honorable thing in any of us is that God has accepted the role as our patron, we will be able to acknowledge the respect that is due to everyone as a child of God.

Alternative Applications

Jeremiah 2:4-13. One wonders where the prophet Jeremiah would have come down in the discussion about God in our public lives. Would he have joined those who see the removal of the words "under God" as forsaking our nation's relationship with the God who, in the words of our Declaration of Independence, as Creator "endowed us with certain inalienable rights"? Or would he have agreed with those who remain in covenant with God but would nevertheless accept the removal of the phrase because it has become in some sense meaningless? In other words, is an expression of "ceremonial deism" in public life itself an expression that we, like the people of ancient Judah, have gone "far from [God], and went after worthless things, and became worthless [ourselves]" (Jeremiah 2:5)?

Jeremiah 2:4-13; Hebrews 13:1-8, 15-16. Many modern Christians have divided their lives into two portions. There is the mundane, day-to-day stuff of living that we consider ourselves more than competent to take care of. We do our jobs, tend to our families, and perhaps (time permitting) even contribute to the broader civic good. Then there are the big things that threaten to overwhelm us. Sometimes they are bad things like catastrophic illness, or they may even be good things like entering into a new marriage or celebrating the birth of a child. When these things happen, we reach beyond ourselves and turn to God for help. Yet these lessons remind us that we are dependent upon God's help for the mundane stuff as well. Even the things we take for granted are there because God's faithfulness to us is "the same yesterday and today and forever." Maybe it is time to take a break from patting ourselves on the back and to thank God for the "fountain of living water" from which we draw on a daily basis.

Proper 18 / Pentecost 16 / Ordinary Time 23
Jeremiah 18:1-11
Philemon 1-21
Luke 14:25-33
Mark Molldrem

Life with attitude

We live in an ever-coarsening culture. The edgy sounds and razor lyrics of punk and rap music have set a cutting edge to what defines our time. It's a raw look at who we are and what we do as a society. The language now deemed acceptable for general broadcast in the public media has reached new depths of baseness, not just with the words that are permissible to air, but also in the way certain topics are talked about. Dress has become more undress, with fashions flaunting undergarments, as well as slovenliness. Rudeness is justified either as "my rights" or "I'm just being honest with you."

Sadly, this coarseness is part of the ethos that defines America at the beginning of this new millennium. It expresses an attitude that is self-absorbed, angry, and dispirited, playing on the threshold of nihilism. Injected into this malaise today are words from scripture that convey an *attitude*, to be sure, but one that is quite different than what arises naturally from the human heart. These words redirect our focus to a more substantial ground on which to stand, from which a healthier and hopeful attitude can arise for the living of our days.

Jeremiah 18:1-11

Jeremiah would have made a great homiletics professor for the eager preacher, more by example than by erudite lectures on the composition and delivery of sermons. Baruch, his faithful scribe, knew this and recorded for posterity many of Jeremiah's sermons. The first twenty chapters of Jeremiah contain sermons delivered during the reigns of Josiah and Jehoiakim, in the last half of the seventh century BC. Each sermon is introduced in a manner like this: "The word that came to Jeremiah from the Lord" (Jeremiah 1:4, 11; 2:1; 3:6; 7:1; 11:1; 14:1; 16:1; 18:1). Notice in this formula that the Lord is the source of Jeremiah's message. The prophet speaks not on his own authority; nor is his message simply what he thought up while burning the midnight oil.

Good sermons have good illustrations, and Jeremiah's sermon in today's text is no exception. The visual image of a potter toiling over a lump of clay is sufficient for Jeremiah to speak about how God is dealing with his people. Just as a potter can take a misshaped lump of clay that at first did not respond to the potter's design and remake it into something else, so too can God rework his people in new ways, "as it seemed good... to do" (18:4). It is God's prerogative to do with the clay of his creation (the house of Israel) as he chooses.

The relationship between God and his people, the clay, is a dynamic one. The response the people offer to the working of the divine hands will make a difference in how those hands work the unfolding creation. When there is repentance in the clay, God, the potter, will not throw the sample away but will continue to work with it and develop a newer, more satisfying design. If, however, there is evil in the clay — a resistance to the potter having his way in shaping the clay, then the potter will not be able to finish the intended design. The clay will be taken off the wheel, and it will no longer have the opportunity to come to life.

Out of this undesirable result comes the exhortation to repent (18:11). Short of this, there can only be judgment, which will disappoint the potter and leave the clay in despair. This message of Jeremiah does more than lift up the threat of judgment; it emphasizes the invitation of a caring potter that the clay remain responsive and thus on the wheel of life. This does not minimize the seriousness of the judgment; what it does more so is motivate a response of returning to the Lord.

Philemon 1-21

It is understandable, though unfortunate, that Philemon gets only one slot in the lectionary. Perhaps every pastor should determine to preach from this text/story this weekend, because this is the only time we will intentionally see Philemon and Onesimus. They have so much to offer us that it would be a shame to pass them over for any reason.

This is a beautiful story of forgiveness and Christian fellowship at its richest. Onesimus was a slave in the household of Philemon. We do not know the circumstances of why he apparently ran away. We learn that Philemon was a faithful Christian who expressed his love for the Lord and for the Christian community. Apparently, however, Onesimus did not convert to the faith while in Philemon's household.

Somehow, Onesimus ends up with Paul and becomes a Christian. Paul wants to send him back to Philemon. He is concerned, though, about everyone's attitude in this matter. He lifts up Onesimus as a valued servant (not slave; vv. 13 and 16) in the Lord. This he makes clear in his choice of words describing Onesimus. The word for "slave" describes his station in life; the word for "servant" (from which we get the word *deacon* and the *deaconite ministry*) describes his status in the Christian community. Paul affirms Onesimus as "a beloved brother." With this new identity, Paul encourages him to return home to his master, most likely with a refreshed vision for serving the family with an attitude of mission, an attitude that transforms Onesimus' station.

Paul, like a master potter, "works" Philemon to reshape his attitude toward the one he had considered useless up until now. Since Paul found Onesimus true to his name (meaning "useful"), he confidently sends him back to Philemon, who will benefit from his service. In fact, Philemon will discover a new attitude in his own heart, a discovery for which Paul prepares him.

One of the angles from which Paul persuades Philemon is that of debt. He recognizes that Onesimus has cost Philemon some financial loss. Paul is willing to assume the debt and promises to pay it. Then, he deftly reminds Philemon of the debt he himself owes Paul (probably for his salvation in Christ through Paul's witness — what price can be put on that?). Paul does not belabor the point, for it is sharp enough to penetrate immediately.

Underlying all of this is the notion of passing on what one has received. Just as Paul received the saving grace of God through Jesus Christ, he passed it on to those who would hear and receive it in turn, like Philemon. He now calls upon Philemon to extend such grace to Onesimus, especially since both of them claim Jesus as Lord in their lives. Between the lines (especially in vv. 14-16), one can sense a hint of what Paul wrote in Philippians 4:17: "Not that I seek the gift, but I seek the profit that accumulates to your account." Paul recognizes that Philemon will grow in his Christian discipleship by exercising the freedom he has in Christ to welcome Onesimus back into the home with forgiveness and new appreciation.

Some interesting comments can be drawn from the conjecture around the word in verse 9 that the Revised Standard Version translates "ambassador" and the New Revised Standard Version renders "an old man." The latter seems the more authentic, but the former makes good sense, even though its attestation in the manuscripts is minimal. The confusion arises over the difference in spelling between the words by one simple letter. It is easy to understand how a change from one to the other could be made in the tedious copy process of those early centuries.

The word for "ambassador," with the extra letter, would be consistent with other language Paul uses in his letters — for example, 2 Corinthians 5:20 and especially Ephesians 6:20. The authority of his witness as commissioned by the risen Christ Jesus is emphasized here. This puts quite a lot of pressure on Philemon to comply with Paul's appeal.

But the word for "an old man" has greater corroboration among the manuscripts. In that case, Paul would seem to be appealing to the charm of his age, like an elder statesman, who is also in prison. How could Philemon refuse a request from such an individual in those circumstances? This may not carry the theological weight of the former word, but it nonetheless comes across as highly motivational.

Luke 14:25-33

Jesus is no stranger to hyperbole, a figure of speech that uses exaggeration to make a point. (The Greek word from which the hyperbole derives means "to exceed." See Matthew 18:6 for an instance of Jesus' strong use of language; also Luke 23:29-31.) *Hate* is an offensively strong word to use in reference to family ties. Jesus uses it freely when talking about the priorities one is to have in life. What Jesus likely means here is that while there are many important relationships in life, there are none more important than the relationship one has with him.

It may be for our sensitive ears that Matthew 10:37 expresses this same thought in a more palliative way. Reference is made to degrees of love. We can comprehend degrees of love, whereas the terminology of hate makes it sound like we must choose one over the other. John 3:20 expresses this, as light and darkness are set in antipathy and those who choose evil do so because they hate the light. The same Greek word for *hate* is used in the Johanine text and the Lukan text.

It may be helpful to reflect on this pericope in light of Jesus' passion predictions in Luke 9:22-23, 43b-45. Jesus knows his destiny is the cross. He will need to give up everything to reveal the fullness of God's love for the world. Therefore, any who follow him must be willing to walk the same road to Calvary, giving up everything for the sake of attaining what Paul calls "the prize of the heavenly call of God in Christ Jesus" (Philippians 3:14).

It is not that we attain it through our efforts; we embrace what Christ has done *for* us. In so doing, we accept his claim on our life, which is a total claim so that he may give to us his total blessings. Hence, the language of "denying self" that Jesus uses in describing how his disciples must follow him. Part of this denying of self is to relegate all other matters into secondary and tertiary positions, even the icon of family.

Jesus offers two very common images to help his hearers understand the *cost* of being his disciple. When one begins a building project, it is important to know just how much it will cost in order to be able to complete it. Constructing a tower is no small enterprise. Neither is following Jesus! One best be prepared to bear the cost, including denial of self, subjection to the will of God, rejection and even possible martyrdom.

In like manner, when an army is set against another, the combatants must have a complete understanding of their resources to determine if this is a cause that can be won. Battles are a matter of total commitment, for they mean life or death. So does following Jesus! It is a matter of life or death. There really is no middle ground. To side with Jesus, one must be willing to give up everything, like a soldier pledging allegiance to his general and offering his life on the front line for victory.

Application

We say we want warnings before things happen. "Forewarned is forearmed." Especially if there is something for which we may be chastised, we say we desire a warning to allow opportunity to change our ways and avoid the discipline. We get angry at those over us when they just "lower the boom" and don't even give us a second chance with "just a warning this time." However, like the people of Israel, we still "do it" even after the warning. The warning does not seem to work. Jeremiah's potter sermon did not turn the people from their ways. Clay just has a hard time listening, even with ears shaped to hear.

God is compelled by our resistance (like the spoiled clay on the potter's wheel) to deal with us in judgment. Rather than rag on God for "hard times" and ask whiney questions like "Why me?" the right attitude is to embrace the judgment, like Jeremiah had to. Ask the difficult but necessary questions in the midst of God's discipline: "What must I learn from this experience? How can I let God have his way with me better?"

This is a more profound attitude to nurture in life, one that can endure the rough edges of experience with character and courage, because it rests in the promise of God. "At one moment I may declare concerning a nation or a kingdom, that I will pluck up and break down and destroy it, but if that nation, concerning which I have spoken, turns from its evil, I will change my mind about the disaster that I intended to bring on it" (Jeremiah 18:7-8). This can certainly apply to individuals also.

In his letter to Philemon, Paul gives some practical direction for how the "clay" can be pliant, and therefore compliant, in the potter's hands, in God's hands. First, it is important to have a good understanding of self. Paul sees himself as "a prisoner for Christ Jesus" (v. 1; very contextual, given his imprisonment). In other letters he describes himself as a "slave of Christ Jesus" (Romans 1:1; Philippians 1:1; Titus 1:1). Paul does not live for himself or unto himself. He belongs to another. "For to me, living is Christ..." he writes in Philippians 1:21. A vital attitude for Christians to maintain in our very ego-centered culture is one that understands the self first and foremost in the hands of God and subject to the will of God.

Second, having a healthy appreciation of others will go far in balancing the deleterious effects of individualistic tendencies. From the very beginning of his letter, Paul lifts up Philemon as beloved, a fellow worker, a lover of people, a man of faith, an inspiration to others. It would be crass to assert that Paul is simply setting up Philemon to be persuaded to do what Paul wants him to do. He builds up Philemon with genuine appreciation, following his own advice "for building up the body of Christ" (Ephesians 4:12). One of the best ways to keep from turning in upon ourselves (*incurvatus se*) is to focus on the gifts that others bring into relationships and offer for the good of the larger community.

Third, acknowledge, encourage, and work for growth in others, not just for their own benefit, but for what they can then contribute for the benefit of others. Paul grew Onesimus from a slave to a servant, from a domestic to a disciple. This is doing in Christian parlance what the prophets called for in ages past — to beat swords into plowshares and do justice (Micah), to seek good and not evil (Amos). Onesimus became a blessing for Paul and now Paul wants to send him back to Philemon that he may be a blessing to him as well. In this way, the words of the psalmist ring so true: "How very good and pleasant it is when kindred live together in unity!" (Psalm 133:1).

It truly is good and pleasant when people can dwell in unity. Unfortunately, the world does not allow this to happen without a struggle. There are hate groups that recruit followers and train them in violent attitudes and behaviors. Neo-Nazi enclaves exemplify this to the chagrin of humanity. Ethnic communities define themselves over against and at the expense of other communities. The strife in the Middle East in an ongoing illustration of this to the bafflement of world leaders, some of whom have been martyred in the search for peace.

How hard it is for us to give up our wills and subject ourselves to the will of God! Dietrich Bonhoeffer said it well when he described what is necessary for this to happen: "When Christ calls a man to follow him, he bids him come and die." It takes nothing less than that, and that is why the world cannot understand it. In the world and of the world, we seize what we deem important to us, what we can tangibly hold on to — like our possessions and our family. We are oriented to the here and now and are often willing to settle for immediate satisfaction without regard to future blessing. In so doing, we miss the point of Jesus' promise that as we seek the kingdom of God first and foremost, these other good things will be added to our experience in ways that bring joy and satisfaction (Matthew 6:33).

Take, for example, the matter of family. Society has elevated the status of family to the position of demigod. "Family is everything" is a cliché that is repeated everywhere. With such a notion imbedded in our minds, it is no wonder that we have difficulty in comprehending Jesus' words about priorities. He is challenging us with a whole new paradigm for life, which places him as Lord in our life. How can we help young families, for example, live in this paradigm, as they struggle with schedules for their children that include wholesome activities that may conflict with the scheduled activities of the Christian community for worship, education, fellowship, and service? Where do we adapt the church schedule to be responsive to the realities of our culture? Where do we challenge our families to make choices when this cannot so easily be done? Having the right attitude will go a long way in shaping right behavior.

Proper 19 / Pentecost 17 / Ordinary Time 24
Jeremiah 4:11-12, 22-28
1 Timothy 1:12-17
Luke 15:1-10
David Kalas

But what if it is broken?

Conventional wisdom says, "If it ain't broke, don't fix it." That's fair advice. But what if it *is* broken? What shall our policy be then?

We make that kind of decision on a regular basis. Some items are so inexpensive or so unimportant to us that we regard them as disposable. If they're broken, we throw them away and replace them. Other items are so valuable to us, however, that we readily invest the time, effort, and money necessary to fix them when they are broken.

Sometimes the choice is not so clear-cut, of course. When the family car is getting old and has a lot of miles on it, and the mechanic says it will cost this much to fix the latest problem, then what should you do? Is it more cost effective to keep putting repair and maintenance money into the car that's already paid off, or is your money better spent on something newer that will require less upkeep?

In the biblical story, we see a God whose creation is broken. It is not his doing, of course, but ours. Indeed, our brokenness seems chronic. The fix is costly beyond estimation. That is the loving, saving choice he made — to remake us rather than to replace us — and at great personal expense.

Our three scripture passages this week bear witness to the brokenness of humanity and to God's costly fix.

Jeremiah was a judgment prophet in the early days of the Babylonian Empire. Like the other judgment prophets, a part of Jeremiah's ministry and message was the identification of the people's sins. In our selected verses from chapter 4, Jeremiah offers a glimpse of the chronic brokenness of humanity — which, in this case, is God's own people.

Our passage from Paul's first letter to Timothy includes a part of Paul's testimony. He articulates the form and depth of his own formerly broken state. Then he bears witness to the gracious and costly "fix" by God that we call salvation.

Finally, the familiar selection from Luke's gospel portrays in story form the beauty of God's approach. The explicit theme is not brokenness but "lostness." God's response to his lost loved ones is to seek, find, and then, rejoice.

The mechanic might tell me that my car isn't worth putting any more money into it, and any impartial observer would have told God that rebellious and fallen humanity was not worth what he intended to invest in us. "You're throwing good grace after bad" might have been the skeptic's counsel.

But love does not count the cost; it just pays the price.

Jeremiah 4:11-12, 22-28

The Old Testament judgment prophets were the bearers of bad news. They did not do much to try to disguise or to soften it. That in itself is something of a lesson to us, for often a fear of confrontation, an instinct toward salesmanship, or a well-meaning pity interferes with our capacity to speak bad news. Jeremiah and his prophetic colleagues, however, did not offer a spoonful of sugar with their medicine. There was bad news for the people, and the people needed to recognize it. "Warning" and "danger" signs do no good if they are in small print.

Here that bad news is represented by "a hot wind" — a provocative image in contrast to the image of a cool breeze. A cool breeze connotes relief and pleasantness for us; a hot wind, therefore, must be a burdensome, destructive thing.

We referenced earlier the chronic brokenness of humanity. God laments it in verse 22, detailing the severity of the problem. He expresses it in three sad observations.

First, God laments that his people "are foolish, they do not know me." Over a century earlier, God had expressed the same kind of bewildered complaint about his people through the prophet Isaiah (1:3). How is it that God's own covenant people should not know him? Throughout their history, he had provided for them, led them, spoken to them, and revealed himself to them. They were uniquely and intimately his, and yet they did not know him. We human beings are surely mystified by the things of God, but he may be even more mystified by us. God's mystery, after all, is due to his vastness and majesty. Our mystery, however, is in our inconsistency and illogic.

Second, God laments that "they are stupid children, they have no understanding." The identification of the people as children carries two great implications. On the one hand, it is no doubt an insult to the pride of the people. They surely did not regard themselves as being like children — particularly like stupid children. It is a harsh criticism to say to an adult, "You're being childish" or "You need to grow up." This was the spirit of God's critique of his own people. On the other hand, we must never lose sight of the beauty in God referring to his people as children. That, after all, is how he always views us. I am an adult with children of my own, and yet my mother still regards me as her child. It is that identification of his people as his children, albeit stupid ones, that moves God's compassion and devotion (see, for example, Hosea 11:1-8).

Third, God laments that "they are skilled in doing evil, but do not know how to do good." This is the great indictment of fallen humanity, and it becomes our own realization about ourselves (see Romans 7:15-19). The question to consider is whether this condition is a matter of degree or a universal state of being. Paul's implication in Romans 7 seems to be that this is a ubiquitous symptom of our "fallenness." On the other hand, one senses in God's words in Jeremiah 4 that he expects better of his people.

Next, the voice of the speaker suddenly changes. After the Lord has expressed what he sees as he looks at his people, Jeremiah then expresses prophetically what he sees as he looks around him. "I looked" is the recurring statement that introduces four descriptions of God's judgment.

The first thing Jeremiah saw was an earth that "was waste and void" and heavens that "had no light." The imagery is reminiscent of Genesis 1, for before God began his creative act there was no light and "the earth was a formless void" (Genesis 1:2). Does the imagery in Jeremiah mean that God's deliberate judgment reverts the universe to its prior, terrible state? Does the imagery suggest that Judah's choice to live without God eventually results in an experience that completely lacks God's gracious influence? Does the state of darkness and void anticipate the saving work of God who will once again bring light and life?

The second thing Jeremiah saw was mountains "quaking" and hills moving "to and fro." It is an eerie sight. I remember flying to the Holy Land some years ago and as our plane passed 35,000 feet over Switzerland, Austria, and Italy, I was awed to see how high above the clouds the mighty mountains of the Alps rose. They seemed to be more a part of the sky than the earth, looking down on the clouds below. I imagine those mighty mountains shaking and quaking, and I have a picture of chaos: Earth is out of control when the largest, most immovable, most stable symbols on earth are quivering.

The third thing Jeremiah saw was "no one at all, and all the birds of the air had fled." There is something peculiarly unnerving about a place that has been completely vacated. That the birds had fled suggests a kind of dread — as though nature itself sensed the terror that was coming and took flight. On the other hand, "there was no one at all" suggests that perhaps the terror had already come. Perhaps the people had not fled and were gone but rather were dead and gone.

Finally, Jeremiah saw that "the fruitful land was a desert, and all its cities were laid in ruins." The prior image was one of desolation. This is an image of devastation. Everything has been ruined, from nature to civilization. We are reminded of Leviticus 26 and the truth that both God's blessings and his curses are thorough. No area of life is untouched by his generosity. Likewise, nothing is shielded from his judgment.

On the tail end of this otherwise unrelenting slideshow of troubles, comes this brief word of hope: "Yet I will not make a full end." How utterly characteristic of God and of his judgments this sounds. In the days of Noah, God did not make a full end but preserved for a fresh start Noah, his family, and two of every kind of animal. In the days of Israel's unfaithfulness at the border of Canaan, God did not make a full end but raised up a new generation to take into the land of his promise. To the people of Jeremiah's day, he promised again not to make a full end. For in the end, his final purpose is not sentencing, but saving.

1 Timothy 1:12-17

In the Jeremiah passage, we saw God's view of the brokenness of his people, and in the end, we also had a glimpse of the mercy that is built into even his judgment, for he does not "make a full end."

In the Luke passage, we see two parables that depict the happy ending of God seeking and saving his people. Both stories are told from the perspective of the "God characters" (i.e., the shepherd of the lost sheep and the woman who lost the coin).

In between the other two lections, in these words from the apostle Paul, we see the other side of the same story. This is the human side: The personal testimony of one who was lost and broken, and who has been sought and saved by God. We do not hear from the people of Judah in the Jeremiah passage. We do not hear from the sheep or the coin in the Luke passage. But we do hear from Paul. He offers the testimonial of all those who have been lost and broken, and who have been the recipients of God's grace.

Paul recalls the specifics of his former condition: He was a blasphemer, a persecutor, a man of violence, and ignorant. Indeed, Paul identifies himself as the "foremost" of sinners. The Greek word translated as "foremost" is *protos*. It is used most often in the New Testament to refer to someone or something that comes first in time or in sequence, which is clearly not what Paul has in mind here. There are a few other uses, however, that lend special insight into Paul's self-identification as the foremost — the *protos* — of sinners.

Jesus told his disciples "whoever wishes to be first among you must be your slave" (Matthew 20:27), and *protos* is the word translated "first." The commandment to love God is cited as the *protos* commandment (Matthew 20:27). The robe that the father of the returning prodigal son calls for is the *protos* robe (Luke 15:22). When Paul calls himself the *protos* of sinners, therefore, he means that he is the blue ribbon, gold-medal sinner.

Lucy once said to Charlie Brown, "Of all the Charlie Browns in the world, you're the Charlie Browniest." Such is the nature of Paul's conclusion about himself. Of all the sinners in the world, he had been the "sinneriest."

This is a little bit of boasting on Paul's part but not boasting about his sinfulness. He is not like the fool who brags about how drunk or wasted he got over the weekend. Rather, Paul is citing his badness as a way of boasting about God's goodness. The magnitude of Paul's sinfulness only serves to bear witness to the magnitude of saving grace.

In this regard, Paul's is a model testimony, for we are rightly struck by the fact that his own testimony is not really about him. Four times in six verses, Paul references Jesus by name. The real headline is not Paul's sin, but the Savior and his love and grace.

Finally, the pattern of the passage is noteworthy, for it begins with thanksgiving and ends with praise. "I am grateful," Paul begins, "to Christ Jesus our Lord." Then, after recalling his sin and God's salvation, his testimony crescendos to a great doxology: "To the king of the ages, immortal, invisible, the only God, be honor and glory, forever and ever. Amen" (1 Timothy 1:17).

If the sheep and the coin could speak, I expect that's what they would say too.

Luke 15:1-10

Luke 15 has often been referred to as the "lost and found chapter" of the Bible. Here we find, in succession, the three great parables of Jesus about someone or something being lost and then found again. First comes the story of the lost sheep, then the lost coin, and then the lost (we call him the prodigal) son.

The three stories escalate in intimacy and value. The lost sheep is just one out of a hundred. The lost coin is one out of just ten. The lost son is, well, a son, and one of only two. Each story ends with the lost item being restored to the proper person, who in turn throws a great celebration.

This whole set of priceless parables, according to Luke, is shared by Jesus in response to some grumbling by the Pharisees and the scribes.

From time to time you get some criticism that assures you that you're doing the right thing. That is surely the nature of what the Pharisees and scribes had to say about Jesus. They thought they were being sharply critical. In fact, however, they were just grouchy evangelists, declaring with a frown the good news about Jesus: "This fellow welcomes sinners and eats with them."

The scribes and Pharisees had the right lyrics. They just didn't realize they were singing them to the wrong tune. They said that Jesus welcomed sinners in the tone that one would say, "This fellow blasphemes God," or "This fellow teaches heresy." Instead, they should have said it with the same tone and expression that one would use to say, "This fellow feeds the hungry," or "This fellow heals the sick." Their critique of Jesus was actually good news.

Jesus responded to their misguided criticism with three stories, two of which are a part of our gospel lesson for this week: the parable of the lost sheep and the parable of the lost coin.

The stories are different, as we observed, in the relative value of the item lost, as well as in the culpability of the item lost. What is identical in the two stories, meanwhile, is the behavior of the "God character." Both the shepherd and the woman devote themselves to finding what has been lost, and both celebrate with others when it has been found.

Such is the heart of God toward his lost loved ones. He does not regard us as disposable — not even one of us. Instead, Christ came "to seek out and to save the lost" (Luke 19:10). Or, as Paul expressed it to Timothy, "The saying is sure and worthy of full acceptance, that Christ Jesus came into the world to save sinners" (1 Timothy 1:15).

Application

What to do with something broken?

Some things are so cheap that there's no point in fixing them, so we simply throw them away. When my shoelace breaks, I buy a new one.

Some things are too difficult to fix, and so we replace those. When I was a little boy, I broke a window or two while playing ball. My dad did not try to gather and reassemble the pieces of broken glass to fix the window; he replaced the window.

Then there are those things that are too costly to fix. It is actually cheaper to replace the item than repair the item, and that's what we do.

See what God does with a broken creation? Surely it would have been less costly to throw us away and create something all new. We don't see any expense to God at the creation; we see a great expense, however, at the cross. Still, he paid the price to fix us.

An Alternative Application

Jeremiah 4:11-12, 22-28. God's emphatic statement — "It is I who speak in judgment against them" — might go unappreciated by the people in our pews. At best, it seems redundant; for the larger context of Jeremiah's message makes it quite obvious that the Lord is speaking judgment against the people. At worst, God's words here may sound bullying or spiteful. In fact, however, there is a great reassurance to be found in this affirmation from God to his threatened people: he is running the show.

The current events of Jeremiah's day were foreboding for Judah and Jerusalem. The Babylonian Empire was a menacing presence, and Judah had little realistic hope of prevailing in any conflict with Babylon. During Jeremiah's lifetime, the Babylonians would conquer Jerusalem, destroy the temple, and take several "shifts" of Jews into exile.

To wonder, in the midst of all the trouble and tragedy, whether God had forgotten his people would have been debilitating to their faith. To think that the gods of Babylon had defeated the God of Israel would have been unbearable. But the Jews faced no such theological crisis, for it was God himself who spoke "in judgment against them."

When I was young, I sometimes objected to my mother's rules and discipline. When I was forced to come home earlier than some friend, I would protest, "His mother doesn't care what time he comes home!" And my mother would answer, "But I do care what time you come home. I do care." That was even her claim in the midst of punishing me: "I only punish you because I care."

That is the nature of the good news hidden in the midst of this judgment message. Judah did not fall to Babylon because God was absent or defeated. Instead, God himself was behind the catastrophe. He declared: "It is I who speak in judgment against them." That means he cares.

Proper 20 / Pentecost 18 / Ordinary Time 25
Jeremiah 8:18—9:1
1 Timothy 2:1-7
Luke 16:1-13
Mark Molldrem

From lamentation to larceny

Our texts today take us over a varied landscape. Any one of them could take the preacher and the congregation in a different direction from the others: Jeremiah to the Wailing Wall, Paul and Timothy to the steps of the capitol, the unrighteous steward to behind-closed-doors dealings.

They all hold together on the theme of how one can intercede with God on behalf of those for whom one cares and shares a common destiny. Jeremiah interceded for "my poor people" (Jeremiah 8:19) with questioning tears. Timothy is urged by Paul to lead the Ephesians in advocating with God on behalf of the civil authorities. Even an unrighteous steward acts as arbiter to avoid small claims court. Finally, of course, Jesus is named the "one mediator between God and humankind" (1 Timothy 2:5) who guarantees the salvation that arises out of the very heart of God.

Jeremiah 8:18—9:1

When God speaks, the prophet speaks. "Thus says the Lord" is the herald cry to perk the ears of those who need to hear. In this text, it appears that we have the words of Jeremiah lamenting the fate of the people. Could it be that when the prophet speaks, God speaks?

Jeremiah has been called "the weeping prophet." He had the uncompromising and unwelcome task of announcing the demise of Judah, the destruction of the temple, and the exile of God's favored ones. Not only was his mouth into his work, but also his heart. In today's text, we see how much his heart is in the prophecy he has been given to deliver. Jeremiah himself shares in the pain of what is happening to the people, whose future will not be in the Promised Land, but in a land of exile. In the statements he has heard and now repeats, we can hear his own questioning and his own dismay: Where is our God? Why have we blatantly disregarded the commands of God? When will we be saved from this catastrophe?

These are questions of lamentation that arise out of a wounded heart. "My heart is sick" (8:18). He would later fill another book with such anguish; but for now, he bears his soul publicly, tear-stained, and dismayed.

Can it be that when we hear the prophet speak, we hear the voice of God? That is to say, do these words from Jeremiah's *angst* express the very turmoil that ravages the heart of the living God, who claims these rebellious children as his own? Are we getting a glimpse into the sorrow of God's wrath, which he exercises in justice but also in pain — God's own pain? What grief God must bear, having to wait with his people for history to clock forward in order to answer the questions raised against heaven: "Is there no balm in Gilead? Is there no physician there?" (8:22). The balm *will* be in Gilead in time, "the fullness of time had come" (Galatians 4:4). The physician *will* stride upon the landscape of a people in need of healing (see Luke 4:23). But until that time arrives, there will be weeping "day and night for the slain of my poor people!" (9:1). Thus says the prophet; thus says the Lord.

1 Timothy 2:1-7

Paul charged Timothy to remain in Ephesus as guardian of the faith (1 Timothy 1:3), for there were some there extrapolating crazy notions. These they were passing on as faithful commentary about Christ's

90

death and resurrection for the salvation of the world. Timothy was to provide oversight for and nurture of the congregation, holding them to the teachings of Paul. We would expect this concern from Paul, who was so clear on the differences between the law and the gospel, between the "myths and... speculations" (1:4) of human minds (see also 2 Peter 1:16) and the revelation of God.

It is refreshing also to receive Paul's very practical concerns for the public life of the Christian community. Complementary to Romans 13:1-7, he expresses his sense of Christian responsibility to engage in prayer for all, especially mentioning those in public office. This is not only a matter of Christian compassion, it is also a matter of Christian citizenship, living "a quiet and peaceable life in all godliness and dignity" (2:2). Our feet need to be grounded below, though our vision is set above.

There is purpose in good citizenship, even beyond a "quiet and peaceable life." That purpose is the same evangelical one that propels the overt preaching of the gospel, namely, that everyone be saved and come to the knowledge of the truth in Jesus Christ (2:4). From the chancel to the curb, the Christian life is to witness to the one, "who gave himself as a ransom for all" (2:6).

Paul's vision for the gospel is quite extensive and inclusive. It is "for all" (2:6 and also expressed in 2:1, 4). In this text for today, he is applying the contemporary notion of *thinking globally and acting locally*, as he advises Timothy to lead the local congregation in Ephesus to pursue the common good in public life in the name of Jesus. For Paul personally, his efforts were to be directed specifically with the Gentiles, wherever they may be. That is why he traveled. His *locus* was the Roman Empire, while Timothy's at this time was Ephesus.

Luke 16:1-13

If we go back to the beginning of chapter 15, we can surmise that the three parables there as well as this parable of the unrighteous steward were spoken to the disciples within earshot of the tax collectors, sinners, and Pharisees. One of the remarkable things about Jesus' teaching is that it is not aimed at a narrow audience, nor is it esoteric in nature such that only a privileged few can truly comprehend what he was talking about. Jesus spoke, for the most part, for all to hear in a way that most could understand, if they had ears to hear.

The theme in Jesus' words for today is stewardship. In the Bible, stewardship means using time-conditioned goods according to timeless values. Jesus applauds the widow who gave so generously (all that she had) out of the abundance of her heart (Luke 21:1-4). Paul applies this principle in one of his best stewardship texts, where he writes, "God is able to provide you with every blessing in abundance [timeless values], so that by always having enough of everything [time-conditioned goods], you may share abundantly in every good work" (2 Corinthians 9:8).

What does Jesus mean when he describes the unrighteous steward as wasting the rich man's goods? Was it that the steward was lax in retrieving what had been loaned to others? Was he foolishly investing the resources in unprofitable ends? Was he stealing from the owner for his own personal gain? Whichever way one may wish to spin this, the steward comes up short in fulfilling his responsibilities to the owner.

It is remarkable that the owner gives the steward the authority to settle matters before he is dismissed. The steward sets out to get back what he can for the owner. He acts like a collection agent, retrieving at least something on outstanding bills, rather than letting them go unsettled. There is advantage in this to the owner, as well as the debtor and also the steward. The owner gets more than he would have gotten if matters were left as is; the debtor satisfies the debt with less than formerly required. The steward comes out of this with a compliment (shrewdness, 1:8) from the owner and with friends on the outside (1:9), where he is now cast.

One of the things to notice about the steward is that he deals with each situation differently. The one who owed oil only had to pay back 50% of the debt. The one who owed wheat, 80%. Do we make of this that the steward had a sense of fairness with the varying circumstances of the debtors? Or, is the steward

91

more concerned to appease the one owing oil, because he will make a better friend after all is said and done? There may be several motivating factors (some even contradictory) in any given act.

What can be made of verse 9? Is Jesus telling us to be wily and get the most use out of "unrighteous mammon" while we can? Or is he speaking tongue-in-cheek about just how far such efforts can really take one? After all, who are these people who can "receive you into the eternal homes"? Are they none other than those who may remember you fondly for a while, and then forget as life takes other directions? Are they those who will pass on your legacy to posterity, until you are but a faded memory at best — as if that is ultimately important?

Jesus finally gets to his point in all of this parable-speak, when he explains how important it is to be faithful in the little things of life as a reflection that one values the truly important things of life. That is to say, one serves God by handling the matters of the world with judicious care, in a way that gives God glory and advances the kingdom, not one's own position. Like the steward, we will get into serious trouble if we try to switch the priorities around and treat the mammon of this world as if it had lasting value.

Application

One of the traditional disciplines that has carried Christians through ages of crises has been meditation on the cross. Peering into the suffering of Christ has the power to shape the soul. Profound mystics in their retreats as well as simple believers in their homes find humility and courage when faced with the suffering of Jesus on the cross. To perceive in some small way the self-giving, self-sacrificing heart of God for his people puts all other human predicaments into a unique perspective. Not that they are diminished or dismissed but they are contextualized into a more grand meaning. They are engulfed by the fullness of God revealed through the life, death, and resurrection of Jesus.

Related to this is the spirit with which so many come to worship these days. Closest to people's heart are such concerns as "How does this relate to my daily life?" "What will I get out of it?" "Will I like what I experience?" "How comfortable do I feel in this setting?" Harder to find is the heart that humbly draws near to God in holy space to present the offerings of praise and adoration, prayer and alms, silence and obedience.

Even when life is collapsing around one, we should bring the hardest of questions before God. It is not necessary to be strong before God; reality actually keeps us rather weak, fragile, sick, and in need of healing from sole to soul. When we can be so honest with ourselves and also transparent before God, we are in a position to receive God's blessing of presence and promise, as expressed in Psalm 23: the deepest, darkest valley need not be cause for fear, for the Lord, like the good shepherd with rod and staff, walks with the vulnerable sheep.

A vital part of the Christian perception of God is that, in Jesus, God assumes the very cries, grief, questions, dismay, and tears of his people, voicing their anguish from the cross, mediating a saving grace through the apparent weakness of the crucifixion itself. Jesus stands in the line of fire between a vulnerable humanity and the enemies of sin and death that would force us out of favor and relationship with God.

Intercessory prayer is a practical application of the intercession Jesus accomplishes for us on behalf of God the Father. Paul writes about this in Romans 8:34 and 2 Corinthians 5:16-21. Jesus is the very expression of God to us and for us. Our intercession on behalf of others is not quite the same as Jesus' role of intercession, because "There is one God" (1 Timothy 2:5). In Jesus, God is not called upon to respond with favor for the sake of the people. In Jesus, God himself is exercising intercession for the ones God loves. Because of this, God does not set up Jesus as a "middleman," similar to the one who is to work out the differences between two contrary parties. Jesus is "God our Savior" (1 Timothy 2:3) who comes to guarantee (the Greek word for "mediator" also carries the sense of "guarantor") that the will of God is characterized by a saving grace that extends to all people. The ransom given by Jesus' life is not a price paid to God to deposit a people into his heavenly account, but is the price God himself paid to buy a people for his own heart.

In contrast to this, when we pray for others, we step forward between those who have our concern and the one who is concerned for them. God's love encompasses all, so we are urged to pray for all leaders in public life, presumably beginning with one's own local officials. Paul becomes an example of this, insofar as he was the apostle to the Gentiles. Just as he stepped outside the box of expectations and expanded his world to include the Gentiles, so is the Christian to step outside the box and reach out with the compassion of Christ to all, whoever they are and wherever they may be. Our prayers will reveal where our hearts are and our prayers will lead us into action in response to the very things for which we ask.

Alternative Applications

In our culture of endless choice, one of the greatest challenges facing the church is to help people keep their priorities in order, so that they can make appropriate decisions in the little things (time-conditioned matters) based upon the big things (timeless values, kingdom goals). In this fall season, with school activities starting and organizations and clubs getting together again after summer vacations, there is tremendous pressure on people for their time, talents, and treasures. Younger and older alike feel this — at school, at work, in volunteer responsibilities, and in ever-increasing recreational opportunities. Individuals and families deal daily with the issue of choosing between so many good options through which to express and enhance themselves. In our increasing secular society, what often happens is that the activities of the church get squeezed out (or at best "squeezed in"). This is symptomatic of how we are becoming more devoted to the pursuit of mammon, rather than God.

Seventy-five years ago, Eberhard Arnold, founder of the Bruderhof communities, raised some serious questions in pre-Nazi Germany that bear hearing today, such as "Are not the state and the organized church, which protect privilege and wealth, diametrically opposed to what is to come: God's new order?" In a lecture delivered in 1923, he offers this challenging description: "Where mammon rules, the possessive will is stronger than the will to community; the struggle to survive by mutual killing is stronger than the urge to love... matter is stronger than spirit, things and circumstances are stronger than God...."

Arnold was neither entranced by socialism nor communism; nor was he captivated by capitalism. He strove to embody an actual fellowship of people organized around the principles of the Sermon on the Mount. His vision was "the new way of communal work and fellowship in things spiritual and material — the voluntary gathering of those who are free of private property and capital." This is a radical view compared to that held by most everyone who is seated in church pews these days. Yet, it calls into question what we are really about in our daily lives and challenges us to look deeper into our confession of sins and how great the love of God must be to still call us his children. Then, we may be inspired to act differently, even if spasmodically, in ways that embody stewardship that is based on kingdom goals (Matthew 6:33), rather than personal ones.

All three of today's texts carry a common theme of citizenship. Jeremiah laments the civil and spiritual disorder that plagues his beloved homeland. Timothy is encouraged to be supportive of those in high places in the community, as a spiritual discipline. Jesus tells a parable about keeping a spiritual perspective on personal affairs. Without that perspective, priorities get skewed and we may fail to handle civil responsibilities appropriately.

Proper 21 / Pentecost 19 / Ordinary Time 26
Jeremiah 32:1-3a, 6-15
1 Timothy 6:6-19
Luke 16:19-31
Mark Molldrem

Blessing the rich man's proceeds

Everybody likes payday. Of course, it's time to pay the bills and set some money aside for a rainy day or retirement; but most enjoyable is putting some of that hard-earned money in the billfold to be used on a whim later in the evening or on the weekend.

Jeremiah, Paul, and Jesus have a very interesting perspective on wealth that may change the way we go to the bank. Through buying a parcel of land, Jeremiah invests in his country when everything was falling apart. Paul urges Timothy and the congregation at Ephesus to be rich in godliness. Jesus tells a parable about material wealth not cutting it, when it comes time for death and the hereafter. The advice each would give us today is to head for the bank with "withdrawal slips" to invest one's assets for the kingdom of God rather than "deposit slips" for one's own benefit.

Jeremiah 32:1-3a, 6-15

Babylon had already trampled the land. Nebuchadnezzer had besieged Jerusalem at the close of the seventh century BC and then again in 598 BC when he plundered the city. Judah was at the mercy of this new empire that had risen over the collapse of the Assyrians (Nineveh was destroyed in 612 BC). When Judah, under the token reign of Zedekiah, revolted against their new overlords, Babylon swept down once again, this time leveling Jerusalem and dismantling the glorious temple built by Solomon. During this time, Jeremiah had been imprisoned and left to starve to death (Jeremiah 37), but King Zedekiah took pity on him and kept him in the court of the guard instead (32:2).

There is no good reason not to include Jeremiah 32:3b-5 in the reading. It provides the reason that Jeremiah was imprisoned in the first place. It also sets in stark contrast Jeremiah's prophecy about the success of the Babylonians against Israel and Jeremiah's action parable of hope, in which he buys the field at Anathoth.

This purchase is a symbol of hope. If "actions speak louder than words," then this transaction demonstrates "loud and clear" that there is cause to hope in the future even in the face of such devastation in the present. Jeremiah took great pains to see that everything was done legally and publicly as a witness to his confidence. The land may be lost to this people, who will be carted off into exile, but the people will not be lost to God. This investment in the land foreshadows the return of the people to again occupy the land that the Lord had promised to Abraham.

What makes this hope so striking is that it is shaped by the same God who in "anger... wrath and... great indignation" (Jeremiah 32:37) is judging the people for unspeakable sins. Not only have they turned their backs on the God of Abraham and Sinai by worshiping Baal, they also turned their children into fodder for the god Moloch, who devoured the little ones in his fiery belly to appease his avaricious appetite for blood. How remarkable that the God of the covenant remains faithful over against his faithless people and holds out for them a hope that will carry them through this time of judgment!

1 Timothy 6:6-19

Paul gives Timothy lots of practical instructions in this letter to help him guide the church at Ephesus. The topics covered include public prayer, the place of women, the office of bishop and deacon, false doctrine, godly living, faithful service, care for widows, and the role of elders and slaves. He accents the importance of what he explains by exhorting Timothy, "Teach and urge these duties" (1 Timothy 6:2c). Then, Paul moves on to his concluding remarks, which form the pericope for today.

Similar to what he wrote in Philippians 4:11, Paul reflects on the basic wisdom of contentment as the companion of godliness (6:6). Since we enter this world naked (literally) and leave it naked (figuratively; "you can't take it with you"), it is best to be concerned with what is truly essential. More than food and clothing (survival minimums), the Christian is to "pursue righteousness..." (6:11). This is the righteousness that comes through faith in Jesus Christ (Romans 1:16-17; Galatians 2:16), to whom Paul offers a doxology (6:15-16). This righteousness means that one's life is understood as existing from, within, under, and toward God.

One stands right with God because one stands in the shadow of the cross of Christ, submitting to the shape of that instrument of certain death and promised life. In the shadow of that cross, there can only be love for the one who gave up his life that we may know the extent of God's love for us. That is why Paul uses cruciform language ("pierced their hearts with many pangs"; 6:10 RSV) when talking about the danger of money-love, seducing one's heart "away from the faith," away from Jesus as one's master.

In a very personal comment to Timothy, Paul commends him to the virtues of the Christian life: "righteousness, godliness, faith, love, endurance, gentleness" (6:11; compare complementary lists in Galatians 5:22-23 and Colossians 3:12f). He charges him to "keep the commandment" (6:14), which is a reference not to any particular commandment among the ten, but to the whole of the divine directive to live according to the will of God — which is love!

Jesus defines it this way when asked about the greatest commandment; it is love for God with one's whole heart and love for the neighbor as for oneself. When in the upper room on the night in which he was betrayed, Jesus bequeaths this commandment to his disciples (John 15:12; the same Greek word for "commandment" is used in these texts cited from 1 Timothy, Matthew, and John).

Paul puts a time reference on this expectation he places on Timothy: "until the manifestation of our Lord Jesus Christ" (6:14). As we learn elsewhere in Paul's letters, he expected the return of Jesus to occur sooner than later (Romans 13:11; 1 Corinthians 7:29). This puts a qualification on how Christians are to live their lives, not pursuing personal wealth and the pride and power and glory that can come with it, but "rich in good deeds" with liberality and generosity (6:18 RSV). In other words, daily life that invests itself in others in many (liberality) intense (generosity) ways "really is life" (6:19). The future is promised us as we stand on a solid foundation; the walls of good works come to rest on the foundation of the grace of God, "who richly provides us with everything for our enjoyment" (6:17).

Luke 16:19-31

The word "Hades" is used only ten times in the New Testament. The synoptic references in Matthew 11:23 and Luke 10:15 refer to Capernaum's fate due to lack of repentance in response to the ministry of Jesus. In Acts 2:27 and 31, Luke cites a psalm and relates it to the resurrection of Jesus, whom Hades could not contain. In Matthew 16:18 and Revelation 1:18, Hades is cast in a subjugated status before Christ. Although Hades gets to ride its day on earth (Revelation 6:8), in the final judgment before God, Hades will be thrown into the lake of fire, an apocalyptic image of final and eternal damnation (Revelation 20:13-14).

In this parable Jesus tells for the Pharisees, a rich man dies and goes to Hades, which is cast as a "place of torment." It is plain why he is there. He was self-absorbed in his earthly life and did not provide for the poor at his gate. This is a parable of simple morality, accentuating the seriousness of how those who have much relate to those who have little. The prophets themselves spoke of these things clearly throughout history. Leviticus 19:18 plainly says to all, "You shall love your neighbor as yourself: I am the Lord." Micah

6:8 describes in no uncertain terms just what God expects: "He has told you, O mortal, what is good; and what does the Lord require of you but to do justice, and to love kindness and to walk humbly with your God?" It does not take someone rising from the dead to convince one of the rightness of such provisions.

If one's heart is hardened to this, repentance will be no easier should someone rise from the dead. One could "fast forward" to Easter morning and the tomorrows beyond, asking the question why the whole world is not converted to egalitarian care, if it were true that "if someone goes to them from the dead, they will repent" (16:30). No! What one sows in this life will have eternal consequences, and it is no secret what the planting should be! It is as distinct as "a great chasm... fixed," so as to distinguish between right and wrong.

In the context of the observation made in Luke 16:14-15, where the Pharisees are noted for their love of money, this parable calls for repentance in the here and now, for after death there will be no chance for recovery. The Pharisees certainly had the resources of blessings at their disposal. When they failed to act with compassion and share with those still in need, they exposed themselves as "an abomination in the sight of God."

Application

One of the fatal features of American culture is the growing gambling industry. The spirit of King Midas broods in our hearts with a "lust for lucre." Paul reminds us that the love of money is the root of all evil. Lotteries and all sorts of ploys are used by states, tribes, and private businesses to seduce us to seek easy wealth by means of frivolous games.

Christians are urged instead to be "rich in good works" (1 Timothy 6:18). True wealth is found in the treasures of kingdom virtues, like righteousness, godliness, faith, love, endurance, gentleness, and so on. Here is where lifestyle will truly reveal one's priorities. It's not that wealth is to be shunned. There are those who know how to make an honest dollar and multiply it by hard work and shrewd investment. If we were all equally poor, we would probably all be equally dead. The wealth of the world has spurred invention, research, and development to advance world civilization to new heights, upon which we can stand and praise and thank God. It is the use of all this wealth that is at issue, whether it is for personal gain or community good. These are not always totally separable but each individual must go to the depth of the soul to search out the core values by which one lives and dies. The good foundation must be laid for the future, which includes eternal life.

This is what Jesus gets at with the story of the rich man and Lazarus. We really do not need to look far to see parallels to this story today. In American cities, many wealthy, gated communities are not far from some of the most poverty-stricken neighborhoods. Vacationers at posh island resorts or third-world getaways can look out over their balconies and the walled enclosure to see people begging in the streets. It is probably the case that those who are reading this column, like the writer, have been privileged to enjoy the proceeds of the rich man. It is also probably the case that there are not too many Lazarus folks in the pews of churches whose pastors, along with the writer, are picking the fruits of this publication.

We cannot necessarily equate the good life with God's benediction upon our lifestyle. If there were but one poor person in the world, we would be called upon "to be rich in good works, generous, and ready to share" (1 Timothy 6:18). How well are we Christians really doing that as individuals, as families, and as congregations?

Allan H. Sager, in his book *Gospel-Centered Spirituality*, describes four spirituality types who listen to the gospel and hear what they are "typed" to hear. These types can be labeled: Societal Regeneration, Theological Renewal, Inner Life, and Personal Renewal. Depending upon one's inclination of mind (knowing God) or of heart (sensing God) and one's response to the mystery of God or to the revealed God, Christians bear a certain type or cast to their spirituality.

With Societal Regeneration types, concerns for justice, peace, and prayer tend toward social action. The Theological Renewal sort want to think correctly about the faith and prayer so as to gain insight. For Inner Life types, the order of the day and night is contemplation, inner peace, and prayer leading to mystical union with God. And those of the Personal Renewal bent seek holiness of life and prayer that leads to experiencing the presence of God. These are not pure types, however, for though we may predominate in one, we may evidence some elements of the others.

What Jesus' parable does for us today is to awaken the Societal Regeneration type that is in each of us, because God calls it out from each of us. (On other Sundays with other texts, there may be other types that need to be awakened and nurtured; but, for today, let us focus on this one, since the texts call us to express ourselves actively, in concrete terms, to embody the word of God.)

It certainly was called out of Millard Fuller, founder of Habitat for Humanity. In his book *The Theology of the Hammer*, he writes, "Putting faith into practice and being relevant is at the very heart of 'the theology of the hammer.'" He goes on to explain how God's love indeed embraced all, but he also observes from scripture that God has "a preferential concern for the poor." Upon this understanding, he set a very lofty and generous goal, which has made his organization wealthy in good deeds: The complete elimination of poverty housing and homelessness.

This is the season of Pentecost, the cycle lifting up the life and ministry of the church, just as the other five seasons of the church year lift up the life and ministry of the Lord of the church. It is time to bear witness in our lifestyle to the very values that God imparts to us. As we mature in Christ (Colossians 1:28), we are equipped, motivated, and empowered to live out the wealth of faith, hope, and love with which the grace of God brings us.

An Alternative Application

You could call this "In Boon and Bane." Flags are burning in the Middle East as Palestinians and Israelis argue over land and governance and independence. The world wonders if there will be any peace in this land of promise. In America, a land where so many promises do come true for so many (read Dan Rather's *The American Dream*), there are families besieged by one catastrophe after another and left wondering how many times can the heart break. Do we have the courage of Jeremiah to still hope in what appears to be a hopeless situation? What field at Anathoth are we willing to invest in as we peer into the future from under storm cloud days?

Jeremiah would have us invest in the promise and power of God, who has shown himself faithful in mighty acts throughout history. To borrow from a Christian hymn penned two-and-a-half millennia later, "When all around my soul gives way, he then is all my hope and stay" (from "My Hope Is Built on Nothing Less").

Venturing deeper into the message of Jeremiah (Jeremiah 32:17ff), we hear him praising God for the great demonstrations of power and compassion that can be recalled from the Exodus event. Courage can be taken when one relies on this one, true God in any and all circumstances, for even when God acts in judgment, there is a word of promise attached. What God decrees comes to pass, both in wrath as well as blessing. The God of exodus and the God of exile are one and the same; he will have his people in boon and bane. Jesus knew this on the cross and committed himself into the hands of God. So too can we all in times of trial find a solid rock on which to stand (Psalm 18).

Proper 22 / Pentecost 20 / Ordinary Time 27
Lamentations 1:1-6
2 Timothy 1:1-14
Luke 17:5-10
David Kalas

System requirements

Before you buy a new piece of software, you check the side of the box where it lists the system requirements. What operating system is assumed? How fast a processor do I need? How much memory? Do I need a CD-ROM drive? Will the program require a certain quality of monitor, a certain card, or a joystick?

Before you buy a new piece of software, you check to see whether or not it will work on your system. Not to check would be foolishness and to buy software that doesn't match your system would be pointless.

Following Christ also comes with its own kind of "system requirements." Jesus spoke several times and in several ways about what is required of a disciple. We have one of those passages before us this week in the excerpt from Luke. When we consider those teachings honestly, we have to admit that the requirements seem to exceed the capacity of our systems. Or, if not the capacity, it at least exceeds the past performance. Jesus' own disciples may have forgotten from time to time the nature of their obligation, and his reminder to them continues to challenge us.

At another level, Paul also gave Timothy a reminder of the system requirements of discipleship. It is a strong word of encouragement and quite different in tone from the selected passage from Lamentations. Paul himself had successfully completed the life Christ called him to live (see 2 Timothy 4:6-7) and from that vantage point he coached young Timothy to that same victory of grace and faithfulness. The author of Lamentations, by contrast, wrote as one whose people had not been faithful. They had not lived according to the requirements, and the result was a terrible crash.

Most of the packaging on a piece of software is devoted to making the sale. In bold and colorful letters and images, all of the features, advantages, and capabilities of the program are listed. The system requirements, meanwhile, are printed small and black on the side.

Jesus himself did not make a splashy pitch for discipleship. It was the requirements and the cost that got the large print from Jesus. This week, the no-nonsense requirements get the large print from us, as well.

Lamentations 1:1-6

In the wake of the several September 11, 2001, terrorist attacks, a few people publicly suggested that the attacks represented the judgment of God upon this nation. Many people regarded that as an offensive interpretation of events. For myself, I thought it was an uninformed interpretation, for what happened in New York City on that tragic day did not have the look of God's judgment. After all, at the end of the day, most of New York City was still standing.

The opening lines from the book of Lamentations paint a picture of a city and a country fresh in the wake of God's judgment. The picture is poignant and tragic, and the level of desolation portrayed is frankly unfamiliar to the citizens of this country.

From the several judgment prophets of the Old Testament, we are familiar with the detailed and threatening descriptions of what *will* become of Jerusalem or Samaria, of Israel or Judah, of Nineveh or

Babylon. That is very much the nature of the judgment prophet's message: to offer a terrifying preview of what is to come on the other side of divine judgment.

In Lamentations, however, the description is no longer a preview. Rather, it is the present reality. God's judgment had passed through like a tornado, and now the author of this lament wanders through the rubble, weeping over all that is ruined and gone.

Walk through a desert or an untamed forest and the absence of people and civilization is a lovely quality and a marvelous experience. Walk through the wreckages of a city, however — a city that once bustled with life and activity — and the absence of people and civilization is haunting. Jerusalem and Judah must have had that "ghost town" look and feel, for all that was left were the ghosts, the thin and pale memories of what used to be.

Even in the context of a happy life, there is something terribly poignant about times and people that are gone. The house and neighborhood where cherished friends or loved ones used to live, school hallways and playgrounds where we spent so many days when we were young, the faded photographs of familiar faces that look so different now — these are all tinged with grief for us, and that comes only with the ordinary passage of time. Imagine, though, if it was not just time that had passed in between, but tragedy. If that house and neighborhood were reduced to debris, if the old school was nothing but charred remains, if the once-happy photos were of people who had since been slaughtered or kidnapped — the grief is almost unthinkable.

Lamentations recalls a time when Judah was filled with life and strength, with vitality and confidence. But that time is gone. Gone, too, are the people who once populated and gave life to the place. They are gone, either because they are dead, or because they were carted off into exile. All that remains, therefore, is grief and suffering.

What shall we make of these grim first verses of Lamentations on this Sunday morning? The passage does not contain a ray of hope, and its only explicit reference to God is a terrifying one: "The Lord has made [Zion] suffer for the multitude of her transgressions." How do we take the poignant and painful lament from a ruined nation from over 2,500 years ago and make it speak to a comfortable American congregation in the middle of the football season?

We might take our cue from Jesus. He was once was presented with two stories of other peoples' ruin and misfortune. He took the stories and brought them close to home for his own audience with exceedingly practical and sober advice: "Unless you repent, you will all perish just as they did" (Luke 13:5).

2 Timothy 1:1-14

Given our theme of "system requirements," it is worth highlighting the "shoulds" and "should nots" of Paul's counsel to Timothy.

There are just two should nots, and they go to the same point. Paul affirms that "God did not give us a spirit of cowardice," and subsequently urges Timothy, "Do not be ashamed, then, of the testimony about our Lord." Cowardly and ashamed — these are the things Timothy must not be.

Such vices may appear harmless in the Christian. They may operate under the guise of being timid, reserved, cautious, or even sensible. But such sensible caution is what drove the third servant to bury his talent in a hole, and his master was not pleased (Matthew 25:14-30).

In contrast to the cowering posture suggested by the two should nots, Paul urges Timothy to a list of strong things. Over against the cowardice that does not come from God, Paul commends these three strong gifts of God: power, love, and self-discipline. Rather than shrinking back in shame, Paul beckons to Timothy to step forward and "join with me."

The three gifts of God listed by Paul are significant terms. In the Greek, *dunamis* is the word we translate power. The word provides a compelling image for us, for it is related to our word "dynamite." Meanwhile, the Greek word Paul uses here for love is the familiar *agape* that is so marvelously explicated in 1 Corinthians 13. Finally, there is *sophronismos*, translated "self-discipline." William Barclay admits that it is "one of these great Greek untranslatable words," but offers this insight into it: "*Sophronismos* is that divinely given self-control that makes a man a great ruler of others because he is first of all the servant of Christ and the master of himself."

We are given more insight into what it means to be a servant of Christ in our gospel lesson. In the meantime, we add these three potent qualities — power, love, and self-discipline — to the "system requirements" of discipleship.

Finally, Paul concludes this section with two imperatives: "hold" and "guard." These are strong terms and picturesque. The would-be man or woman of God cannot afford to be either timid or casual. Rather, he or she must live with a firm and careful grip on the teaching and the treasure of the truth.

When someone appears to be faltering, we say that he is "losing his grip" or that he needs to "get a grip." So it is that, for the Christian to avoid faltering, he must get a firm grip on the truth of the gospel of Christ.

Luke 17:5-10

The apostles' request seems to be an utterly commendable one. They want more faith, and they come to Jesus to get it. It's hard to argue with either their desire or their method.

One wonders, though, how they expected Jesus to respond. Exactly what did they think he was going to do? Could he give them more faith miraculously, like giving sight to the blind? Could he give them more faith didactically, like giving knowledge to a student?

The apostles asked Jesus for increased faith, and he responded by suggesting that even the tiniest faith works great works. The illustration Jesus used is a spectacular one: commanding a tree to be uprooted from the ground and replanted in the sea. Leon Morris observes that the kind of tree Jesus cited was notorious for being firmly rooted, and so "Jesus is not suggesting that his followers occupy themselves with pointless things like transferring a tree into the sea. His concern is with difficulty. He is saying that nothing is impossible to faith."

The pages of scripture are replete with proofs of the principle that nothing is impossible to faith. Surely the disciples were familiar with the stories of Joshua commanding the sun to stand still, David facing Goliath, and Elijah's showdown with the priests and prophets of Baal. Their mistake, however, was apparently a misunderstanding of just where the power to do great things resides.

The disciples assumed that big faith was needed to accomplish big things, and so they wanted their faith increased. Jesus responded, however, that only a mustard-seed-size faith is required to do big things. The final issue is not the bigness of the faith, but rather the bigness of the one in whom our faith is placed.

On the one hand, Jesus' words are a great encouragement to us. Faith is able to do big and impossible things, but the faith itself is not a big and impossible thing. His image of what faith can do is a grand and uncommon picture — a tree transplanted to the sea. His image of the faith itself, however, is an altogether little and common one — a mustard seed.

On the other hand, Jesus' words imply a certain critique of the disciples. They say that they want more faith, but he indicates that they need only a little faith. What did he mean? That they had no faith at all?

Next comes the fascinating transition to what seems to be an entirely different topic. Actually, it doesn't even really qualify as a transition; it's just a sudden shift. Without warning, Jesus moved from talking about faith to talking about servitude. If conversation were a car ride, the disciples would need to be treated for whiplash injuries after the sudden and drastic turn Jesus made.

Of course, that kind of sudden turn is rather characteristic of Jesus. It is something of a pattern in his conversations with people. The Samaritan woman at the well was content to talk about theoretical things, but Jesus suddenly forced the conversation into personal territory (see John 4:7-20). The crowd was naturally concerned with the theological questions of why misfortune and tragedy had befallen the

Galileans slaughtered by Pilate or the victims of Siloam's falling tower, but Jesus turned the emphasis to the people's personal need to repent (Luke 13:1-5).

It may be part of Jesus' tough and wise love that he regularly changes the subject from what we want to talk about to what we need to talk about. While the disciples wanted to talk about big faith, perhaps they needed to talk about humble servitude.

It may be, of course, that the apostles' desire for more faith was not so completely well intentioned. Perhaps they had come to recognize in what Jesus did (e.g., Matthew 17:14-20) and what Jesus said (e.g., Mark 5:34) that faith was the key to miracles and great manifestations of power. Accordingly, they may have wanted faith like a teenager wants the keys to the car — it was exciting, new, and full of possibilities. Perhaps, therefore, it was not the faith that they wanted, but the accompanying power, and that may have been touched with self-importance.

We know that the disciples struggled from time to time with issues of self-importance (see, for example, Luke 9:46-48). We also know from Simon the magician the intoxicating appeal of God-given miraculous power (Acts 8:5-24). It would not be surprising, therefore, for the disciples to crave more faith for somewhat selfish reasons.

One of the compelling characteristics of Jesus' ministry, however, is how selfless his manifestations of power were. He did not use his power or authority to meet his own needs (e.g., Luke 4:1-4) or to save himself (e.g., Matthew 26:51-53). Similarly, though people were clearly impressed by his miracles, he did not work any miracles to prove himself or to spread his reputation (see Matthew 12:38-39; Mark 8:11-12). On the contrary, he often sought to keep his miracles a secret (e.g., Mark 7:36; Luke 5:14, 8:56).

If it was a "self-serving self-importance" that motivated the disciples to ask for more faith, then it is quite natural that Jesus should make the transition that he does. Perhaps he knew the real issue that the disciples needed to understand at that moment was neither miracles nor faith, but selfless servitude. He called upon their own experience with human servants to challenge them to servant-discipleship.

Servants and slaves were a familiar part of the cultural landscape for the first-century Roman Empire. Jesus' disciples, therefore, were no doubt familiar with the life of a servant or a slave. What Jesus said to them here about the lifestyle of a slave was not new or surprising — it was a matter of fact.

The part that was perhaps new and surprising to them — and almost certainly to us — was the equating of the life of a slave with the life of a disciple. The followers of Jesus had already willingly made dramatic sacrifices (see, for example, Luke 18:28-30). But perhaps, in the glare of the spotlight that was on Jesus, the disciples lost sight of the cost of discipleship. Perhaps in the escalating swirl of excitement and speculation about Jesus, this miracle worker with surging momentum and growing support, the disciples needed to be reminded about this basic fact: The job of a slave is to serve his master. He does not live for attention or applause. He does not live for decorations and ticker tape parades. He lives to serve.

Miracles do not require big faith; just a big God. Likewise, the disciple is not called to be big, significant, and important. Rather, the disciple has the privilege of serving the one who is big, significant, and important. The faith we have is in him, and the works we do are for him.

Application

Look at the system requirements for a piece of software and you'll see details of operating systems, processor speed, memory, and such. Look at the requirements for being a man or woman of God, and you discover a daunting list. The shoulds and should-nots of Paul's counsel to Timothy explored above are on the list. Near the very top is this: You must be a servant.

Servants and slaves were commonplace in the New Testament world. You and I, by contrast, live and work in a world of employer and employees, not slaves and masters. We may be somewhat limited, therefore, in our ability to understand this truth of the Christian life.

Of course, the real obstacle to our appreciating and appropriating this truth of discipleship is the "uncrucified" self. Pride does not aspire to serve. Washing feet is not the ego's natural ambition. But an attitude of servitude — "We are worthless slaves; we have done only what we ought to have done!" — is one of the basic system requirements. Try to run the software of discipleship without servitude in place, and the program just won't work right.

The hard message of servant-Christianity is largely unheard in our culture, but it is essential in order for us to understand the relationship — and the life — into which we are invited. After all, we do call him "Lord."

An Alternative Application

2 Timothy 1:1-14. "From Strength to Strength Go On." Strength comes in many forms. On the one hand, there is the strength of the thing that cannot be stopped. On the other hand, there is the strength of the thing that cannot be moved.

Paul urged Timothy to have, and to exercise, both brands of strength. We take his admonition as our own.

On the one hand, we must have the strength that keeps us undeterred from following God's call. Paul encouraged Timothy to be unafraid and unashamed. We know how fear, timidity, embarrassment, and self-consciousness keep us from going full-speed forward in Christ's service. We aspire to that brand of strength that presses on, bold and unstoppable.

On the other hand, faithfulness to God also requires a strength that is immovable, unshakable. Paul challenged Timothy to "hold" and to "guard." The ball is easily knocked away from the player who carries it loosely and lightly. Likewise, if we hold casually what has been entrusted to us, some trial or some temptation will knock it away. We need the strength of a sure grip, fixed and tenacious.

Christianity, the basic course

A survey of Christian education resources reveals a trend toward an increasing number of programs featuring a back-to-basics theme. No doubt this is the result of realizing that despite all previous attempts, many Christians have something less than a working knowledge of the Christian faith. Perhaps it is because in many corners an academic knowledge that reflects more the need to work through the big questions rather than how to get through the day has derailed us. There is no doubt plenty of blame to go around. As I write this, I do see the anti-intellectual red light flickering on my warning panel. Do we ever get to the big talk without engaging what seems to be carrying on the small talk? Perhaps our longing is for a way to go from one to the other effectively and faithfully. On the other hand, the big questions do come at us fast and furiously with a rapacity that few have experienced. The morning paper, the afternoon blog, and the evening news put global warming, energy depletion, biological science, global terrorism, and economic and business ethics on our plate in ways we have never seen before. I long for the good old days of my youth when it all boiled down to beat the Communists. Scary, yes, but it was a clear enemy who, however treacherous, was still known and had a discernable history.

In the light of change of such global proportions we find ourselves searching for answers of clear biblical proportions that can reassure and guide us. Even the mantra that "it is the economy, stupid" has not reassured us. Despite high levels of prosperity and income, political leaders in Great Britain and the United States find their tenures threatened. Some of us see in other faith traditions the joy and vitality that comes from their answers to the difficult questions and wonder where the vigor in using many of our words lies: salvation, election, and praise. Like the letter writer of Timothy, we long to know that though we seem to be bound up in difficult days, the word of God is unchained.

Each of these texts brings us to a place where we must consider basic words and what we believe are the fundamental building blocks of our faith. What could be more basic than Jeremiah's call to, "Take wives and have sons and daughters; take wives for your sons, and give your daughters in marriage, that they may bear sons and daughters; multiply there, and do not decrease"? Yet, it seems in our day that we are bound up in deep controversy over the meaning of appropriate domestic relationships and what it means to seek the welfare of the city. We seem to be far away from the objective that the letter writer of Timothy envisioned, "Remind them of this, and warn them before God that they are to avoid wrangling over words, which does no good but only ruins those who are listening." If anything, we struggle with the meaning of the most basic words. Classroom, political, and business life often feel like minefields with the potential irruption of political incorrectness every step of the way. Jesus' story, recounted in the gospel lesson, ends on the proclamation that the faith of the Samaritan has made him well. In our day, many have found the faith community a source of abuse and a narrowing of human options. Getting back to basics may be a more difficult ride than many had imagined it would be.

Jeremiah 29:1, 4-7

Jeremiah's prophecy is delivered to those who find themselves living out their life options in exile. This sense of dislocation and disorientation that comes with exile certainly characterizes the experience of many in today's Christian community. Many long for an apocalyptic resolution of the dilemma of living in a world where the power and authority that the faith community once thought it had has slipped away. Others seek the more mundane hopes of participating in the political process to usher in the kingdom. Others take to the hills rather than take action — take on an indifference to the welfare of the city rather than a commitment to its welfare. These seem to be the basic options available to faith communities who have found that they are living in exile.

Jeremiah speaks of another path that God may be calling people of exile to follow. Jeremiah writes an open letter but mentions specifically the leaders of the faith community. "These are the words of the letter that the prophet Jeremiah sent from Jerusalem to the remaining elders among the exiles, and to the priests, the prophets, and all the people, whom Nebuchadnezzar had taken into exile from Jerusalem to Babylon." He gives elders, priests, and prophets a call to embody their usual roles but by "being the change they seek in the world." Gilbert Rendle of the Alban Institute, in the *Leading Change in the Congregation* has written, "Yet as far back as 1960, Thomas Merton published a little book called *Bread for the Wilderness.* The title of the book came from the gospel story in Mark 8 in which Jesus instructed the disciples to feed the great crowd of people who had gathered for three days to listen to him. The disciples asked, 'How can one feed these people with bread here in the wilderness?' Merton's response to that question was this book on the Psalms; which he offered as nourishment for the inner life of faith for those who deal with the mix and the mess of the journey. Merton observed that in truly creative times, which prompt new behaviors and new forms of ministry, what we often need from our God, and what our congregations often need from their leaders, is not a quick map to the final destination, the Promised Land, but 'bread for the wilderness' — sustenance and strategies to help us find our ways."

Jeremiah's letter, in calling to the faith community to enter into the process of building homes, planting gardens, and raising families is calling them to enter into a process where they may find bread for the journey. In the long haul that Jeremiah sees ahead for the exiles, the richest blessing that the faith community may offer to the city is the bread that they do find on the journey.

This poses the question, what bread do we find on the journey in the planting, building, and raising that Jeremiah sees as the task that God is calling the exiles to? The fundamental question is: Have we found bread for the journey? Have we found ways of candor of living with and learning from each other in faith communities that will bless the city? Can we show them a more excellent way as we live out our exile in faithfulness?

Perhaps, once people thought that we could bless the world with a sense of certainty, now in exile our task is to be a blessing by walking faithfully in the midst of uncertainty. The challenge of the faith community is to find bread for the journey in the basic task of life. It is interesting that Jeremiah does not call for more plans, more visions, more ideology, and more theology, but more living, learning, and building wherever that may lead.

Wherever this may lead, we will know when we get there. Basically, this is our situation.

2 Timothy 2:8-15

It is somewhat reassuring to realize that we are not to find ourselves the first to wrangle over words that do no good but only ruin those who are listening. All of us have had the experience of finding ourselves in the words we speak and the words that we hear serving the function more of hiding than revealing the truth that needs to be spoken. Churches get into all kinds of fights that serve the function of avoiding the truth that will move us closer to the kingdom of God. The color of the restroom curtains, length of the pastor's hair, or the volume of the sound system seem safer to talk about than our deepest hungers or greatest fears. The letter writer is saying, "Don't go there." The letter gets down to the basic question of what spoken words get us beyond wrangling to the basic words of our faith.

Verse 11 lays the foundation of the basics of getting beyond wrangling. The saying is sure: "If we have died with him, we will also live with him." The author echoes sentiments here found elsewhere in the Christian scripture, "For if we have been united with him in a death like his, we will certainly be united with him in a resurrection like his" (Romans 6:5) "and I want to know Christ and the power of his resurrection and the sharing of his sufferings by becoming like him in his death" (Philippians 3:10). In John's gospel, Thomas pledges his commitment to die with Jesus. Thomas, who was called the "twin," said to his fellow disciples, "Let us also go, that we may die with him." It remains unclear in John's way of ironically telling the story whether Thomas has the full import of what he is saying. We also have Peter's incredulous response to Jesus' announcement that he is going to Jerusalem to suffer and die.

The basic reality we have do deal with is death, which in the end is not something we can wrangle about for very long. However, asserting this reality into congregational conversations can be difficult. Yet it is the congregation that knows how to go through the death process that is able to speak an authoritative word to me. It is the congregation that cannot let false images die or that lives in the past, or lives for an outside image that is most prone to wrangling in a way that does "no good but only ruins those who are listening."

What commands my attention is the church that does know how to die a death like his so that by doing so it might live as Jesus does. The expectation that confirmation programs or pedagogical styles of the past can be counted on to serve us well, forever, may have to die in order to journey to that place where our children can have faith and our faith have children. Old styles of missionary work where we are always the givers and articulators of faith while others are the passive recipients will need to die in order to make way for our journey to the place where God wants us to be. Old expectations about what a denomination is or membership means will need to be examined to see if they have any signs of life in a new age. My own denomination has shifted its central color scheme from a red, white, and blue denominational seal to a reliance on red and black as the central coloring of the celebration of its fiftieth anniversary. It has been fifty years, not of smooth reincarnations, but deaths along the way of many cherished old loyalties that has made way for the emergence of new life under far different circumstances than anyone would have imagined fifty years ago. I imagine this is the basic reality of most churches and larger church organizations that have endured over time.

As I reflect on the past, the truth emerges that even despite times of unfaithfulness, God has been faithful to us in setting before us challenges that give us an opportunity to grow in wisdom and stature. I suspect when we get down to this basic truth there will be a lot less ruinous wrangling.

Luke 17:11-19

Why does it seem basic in the gospel narrative that the foreigners understand in a way that brings a fuller benefit than is available to those who are insiders? Of course, that is the way an insider might ask the question. However, to put it another way, it is the insider who is more at risk in their faith journey than the outsider. The insider is in the position of saying, "We have never done it that way before." The insider can find themselves shifting from what God can do for them to what they have done — from how great God is to how good they are. The insider can find themselves with a history they believe they have to live up to or live down. The ties that bind insiders can become bars to those on the outside.

The outsider knows that some boundary they, themselves, could not cross has been crossed to bring about their healing. The insider has the opportunity to pull rank in a way that is unavailable to the outsider. The outsider knows they must pool together on the face of what threatens. The Samaritan and the Jews, as outsiders when they have leprosy, pull together in their begging. However, once they are healed, there seems to be a parting of the ways that divides the group. Now it is the Samaritan who remains the outsider by virtue of his ethnicity.

The insider is at risk in a way that the outsider is not. Often the things we value on the inside of church become the things that can prove to be a barrier to the advancement of the kingdom of God. Seniority, unit cohesiveness, and success can cause us to turn inward.

In some ways, this story ought to be titled "The Good Samaritan." What we have here is more than mere gratitude but a crossing of boundaries and recognition of what dangers might be incurred on crossing over from outsider to insider. The Samaritan goes from one who must beg to one who finds himself propelled to center stage. Imagine, in the years to come, how one who has known Jesus and been healed by Jesus would be revered by the community of Jesus. One who was on the margins now finds himself with power and authority of being at the center of attention. Moving from the margins to the center can be every bit as dangerous as moving in the opposite direction. Perhaps it is even more dangerous. A survey of the gospels tends to confirm the treacherousness of this path. Jesus' story of the wicked slave whose own debt was forgiven but who pounces on the one who owed him money makes clear the danger of being one of the insiders who has experienced forgiveness. The parable of the talents suggests that the joy of the center is that those who have much get more leaving others shut out. The good, dutiful, elder son in the story of the prodigal son has done all the things that make him the center of attention, yet he finds that there is no party for him. The gospels portray Peter as one who is at the center of things but he finds himself thinking more like men than like God as he maintains his hold on his role.

The lepers in this story are well on their way to moving from the margins of their society to being the center of conversation and admiration because they were so favored. As they leave, they were made clean. Yet, Christian people are at risk in their cleanliness so that they may make others feel dirty who have not shared in the experience of being cleansed. Watching the lepers walk down the road, we know they are at risk. One instinctively feels that the story is not over yet.

It is not until the Samaritan acts that the action is completed. "Then he said to him, 'Get up and go on your way; your faith has made you well.' " This wellness is described in the story of Zacchaeus as the reason that Jesus has come into the world. The measure of the Samaritan is not that he is at the center of things but wherever he is, he has centered on the activity and work of Jesus.

Application

The texts, each in their own way, take up some basic features of the Christian faith. While in our time many see the need for a return to the basics of doctrine, no doubt a laudatory aim, these texts push us toward a different understanding of what the basics of Christian faith are. Jeremiah lived in a context not unlike our own, in which we live in exile in a culture that is often either indifferent or hostile to the faith community. Jeremiah measures our response not by doctrinal purity but by how well we can bless the society in which we live. Timothy reminds us of the basic fact of the journey is that we die. Of course, we understand this intellectually, but the practical reality of the deaths that we must die along the way as part of the journey often eludes us. Celebrating thirty years of ministry this year, I look back in amazement at the number of deaths along the way that have made me more alive. Good Friday before Easter is basic to the journey of faith. Luke's account of the ten lepers reminds us that it is a basic part of the faith to find ourselves at spiritual risk when we move from the margins to the center. It often makes it difficult to reverse gears and journey the other way.

I get the feeling that these basics are not always fully covered in our faith conversations. However, if we get them right, they will help us cover the ground we need to traverse in our pilgrimage.

An Alternative Application

Luke 17:11-19. Three cheers for the lepers who approached Jesus. They do the dance of approaching yet keeping their distance at the same time. When you are on the margins, you need to learn such a dance.

They call Jesus master, which might seem to be a part of the dance to get Jesus' attention without getting embroiled in too much theological controversy.

However, the lepers are on to something here. The description of Jesus as master is a favorite of Luke's, meaning superintendent or overseer. The word is used in Luke when the disciples' fishing produces no results and when it seems that they are going under in the midst of the wind and the waves. We have many names for Jesus — prophet, priest, king, friend, savior, but overseer?

Perhaps we avoid this name because it takes us in a different direction than we are accustomed. If Jesus is master and overseer then we are workers and laborers. The gospel, then, is about our work orders as well as our salvation. It is about Jesus overseeing our lives. Can there be any part social, political, or economic that does not come under his purview?

Proper 24 / Pentecost 22 / Ordinary Time 29
Jeremiah 31:27-34
2 Timothy 3:14—4:5
Luke 18:1-8
David Kalas

The easiest way to lose

Most televised sporting events now feature some pre-game analysis by the commentators. That analysis usually includes some "keys to victory" segment. The different broadcasts have their own catchy names — sometimes even corporate-sponsored names — for those segments, but they are all essentially the same. Namely, the commentators identify what are the two or three things each team needs to do in order to win the game.

Meanwhile, just as the commentators evaluate beforehand what it takes to win a game, any good coach will analyze and evaluate afterward why his team lost the game. Too many turnovers? Too few rebounds? Chasing balls out of the strike zone? Too many penalties? Missed gap assignments on defense?

Whatever the case, the coach wants to minimize his team's losses, and so he is obliged to evaluate the reasons for those losses. If the coach can identify the two or three things most responsible for his team's losses, he can work to improve those areas of the team's performance and that translates into winning.

Perhaps we, as Christians, should be equally deliberate and purposeful in spiritual matters. Perhaps we should recognize both the wins and losses of our Christian lives and be a bit more analytical about those losses.

Of course, in the world of sports, there is one key to victory that is seldom mentioned in the pre-game analysis. It's a huge key — essential, really — but it's almost never mentioned because it's too obvious. Yet, when it comes to the wins and losses of the Christian life, it may account for a majority of our defeats.

It is the easiest way to lose. Giving up.

It is axiomatic: You can't win if you give up. The sports team can't. The individual athlete can't. The candidate for political office can't. And the Christian can't.

Yet giving up may be the most common cause of defeat in the Christian life. One man gives up in a battle with temptation. This woman gives up in her praying for her disappointing marriage. This teenager gives up in his efforts to share his faith with his unbelieving friend.

In our two New Testament passages this week, we will be encouraged not to give up. And that is a message worth proclaiming — and worth hearing — because any coach, player, or analyst will tell you that you can't win if you don't keep trying.

Jeremiah 31:27-34

I had a friend years ago whose standard greeting was, "What's new?" Not "Hi" or "Hello." Not "How are you?" But "What's new?"

Perhaps I took the greeting too literally, but I found it something of a struggle to respond. If we had seen each other less regularly, it would not have been such a challenge to me. But our schedules were such that we saw each other several times a week, and frankly I didn't have that much newness to report.

Well, the prophet Jeremiah has an answer to that question. In our selected Old Testament lection, Jeremiah is here to tell us exactly what's new.

The newness described in this famous passage might be divided — and preached — in three parts. First, there is a new covenant. Second, there are new people. Third, there is a new reality.

All of the newness is a promise from God: "The days are surely coming, says the Lord." The phrase is characteristic of the prophet Jeremiah, appearing eleven different times in his book (including two times in this passage alone). It is used in Jeremiah to guarantee both coming judgment and future restoration.

Another theme in Jeremiah that recurs here in our passage is God's statement that he has "watched over" and "will watch over" the people. The reader whose memory can go back thirty chapters will recall this theme being introduced at the very beginning of Jeremiah's message. God puts his words in Jeremiah's mouth, and then appoints him "over nations and over kingdoms, to pluck up and to pull down, to destroy and to overthrow, to build and to plant" (Jeremiah 1:10). Then, using a brief and simple vision, God assures Jeremiah, "I am watching over my word to perform it" (Jeremiah 1:12).

That image is revisited here but with a favorable twist. Typical of the judgment prophets, God's message for his people is not exclusively bad news. The near future features judgment, to be sure, but judgment will not be the final word. Just as God had "watched over them" to destroy, so now "I will watch over them to build and to plant, says the Lord."

Meanwhile, "the days are surely coming" and "watching over" are phrases characteristic of the book of Jeremiah, the promise of newness is characteristic of God. He is the one who gives new names (Genesis 32:28), who does new things (Isaiah 43:19), whose mercies are ever new (Lamentations 3:22-23), and who in the end will make all things new (Revelation 21:5).

The first particular of this promised newness is the new covenant. If the promise did not come from God himself, of course, it would have been a blasphemous proposition. After all, the covenant between God and Israel was his initiation and to propose a new covenant would not have been within Israel's scope or authority. So it is God who proposes a new one.

Interestingly, God proposes this new covenant in the context of his people having failed to comply faithfully with the original covenant, like a cuckolded husband suggesting that the couple renew their vows. That's why the other two elements of newness are necessary: new people and a new reality.

The people are new here, not in the sense that God has traded in one group for another, but in the sense that he will make them new. That, at least, is the implication of the new covenant's focus on an inner work by God. While the first covenant was written on stone, this new covenant will be written upon the human heart. Interestingly, the covenant is still expressed in terms of law, but now it is not portrayed as a thing imposed from outside, but rather as a thing that lives within.

That, in turn, suggests a larger new reality. The whole situation will be different, for "no longer shall they teach one another," but rather "they shall all know me."

The first detail is reminiscent of Paul's observations about love in relation to the other gifts of the Spirit. Prophecies, tongues, and knowledge will all come to an end, Paul says, but "love never ends" (1 Corinthians 13:8). Such things as prophecy and teaching are necessarily limited, you see, to a time and place where there is a need for such things but that need will not be eternal. The need for people to "say to each other, 'Know the Lord,' " will not last forever, either.

Instead, "they shall all know me." This newness, obviously, is not an immediate byproduct of what we know as the new covenant of the New Testament. For there remains a need to teach and to encourage one another to know the Lord. Clearly not all people know him. But those days are surely coming and that is good news for us as it was for Jeremiah's generation.

What's new? Virtually everything! A new covenant, a new people, and a whole new reality.

2 Timothy 3:14—4:5

If scripture were music, we would listen for motifs. We'd observe how the composer introduced the motif near the beginning, and then how he wove it through the piece with artistic twists and creative interpretations.

If this New Testament reading were a musical composition, we would recognize immediately the motif Paul introduces with his very first verb: "continue." Therein lies the great recurring theme and message of this counsel to Timothy: continue.

Listen through the passage and hear the composer's variations on that motif. "Continue in what you have learned." "Be persistent." "With the utmost patience." "Always." "Endure." "Carry out." "Fully." These belong together. They are images of perseverance, and Paul is persistent in presenting them.

We remember Joseph's word to Pharaoh about his twin dreams: "The doubling of Pharaoh's dream means that the thing is fixed by God" (Genesis 41:32). So here, the repetition makes the message an emphatic one.

On a time line, we are presented with a kind of relay race image, and Timothy is running a middle leg. The baton — in this case might broadly be called the message — neither begins with him nor ends with him. (We resemble Timothy, in this regard.) He is to continue in what he has learned and believed, bearing in mind "from whom you learned it." So it is that Timothy has been the recipient of a message from someone who ran before him and now he is to pass it along to those who follow him: proclaiming at all times, patiently teaching, and carrying out his ministry fully. This middle leg he runs requires persistence and perseverance.

Another theme — a secondary motif, if you will — is the matter of correction. This is perhaps a lost virtue in American Christianity. We are so much the products of a mind-your-own-business culture, and so fearful of the "holier-than-thou" moniker, that we resist all correction. We resist being corrected, for that seems to us insulting and judgmental. We resist correcting, for that seems unsolicited and intrusive.

Yet, Paul is very concerned about the importance of correction. "All scripture," after all, "is useful" for it. Furthermore, Timothy is called, among other things, to rebuke. The imminent context in which he will fulfill his ministry will be marked by a rejection of sound doctrine and truth in favor of more convenient teachings and myths. In such a setting, correction is necessary — albeit unwelcome.

In our day, our knee-jerk response to correction is one of defiance. It is the ego's reflex: we don't like to be told that we're wrong. The person who never allows himself to be corrected never learns. Set aside the relativism that has poisoned theology, philosophy, and ethics and consider instead virtually any other field of endeavor. Correction is assumed; indeed, welcomed. If I do not accept correction from my math instructor, I shall never calculate properly. If I do not accept correction from the craftsman, I shall never learn the craft. If I do not accept correction from God's word or spokesperson, then I shall be left to wander in some amalgam of incomplete knowledge, unfiltered exposure, and personal opinion. Plus, according to the writer of Proverbs, I shall be on the short end of wisdom (Proverbs 9:8; 12:1).

Luke 18:1-8

The older members of our congregations will remember very dignified portraits of prayer from their younger years. There is the classic painting of praying hands that hung in so many churches. Perhaps a familiar picture of a staid Christ praying in Gethsemane. Or a widespread portrait of an old, bearded man quietly praying at his table over a loaf of bread.

Meanwhile, many of us were also taught to pray with a certain dignity. Whether by tacit example or by explicit instruction, it became clear to us that the posture, the tone, and even the language of prayer should be marked by a certain reserve, a quietness, and above all reverence.

Into the midst of all that orthodoxy and propriety, comes Jesus. Here in our gospel lection, he presents us with a most unsettling picture of prayer. So far removed from those sober and still praying hands; so different from the serene face of Christ in the Garden, Jesus paints us a new picture to hang on the walls of our parlors, hallways, and Sunday school rooms. It is a picture of a woman who will not take no for an answer.

Perhaps her first appearance before this notorious judge was marked by the kind of decorum and deference that we traditionally associate with prayer. Perhaps the first time she appealed her case to him, she did so with a posture and tone that would make her a conventional model for prayer. By the end, she is no portrait of quietness and reserve. Quite the contrary: She has become a conspicuous pest.

Take down the picture of the praying hands and the gentle old man at the table. Replace them with pictures of this woman: knocking at the door, calling out, pressing her face against the windows, refusing to go away. That, according to Jesus, is how we should pray.

While Jesus is not proposing that God resembles the unjust judge, he is confirming that our experience may resemble the woman's experience. For example, we can imagine the discouragement she must have felt when "for a while he refused." We know all about the "while" of an unanswered prayer. We have walked — or shall we say waited — in that woman's shoes.

That is the point at which we may part company from the woman: namely, how we respond to disappointment and refusal. Do we resign ourselves? Walk away from the altar with our tail between our legs? Wave the white flag and surrender hope?

Here is where the woman in Jesus' parable becomes exemplary, if not obnoxious. She does not let delay or disappointment deter her from her destination. Instead, she pursues — indeed, bothers — this judge until he gives her what she seeks.

So it is that Jesus himself encourages us to persevere in prayer, even when that persistence seems to turn prayer into something quite far from our traditionally reverent pictures. So be it. If prayer looks like a bowed head and folded hands, then that's lovely. But prayer can also look like determination, like perseverance, and even like nagging.

Lest we still recoil a bit from such an unorthodox picture of prayer, we may remind ourselves of this truth about nagging in our human relationships. If my wife persists in asking me to complete some project around the house, and I still delay, she may become discouraged. But if she stops pestering me about it, then that suggests she has not only given up on the project; she has also, in that particular matter, given up on me.

I do not want to be the person who gives up on God. So let me knock, pester, and nag — for those are, at their core, acts of faith.

Application

If Moses had given up after that initial, disheartening encounter with Pharaoh, the Hebrews would not have been freed. If the people had given up marching around Jericho after five days, the walls would not have fallen. If the Canaanite woman had given up when she received no response — or a negative one — her daughter would not have been healed. If the apostles in Jerusalem had given up at the first sign of opposition, the church there would have floundered while they cowered. If Paul had given up his missionary efforts as soon as he encountered difficulty, untold numbers of individuals and communities would not have heard the good news.

In short, giving up is the easiest, quickest way to lose. And not giving up is a basic key to victory.

It is worth pondering what losses we have suffered — individually or as a church — simply because we have given up in some of the areas where Paul urged perseverance: in sound doctrine, in the proclamation of the gospel, in patient teaching, in the experience of suffering, or in some particular calling or ministry. Perhaps more sobering still, how many losses have we suffered because we have, unlike the importunate widow, given up in prayer?

This Sunday, we play the part of coaches. Setting aside all the nuances of strategy, all the details of individual plays, we simply remind the team that the single greatest key to victory is, simply, not to give up.

2 Timothy 3:14—4:5. "The Neglected Testament." In my years of ministry, I have observed a common and sometimes deeply ingrained prejudice against the Old Testament. In some cases, the dislike is rather innocuous: "It's boring" or "I don't understand it." In other cases, though, the objections are quite insidious, for they undermine our basic affirmations about scripture as canon, as God's word, and as authoritative.

The prejudice displays itself in dismissive remarks, like, "but that's in the *Old* Testament" and in the sloppy hermeneutic that draws a sharp distinction between the revelation of God in the Old Testament and in the New Testament. To assume wholesale differences in God's nature, actions, and will from one Testament to the other is either to suggest that God changed or that one whole section of scripture is unreliable. Either assertion cuts deeply and carelessly into one of the legs on the stool of our faith.

In response to the modern-day Marcionism, and in affirmation of that two thirds of our Bible that we call the Old Testament, we might do well to preach about Paul's remarkable statements in the passage from 2 Timothy.

The key question is this: When the apostle Paul refers to "the sacred writings" and "all scripture," what does he have in mind? Was there, at the time of this letter, any sense yet of a new corpus of writings that he would have referred to so deferentially? Or are these simply references to the writings that were recognized as canonical in first-century Judaism and that we know as the Old Testament?

If we assume the latter, then Paul is saying two things that some contemporary Christians might choke on. First, the Old Testament is "able to instruct you for salvation through faith in Christ Jesus." And, second, the Old Testament is "useful for teaching, for reproof, for correction, and for training in righteousness."

There is nothing in that second affirmation about the Old Testament that would have been anything other than standard orthodoxy for Paul the Pharisee. For him, it was not at all a remarkable thing to say, even though many in our churches might find it hard to say about the Old Testament.

Meanwhile, the first statement — that the Old Testament is sufficient to lead a person to salvation through faith in Christ — may seem oxymoronic to the uninformed, but this is clearly supported elsewhere in the New Testament. It is supported in the ministry of Jesus (Luke 24:25-27, 44-47) and in the preaching of the early church (Acts 17:2-3; 18:24-28).

Preaching the relevance and significance of the Old Testament is not glamorous stuff, but it may be the first step in some of our people recovering and rediscovering the neglected part of their Bible.

Keep looking up

In my childhood home, there was a wall plaque, unadorned except for three words: "Keep Looking Up." For us young ones it was a comic command, and we would stumble about with our eyes glued to the ceiling. But for those who have known any kind of adult anguish, there is no other hope or help.

Sir James Simpson, the Scottish physician who discovered the anesthetic properties of chloroform, freed his world from much pain. But his own heart was anguished by the death of a little daughter. When she was buried in a lonely Edinburgh cemetery, Simpson had a single word carved on the headstone: *Nevertheless*. In that small act of devotion he placed his grief in the hands of God. It was his affirmation that he would "keep looking up."

Bertrand Russell once said, "The only adequate way to endure large stresses is to find large consolation." This is the theme for today. Joel helps his community see through the stark tragedy of a locust plague to find divine consolation and anticipation. Paul faces the executioner's blade with confidence of a coronation to come. And the despised tax collector of Jesus' parable reaches for heaven from down on his knees. "Keep looking up!"

Joel 2:23-32

When did Joel live and command attention as the mouthpiece of God? For a prophecy that plays so prominently in biblical theology, we simply don't know. Joel references no king, as do most of the other prophets, causing some to place his dates early in Israel's history (either in the eleventh century, prior to the development of the monarchy, or perhaps in the ninth century at a time when the king was ineffective because of age or other political circumstances) and others to inject him into the post-exilic community (third century) that was trying to find its way after the years of displacement turmoil. Another theory makes Joel a contemporary of Jeremiah, mainly because the first half of Joel's prophecy is stridently apocalyptic with its warnings of impending judgment by way of enemy invaders, a scene that connects well with the Babylonian destruction of Jerusalem in 586 BC.

Unfortunately for the historians among us, the only actual hook on which we can begin to hang a date for this short message is an unusually severe plague of locusts that prompted visions of a looming divine holocaust meted out by some horrible massacring army. But the swarming invasion could have happened during any decade of life in the Middle East, so we are left with a treasury of dating dust. Recent interpreters tend to peg Joel later rather than earlier, primarily because of the words and stylistics of the Hebrew language he uses.

None of this detracts from his powerful message. For one thing, perhaps as much as any and certainly more than most among the prophets, Joel clarifies the meaning of the term "the day of the Lord." This catchphrase and its variations ("that day," "the day of judgment," "the day of Yahweh's visitation," and so on) collectively begin to hold three significant themes as it is rehearsed among the prophets. First, because of the heightened state of wickedness within the covenant community and also among the nations that surround it, Yahweh will have to break decisively into human history as before when battling Egypt for possession of Israel. This time, Yahweh will judge the nations and destroy the rampant evil that has messed up every culture, including that within the societies of Israel and Judah. Second, although the trauma of this visitation will be severe and painful, Yahweh will spare a remnant of the covenant community as a witness to divine grace and as the starter piece in a global renewal effort. This, thirdly, is the culmination of the day of the Lord: the blossoming of the eternal messianic kingdom in which the divine will holds sway again, and life becomes what God intended all along that it should be. All three of these themes — pervasive divine judgment, restoration of a remnant, and ushering in of the marvelous messianic age — are clearly articulated by Joel.

Another brilliant aspect of Joel's timeless message is the manner in which he connects it to current affairs. As Jesus noted when challenged one day by a tragedy in Palestine (Luke 13:1-5), every awful news report is an occasion for spiritual reflection. This Joel does well. He leverages the powerful plague that is devastating the countryside and rides it to new heights of meaning. Although this disaster affects everyone in significant ways, all will soon be traumatized more terribly by a divine judgment that will make this horrible scene seem pastorally idyllic. Joel is a preacher with contemporary significance in his weekly sermon.

Mostly there is the powerful message itself. Joel paints the word of God with lively hues and stark contrasts that call attention to themselves. God will not merely end the nasty locust plight; God will send "autumn rains in righteousness" and "vats will overflow with new wine and oil." God will not only flip a page on the calendar, but instead "will repay you for the years the locusts have eaten," so that "you will have plenty to eat, until you are full," and "you will praise the name of the Lord your God."

If that is not yet enough, Joel sees signs in the heavens, portents among the planets, and the complete refabrication of the warp and woof of the universe. The specific references of verses 28-32 can never be pinned to anything in our realm of experiences, and yet they are accessible at all times and in all circumstances, as Peter would show on Pentecost Sunday when the power of the divine Spirit overwhelmed the crowd in Jerusalem (Acts 2).

How should we preach Joel's message? First, we need to contextualize it by setting it against any locust plagues or other disasters that scream from the headlines of our current newspapers. The message from Yahweh that Joel brings is always lodged in the leading stories that trouble our times. These serve as the powerful mirrors on which the invading judgment of God is momentarily reflected, and we need to make the most of the times because the days are evil.

Second, we need to ride all three dimensions of Joel's understanding of the code term, "the day of the Lord." It is a moment of cataclysmic judgment on our lives and our societies, to be sure, but it is also an episode of gracious care as God notices and succors the lost and the last and the least, the helpless and the homeless, the worn and the wearied. This is a message that reaches into the kitchens of broken homes and puts family members at odds with each other around the same table again for dinner. This is a message that searches the battlefield conflagrations in the wee hours of the morning and binds the wounds of the fallen and rescues the children from collapsing debris. This is a message that probes the psyche of the troubled and marginalized and helps them find healing.

Third, we need to paint this message in bold colors of a present and coming kingdom of God that transforms the ordinary into the extraordinary. Joel uses a few wonderful words to cast a very big vision. We ought to follow suit and give our people a taste of heaven that makes them hunger and thirst after righteousness.

2 Timothy 4:6-8, 16-18

Paul was under arrest again. It had happened many times before (see 2 Corinthians 4), but this time was different. Nero was emperor in Rome, and he had chosen to target the Christian community for the ills of his realm. The church in Rome had felt the scourge of his wrath in a powerful way, becoming the scapegoat for Nero's civic restoration plan begun by an arsonist conflagration. Several years before, the apostle Peter, known widely as the key church leader in the city, had been crucified upside down. Now the empire's prime mover had netted Christianity's dominant evangelist, and his fate was sealed. Paul would die soon, beheaded outside of the capital city in the compassionate execution method reserved for citizens of the empire. Shortly before, in a final gesture of tenderness and testimony, Paul wrote this letter to his protégé installed as senior pastor in the church of Ephesus. Paul was about to die and these would be his final words of encouragement and request.

Even though these verses rehearse painful difficulties Paul has experienced along the way, his closing message is one of powerful trust in the providence of God. This is the echo of a lifetime of faith. Such testimonies are built on the few but near-miraculous signposts of grace that keep us hanging on to religious commitments.

One of the most amazing stories to come out of World War II is told by a chaplain with the US Air Force. A bombing mission in the South Pacific turned into a grueling night of terror for one B-52 crew. The fuel tanks began leaking when hit by enemy fire, and the plane barely managed an emergency landing on the beach of a small island. In the darkness their location was hidden from the Japanese soldiers who held the island but dawn would make them prisoners of war.

"Chaplain," said the flight leader, "you've been telling us for months about the power of prayer. We're out of fuel! We're surrounded by the enemy! If you've ever prayed, pray now!"

While the rest of the crew patched the fuel tanks, the chaplain knelt in the sands to pray. Even when the others knocked off for a couple hours' rest, the chaplain kept to his post. About 2 a.m., a sentry heard something scrape against the sand at the water's edge. A cautious investigation revealed a large metal floating object — a barge — piled high with barrels. Each one contained gasoline — high-octane gasoline — airplane fuel. In a matter of minutes, the crew was roused, the tanks filled, and they were in the air again, bound for home!

Where had the fuel come from? Later investigations told the story. A supply ship captain, surrounded by enemy submarines 600 miles and several weeks away, had set his cargo of aircraft fuel afloat in hopes of saving lives. It landed fifty feet away from the bomber crew *exactly* when they needed it. What an answer to prayer!

"As luck would have it, providence was on my side!" wrote Samuel Butler. A bit more reverent is Paul's statement: "The Lord stood at my side and gave me strength." But what does that mean? Is it a good luck charm? Will it get you out of any scrape, even those of your own foolish doing? Hardly. We know of too many tragedies and cruelties and unrequited injustices even in the Christian community to believe that. A young Christian girl whose sister was sick and whose family was troubled by a long list of difficulties, once wrote to me: "I am angry with God right now... Sometimes I even think our family is cursed. When something goes wrong I think, 'Oh no! *Another* curse!' "

Nor can Paul's trust in God be mere fatalism. The message of the Bible is not compatible with the idea that evil forces are either God's delight or his intent. No one can thank God for providential leading when a drunk driver crushes the body of a child. No one can praise God for providential direction when an airplane crashes or a mine collapses. These are not the things of which providence is made.

Thus it is difficult to read the times we live in or to easily identify the exact way God is moving with power or shaping destinies. The dangers are all too evident when we read the statement signed by 600 German pastors and fourteen theology professors in 1934: "We are thankful to God that he, as Lord of history, has given us Adolf Hitler, our leader and savior from our difficult lot." Such a confession seems demonic now!

In a sense, Paul's testimony is more a confession than a theological treatise. I *believe* God exists. I *know* that God can control the destinies of peoples and nations. I am *confident* that God has a direction, a purpose for this world, and I *want* to be a part of that leading. Even when things go "wrong" (from my own point of view) — even when tragedy strikes — even when no miracles happen — "The Lord will rescue me from every evil attack and will bring me safely to his heavenly kingdom." That's the confession of faith! That's the confidence of trust!

A young schoolteacher named Ray Palmer thought about that one night in 1830. He sat at his desk in the darkness and wrote a little poem to God. It was a prayer of trust, a statement of faith. One day he met Dr. Lowell Mason, a brilliant musician. Looking for verses to set to hymn tunes, Dr. Mason scanned Ray's poetry. It was all quite good but one poem moved him to tears. It was the nighttime prayer. With a melody of simple majesty, Mason published the hymn that spoke with the convictions of Paul. It still grabs hearts. It still brings tears. Its opening line goes like this: My faith looks up to thee!

Luke 18:9-14

A rather distinguished matron of high society felt the need to commission a lavish portrait of herself. But her demands and desires drove her from one artist to the next. None could do it right! Finally she stormed into the studio of still another candidate. As they settled on a fee, she told of her disappointment with others of his profession. "Young man!" she said, "I want you to do me justice!"

By now, the artist was having second thoughts. He looked her up and down and finally let it slip: "Madam," he said, "it's not *justice* you need. It's *mercy*!"

This may well help us think through Jesus' marvelous parable in a fresh way. Who do we think we are? What do we think we need? Why does Jesus take a bad man and make him a model for our prayers?

"Mercy is a beggar's refuge," said George Bernard Shaw, "a man must pay his debts!" That's how we feel when someone hurts us. Can you imagine a rape victim suffering a lifetime of psychological scars while her attacker gets a mild reprimand? Or a family carrying on with the knowledge that the drunk driver who senselessly slaughtered their son didn't even have his license suspended? "It isn't fair!" we shout. A cry for mercy from such trash is a beggar's refuge. We spit on it.

When Austrian Prince Schwarzenberg put down the Hungarian rebellion of 1849, some counselors advised mercy for the captives. "Yes, indeed," he replied, "a good idea; but first we will have a little hanging!" Often our hearts nod in assent.

Even our mercy can be laced with spite. When the first Elizabeth finally came to England's throne after the political and religious wrangling of the sixteenth century, a knight who had formerly despised her came seeking pardon. He threw himself at her feet begging mercy. With a flick of her hand she dismissed him, saying, "Do you not know that we are descended of the lion, whose nature is not to prey upon the mouse or any other such small vermin?"

A royal put-down indeed! But husbands do it to wives and vice versa, neighbors condescendingly do it to each other, church members justify their cases and offer mean-spirited "forgiveness." "Community" becomes a shining ideal that we can't buy with our smoldering bitterness.

In Shakespeare's *The Merchant of Venice*, the main character borrows a great sum of money from Shylock. Due to adverse circumstances, he is unable to pay it back. Shylock demands justice, but seethes with vengeance. And, in a marvelous speech, Portia slices to the heart of human need:

> *The quality of mercy is not strain'd,*
> *It droppeth as the gentle rain from heaven....*
> *Though justice be thy plea, consider this,*
> *That in the course of justice none of us*
> *Should see salvation. We do pray for mercy,*
> *And that same prayer doth teach us all to render*
> *The deeds of mercy.*
> — Act IV, Scene 1

That's the kind of mercy the tax collector mutters about in Jesus' story. The great and good religious leaders stand to strut and pose and behind him all this man feels is the blazing wrath of God. He knows he deserves divine anger. He knows he's not caught in an unfair tragedy of blind circumstances but wrapped up in the fair balances of justice.

Will he stand like a man and pay his debts? No, for in this courtroom there is no limit to the punishment and no door marked "Exit." All that's left is love's second name: mercy! And in the scent of that whisper, life begins again.

Application

Both the epistle and gospel lessons are intensely personal. They could be used to call out experiential reflections on how each person present came to faith and grew in grace. It might even be appropriate, using the 2 Timothy passage, to get people to think about what their obituaries might say and why. Did others catch from them that they indeed spent a life "Looking Up"?

An Alternative Application

Joel 2:23-32; 2 Timothy 4:6-8, 16-18; Luke 18:9-14. There are many great hymns of faith connected to the passages in today's lectionary readings. These could shape segments of a message in which the testimonies of the past might inspire the singing of powerful songs that would renew the personal reflections of those gathered. They deepen their understanding of the journey of faith as they are traveling in pilgrim company.

Forming, deforming, reforming

For many years we drove a small Volvo wagon. It fit the needs of our young family, with its safety features and good cargo space.

When we needed a second car, a friend who deals in used autos and parts found a car he thought I would like. It was a brand new Volvo sedan, available for a used car price.

How could this be, I asked. Here's the story: a young couple ordered a new Volvo sedan to their expressed tastes, including color and interior appointments. Taking delivery of it in late November, the couple was driving it off the dealer's lot during the season's first snowstorm, when a car on the street slid out of control. Twisting and spinning, the street driver spun right onto the dealership lot and smashed into the front end of the young couple's brand new Volvo.

Since the car had not yet left the dealer's lot, the dealer's insurance had to cover the restoration costs. And because the couple had purchased a factory-perfect new vehicle, they demanded not just a restored broken car, but a freshly built sedan. So the insurance company purchased the compromised vehicle and the dealership ordered another one to be built for the couple. The insurance company sold the damaged car to a repair shop, where the front end of the new-but-undrivable sedan was rebuilt. Then my friend, who is connected to that market, bought the car and resold it to me.

When I took possession, my "used" car had 800 miles on it. Was it new? Was it used? Perhaps the best way I could describe it was that my car had been formed, deformed, and reformed.

This idea of restoration is behind each lectionary passage on this Reformation Day. Jeremiah delivers the word of Yahweh declaring that the Sinai Covenant, once formed to give identity and missional purpose to Israel, has been deformed and needs to be reformed so that the best the Creator can offer will blossom again in our world. Paul uses the scare tactic of sin's deformation to urge reformation under God's gracious offer of salvation. And Jesus locks horns, briefly, with the religious leaders of his day in order to point out where true reform can point past the deceptions of deform to the original purposes of humankind as God formed us.

Jeremiah 31:31-34

The theme of the Sinai Covenant is very prominent in Jeremiah's prophecies and central to today's lectionary passage. Most striking is Jeremiah's recognition that this covenant governs Israel's success and its demise, and that one day soon Yahweh will find a way to renew that covenant in a manner that will keep the restored nation more faithful to its identity and true to its mission.

Jeremiah lived almost a century after Isaiah. By his time, Assyria had long ago destroyed Judah's northern neighbor Israel (722 BC). Judah was itself only a tiny community now, limping along with diminishing resources, and constantly tossed around by the bigger nations of its world.

But things were changing rapidly on the international scene. Assyria was being beaten down in 612 BC by its eastern bully province, Babylon. After snapping the backbone of Assyrian forces at Carchemish and wrestling the capital city of Nineveh to the ground, Babylon immediately took over Palestine, the newer name for the old region of Canaan.

Judah was experiencing a rapid turnover of kings, many of whom were puppets of Babylon. Already the country was expected to pay yearly tribute or security bribes to Babylon, and since 606 BC had been forced to turn over some of its promising young men for propaganda retraining exile in the capital of the superpower, in anticipation that they would return to rule Judah as regents of Babylon.

Into these times and circumstances Jeremiah was born. From his earliest thoughts he was aware of Yahweh's special call on his life (1:4-10). This knowledge only made his prophetic ministry more gloomy, for it gave him no out in a game where the deck was stacked against him (chs. 12, 16). So he brooded through his life, deeply introspective. He fulfilled his role as gadfly to most of the kings who reigned during his life, even though it took eminent courage to do so. Although he lived an exemplary life, political officials constantly took offence at his theologically charged political commentaries, and regularly arrested him and treated him badly. Jeremiah was passionately moral, never allowing compromise as a suitable temporary alternative in the shady waters of international relations or the roiling quicksand of fading religious devotion. He remained pastorally sensitive, especially to the poor and oppressed in Jerusalem, weeping in anguish as families boiled sandals and old leather to find a few nutrients during Babylonian sieges, and when he saw mothers willing to cannibalize their dying babies to keep other children alive. Above all, Jeremiah found the grace to be unshakably hopeful, truly believing to the very end that though destruction would raze Jerusalem and the temple, Yahweh would keep covenant promises and one day soon restore the fortunes of this wayward partner in the divine missional enterprise.

Jeremiah's prophecies are not collected in a chronological order. When tracked against the reigns and events of various kings, it becomes clear that chapters 30-31 were received and written during the reign of King Josiah (640-609). These were the days of promising renewal and hope was in the air. Perhaps the covenant relationship with God might be restored and reaffirmed, and there is a sense in which these lines hint in that direction. But deeper still is the acknowledgement that any reformation movements are destined to fail unless they are initiated by God's restorative grace. The "Day of the Lord" belongs to God, not us. But those who are open to the winds of divine grace are aware of the great reformation that happens in God's time.

Romans 3:19-28

At the end of Paul's second mission journey, he traveled to Corinth from Ephesus, either late in 53 or early in 54, and stayed three months with his friend Gaius (Acts 19:1-3; Romans 16:23). When he learned that a good friend (and a leader in the Christian congregation located in Cenchrea, one of Corinth's seaport suburbs) named Phoebe was making a trip to Rome (Romans 16:1), Paul quickly penned what has become the most orderly summary of early Christian theology.

Since Paul had not yet made a visit to Rome, his letter to that congregation was less personal and more rationally organized than was true of most of his other letters. Paul intended this missive to be a working document that the congregation already established in the capital city of the empire would be able to read and discuss together in anticipation of his arrival, which was planned for some months ahead (Romans 1:6-15). Paul's working theme and emphasis was the new expression of the "righteousness of God," which had been recently revealed with power through the coming of Jesus Christ (Romans 1:17).

Because Paul moved directly from a brief statement about the righteousness of God into an extended explication of the wrath of God revealed against wickedness (Romans 1:18), many have interpreted Paul's understanding of God's righteousness as an unattainable standard against which the whole of the human race is measured and fails. Only in the context of this desperate human situation would the grand salvation of Christ then be appreciated and enjoyed.

But more scholars believe that Paul's assertions of the righteousness of God, central to today's lectionary reading, have a positive and missional thrust. In their understanding of what Paul says, it is because of the corruption and sinfulness that is demeaning and destroying humanity that God needed again, as

God did through Israel, to re-assert the divine will. In so doing, God's focus was not on heaping judgment upon humankind, but instead that of drawing people back to the creational goodness God had intended for them. This was, in essence, the same missional purpose that God had planned for Israel during the Old Testament.

This more positive perspective on the righteousness of God fits well with the flow of Paul's message and certainly seems to come to expression in today's transitional pericope. In chapters 1:18—3:20 Paul describes the crippling effect of sin. But once the stage has been set for his readers to realize again the pervasive grip of evil in this world, including within their own divided and deluded hearts, Paul marches Abraham out onto the stage as a model of divine religious reconstruction. God does not wish to be distant from the world, judgmental and vengeful. Instead, as shown to Abraham, God desires an ever-renewing relationship with the people God made. Thus, as exhibited in Abraham's life (Romans 4), God initiates a relationship of favor and grace with us. In fact, according to Paul, this purpose of God is no less spectacular than the divine quest to re-create the world and undoing the effects that the cancer of sin has blighted upon us (Romans 5).

One important idea to keep in mind is that righteousness is not the same as innocence. Innocence is devoid of the knowledge of evil, while righteousness is a deliberate reaction to experienced evil. Thus it is important for Paul to make explicit that righteousness is God's response to evil rather than our attainment. The reformation of a world gone sordid is completely the initiative and accomplishment of God. But in its wake comes the reformation of our lives and societies.

John 8:31-36

Fred Craddock and his wife were on vacation in the Great Smoky Mountains of eastern Tennessee when they stumbled onto an out-of-the-way restaurant called the Black Bear Inn. It proved to be a good place to eat, besides offering the possibility of actually seeing one of those black bears. An entire wall was glass, opening out onto a wild and rugged valley.

As they sat at supper, quietly communing with nature and each other, their solitude was broken by a tall man with a shock of white hair who ambled over. They could see he was well along in years, probably past the fourscore allotted by the Psalmist.

He was hard of hearing as well, since he rudely interrupted their quiet reverie with noisy and nosy questions at least twenty decibels too loud. When he found that Fred taught at a seminary he suddenly had a story to tell about preachers. Without an invitation he pulled up a chair and invaded their space.

Nodding out the great glass window, he said, "I was born back here in these mountains."

But the story was not to be a pretty one. "My mother was not married," he went on, "and the reproach that fell upon her, fell upon me. The children at school had a name for me, and it hurt. It hurt very much."

In fact, he said, "During recess I would go hide in the weeds until the bell rang. At noon hour I took my lunch and went behind a tree to avoid them. And when I went to town with my mamma, all the grownups would stop and stare at us. They'd look at my mamma, and then they'd look at me, and I could see they were trying to guess who my daddy might have been. Painful years, those."

Something big was about to happen. "I guess it was about the seventh or eighth grade," he continued, "when a preacher came to town. He frightened me when he preached, and he attracted me, all at the same time. He was a big man. Thundered when he preached. But he caught me. Every time he preached he caught me with his words.

"I didn't want the people to catch me, though. So I never went to church on time. Waited around outside till they sang the hymn before the sermon. Then I'd sneak in just as he was getting warmed up. When he was finished I'd rush right out. Didn't want to hear the people say, 'What's a boy like you doin' in church?'

"But one morning I got caught. A bunch of women lined up in the aisle, and I couldn't get out. And I got all nervous and cold and sweaty. And I knew somebody was going to see me and say, 'Whatchadoin' here, boy? What's a boy like you doin' in church?'

"And sure enough, suddenly a hand clamped down on my shoulder. Out of the corner of my eye I could see the preacher's face.

" 'Whoa, boy!' he says to me. And he turns me around, and he looks me in the face. And he studies me for a while. And I can just see he's trying to find the family resemblance. And finally he says, 'Well, boy...! I can see it now...! I can see you're a child of... You're a child of... Wait now...'

"And he stared me right in the face. 'Yep!' he says. 'I can see it now! You're a child of... God! There's a striking resemblance!'

"Then that preacher man swatted me on the bottom, and he said, 'Go on, boy! Go claim your family inheritance!' "

The Craddock's were quite taken by the story the old man had to tell. Fred thought there was something familiar about it, so he asked the elderly gent, "Sir, what's your name?"

The man replied, proudly, "Ben Hooper!"

It was then that Fred Craddock remembered his daddy telling him the story of the time the people of Tennessee twice elected an illegitimate bastard boy as governor, and how Ben Hooper had done the state proud.

Ben Hooper had faith. He gained faith when a preacher told him he was child of God. He proved his faith when he carved a future of grace out of a mixed inheritance. This is what Jesus was looking for in the faces of those who surrounded him during the dialogues of today's lectionary passage.

Application

In 1923 Karl Barth was asked to speak on the topic "What Does It Mean to Be Reformed?" at an assembly of the Reformed Churches in Emden, Germany. He said that to be Reformed means to know your history and your community. All Christians are part of the family of God, he observed, but we cannot experience relationships of significance or intimacy with the whole of the Body of Christ, simply because it is too expansive and we are too finite and limited in the scope of our relational abilities.

Just as it is impossible to understand humanity in general until we begin to live with and experience a small collective of humans called family and neighborhood, so we cannot appreciate the whole church of God without nurturing meaningful associations with a particular congregation or denominational culture. It is only through the smaller conglomerate, by learning its language and its habits and its values and its goals, that the meaning and purpose of the larger entity at last becomes manageable and accessible.

You do not understand the body of Christ or the church of God by embracing the whole, said Barth, but you begin to comprehend it through engagement with the community of Christ closest too you. That is why there can never be free-floating Christians or isolated believers. I can never be a child of God all by myself if I am not cognizant of the family of God and interact meaningfully with it. And I cannot interact meaningfully with the whole of God's family apart from deep and profound attachments to that portion of the family that surrounds and nurtures me.

Hence the idea of "reform" or "Reformation" is essentially a historical and cultural acknowledgment of participation in the dynamics of family life. A family grows through changes and alterations that sometimes move it away from its values and identity, and other times restore it to its deepest connections. "Reformation" is always related to "Deformation" that arises out of "Formation." Thus, today's celebration of reform is essentially a means by which to affirm the elasticity that holds the whole of the Body of Christ to its head, and all of God's children in relationship with each other.

Alternative Application

John 8:31-36. During the heated times of the Reformation, when Martin Luther and Ulrich Zwingli were exchanging strong words about biblical interpretations and ecclesiastical practices, Zwingli spent a troubled morning walking the mountain trails of his beloved Switzerland. From a distance he observed two goats making their way in opposite directions on a path barely stitched to the side of a cliff. It was obvious that not even these nimble creatures would be able to negotiate past one another as they met.

Zwingli watched them round a corner and come face-to-face. There was a moment of uncertainty as each feinted a power move at the other. Both goats took several steps backward and set hind legs in a posture of attack. In a surprise twist, however, the goat at the lower level suddenly collapsed onto the narrow ledge until the other goat could walk quickly over its back. Then each danced on.

Zwingli was impressed. Here was strength defined by submission. It allowed two opponents to survive a little crisis in order to get on with the larger dimensions of their lives. Zwingli considered this moment a divine parable and brought it into his next encounter with Luther.

Submission is at the heart of Jesus' short teaching in today's lectionary passage. John Maxwell noted that there are five different levels of authority that a person can attain in life but each is based on an increasing willingness to submit to outside forces or influences.

The first is "position," where people are challenged to respect you for your rank in society. Second, there is the authority of "permission" that happens when you enter a relationship of significance with someone else, and that person allows you to have a say in his affairs. Third comes the authority of "production" in which you are honored for the results you can get. Fourth, there is the authority of "people development" that recognizes the empowerment you have given others. Finally arises the quality of "personhood" where the very character of your life demands respect.

We can all name people who gather one or another of these forms of authority to themselves: a judge, for instance, fits the first; a dating partner, the second; my neighbor across the street did such a good job of bringing up the production in his factory in our town that he was transferred to tackle the development of an even larger plant in another state — that is an example of number three; my uncle who retired as a high school guidance counselor got the accolades of the fourth; and we only have to say names like "Billy Graham" and "Mother Teresa" to explore the last.

Interestingly, the source of all five of these forms of authority exists in our relationship with our parents. A mother has position over us when we are young children. She can abuse that position, as some have, or she can also use it to give us a wholesome sense of ourselves, as many others have.

A father has our permission, early in life, to direct and guide us. We look for support and advice from him. A mother holds over us the authority of production. Before we can tie our shoes or dress ourselves, she is doing things for us we could not begin to handle on our own. So it is with level four — a good parent is able to serve in developing our characters. When we sat around at my grandmother's funeral, some years ago, my dad and all his siblings said the same thing: "Mom always believed in us. She always prayed for us. We wouldn't be the people we are without her care."

In fact, when all these forms of authority are rolled up in a single package it is that fifth form, the one that is particularly hard to earn, which epitomizes the best of what great parenting is about. There is no higher tribute that can be paid a person than to say that he was a father to me, or she was like my own mother. In our brief years of life, as we meander through strange and familiar paths, both untried and yet as ancient as time itself, no one can help us find our truest selves better than a wise and loving parent.

This is the mystery of submission. The best of ourselves rarely comes when we fight it out on our own. Instead, it is brought to life when someone who loves me takes my hand and helps me to reach higher than I thought I could. This is what Jesus is looking for when he talks about lines of parentage.

The ancients always compared our wills to horses. It is a fitting comparison, I think. There is a stallion inside each of us, snorting and restless, and nervously pacing. That energy and strength of character can be thrown about with the destructive power of a mad horse that will not be mastered, or it can be harnessed by a rider and a bit and channeled into speed and purpose and direction.

Your will is strong. You need it to survive. But you also need it to be brought under submission to a higher power if you would be fully human.

All Saints
Daniel 7:1-3, 15-18
Ephesians 1:11-23
Luke 6:20-31
Craig MacCreary

The twilight zone

Many will remember the television series *Twilight Zone* that aired in the early '60s and in various formats in succeeding years. At the center of the series was always a sudden plot twist that gave a jolt to the characters living in the twilight zone and to the audience that came for their weekly visit to a land beyond normal imagination.

Many of us find ourselves beginning to believe that we have never quite gotten out of the twilight zone. National and world events seem to mimic many of the events foretold in the series including one episode where the earth begins to get hotter and hotter. The capacity to sit at a computer and go online and enter into virtual reality, defying all known time zones, and read newspapers that have not yet hit the streets where they are published makes the twilight zone the next stop on your journey.

Writing about All Saints day after having watched a *Twilight Zone* TV marathon leaves me wondering if the twilight zone is not just a stopover but my permanent residence.

Over the years there were several imitators of the *Twilight Zone*. Most of them were able to capture to some degree the eeriness of the original but none of them were able to capture the moral force of Rod Serling's seminal effort. His agenda was not merely to tantalize the viewer each week with thoughts of how reality might be twisted out of shape into a mysterious plot line.

What was particularly chilling was how the macabre and distorted might break out in the lives of ordinary folks going about their business in familiar contexts. In most of the episodes, we see the principals as people very much like us. Who would ever have thought that they would be candidates to find themselves wresting with the dark side that is about to be revealed in the twilight zone? This was Serling's point — that ordinary people were actually, even in the prosperity and calm of the late '50s and early '60s, living in the twilight of a vulnerable way of life that had not yet risen to the reality of racism, materialism, violence, and dehumanizing technology. Serling was protesting in his own way against the complacency that comes from having other god's before the one, true God. His writing was not the first nor will it be the last to use science fiction to gain a hearing for a message that might otherwise be rejected.

Certainly the apocalyptic writings of scripture such as Daniel are attempting to convey a message that otherwise might not get a hearing. Daniel warns his readers that soon they will be living in the twilight zone of the last of the fallen empires. However, for the saints, the twilight is also the time of daybreak when the cock crows its message that despite our betrayals, denials, faithlessness, and the impending darkness, the Sun (Son) is raised.

The saints are those who live in the context of both of these realities. They live in the context that the powers that be are on shaky grounds to the degree that they diverge from the intentions of God. Secondly, such times are not merely times of the verdict being rendered but of people being empowered by a new reality that is trying to break into the world.

Each of these texts give definition to the term saint as one who sees the fading reality while recognizing the impending dawn and is able to live faithfully in the tension between the two. Most of the people who I would define as saints have a dual capacity to see others as they are and as they might become, an ability to live in the tension between the now and the not yet, and the capacity to stand with the hurting and up to the hurters. "God put this power to work in Christ when he raised him from the dead and seated him at his right hand in the heavenly places, far above all rule and authority and power and dominion, and above every name that is named, not only in this age but also in the age to come" (Ephesians 1:20-21).

Daniel 7:1-3, 15-18

Watching the *Twilight Zone* marathon I quickly became aware of the basic sensitivity that motivated Rod Serling. In the face of fear and stripped of the comforting trappings and services of the empire, normally reasonable people would become an irrational mob. In an episode titled, "Shelter," nuclear war breaks out, and the only shelter available in a respectable neighborhood is the home shelter of a doctor and his family. Of course, the shelter is only big enough for the doctor's family. The neighbors cannot come. The story narrated the breakdown of human decency as neighbor rises against neighbor to save themselves. As Rod Serling says in his closing narration "No moral, no message, no prophetic tract. Just a simple statement of fact. For civilization to survive, the human race must to remain civilized. Tonight's very small exercise in logic from the *Twilight Zone*."

What stands between us and annihilation is the ability to move beyond being a mob to being a community of saints. Sainthood, here, does not mean moral perfection but the ability to recognize that we are all in it together and that we need to tend the garden of the things that make us more alike than different. Choosing to be part of the community of saints over the mob is to acknowledge that the greatest human victories come not from the force of arms but the force of open arms.

Rod Serling's moral compass intrigued and frightened the viewer at the same time. The truth found in the episode where earthlings surrender their responsibilities and sensibilities to travel to a planet hosted by aliens who have promised to "serve man" are shocked when they discover that the book bearing this title is a cookbook. How easily do we become a mob when we believe that all our needs will be met, and we are afraid that we will be left out of the coming good times? One need only think of those who will stand in line or fight in line for the latest Christmas fad or the most recent version of the iPhone. Watching the *Twilight Zone*, I find myself feeling like Daniel, who saw in his "vision by night the four winds of heaven stirring up the great sea, and four great beasts came up out of the sea, different from one another ... As for me, Daniel, my spirit was troubled within me, and the visions of my head terrified me" (Daniel 7:2-3, 15).

It takes a community of saints to help us value ourselves not for what we have but who we are. To value us even at our worst, we need a community that is strong enough and that we trust enough, we can be enough of ourselves that we do not seek status through fads and the getting of things.

One of the themes of Serling's work is the readiness of the mob to seek out a scapegoat for its fears and failures. The episode titled "The Monsters on Main Street" has the residents of a *Leave It To Beaver* street quickly turning on each other in the midst of the sudden loss of all forms of power. They cite each other's eccentricities as clear evidence of guilt. The mob always has a clear profile of the guilty: particularly in the twilight of fear. The saints know that "there is no fear in love, but perfect love casts out fear" (1 John 4:18). The mob thinks that the perfect profile will cast out all fear. The saints proclaim love that seeks to know and be known.

The vision given to Daniel is disturbing in its form and content. However, it is also promising. As the psalmist puts it, "The nations are in an uproar, the kingdoms totter; he utters his voice, the earth melts. The Lord of hosts is with us; the God of Jacob is our refuge" (Psalm 46:6-7). Daniel seems to have gotten over his fear. Though he may, as we do, live in the twilight zone, the community need not surrender to the impulse of the mob for, "As for these four great beasts, four kings shall arise out of the earth. But the holy ones of the Most High shall receive the kingdom and possess the kingdom forever—forever and ever" (Daniel 7:17-18).

Ephesians 1:11-23

The letter writer gives thanks for the faith of the Ephesian community. They persist in living faithfully in the midst of their own twilight zone where life is liminal between the decay of the Roman Empire and the dawn of the present and coming rule of Jesus. Many have criticized the early church for the kinds of compromises it made in the process of trying to get along by going along. We are naturally troubled by passages from the Christian scripture such as this from Romans 13, "Let every person be subject to the governing authorities; for there is no authority except from God, and those authorities that exist have been instituted by God. Therefore whoever resists authority resists what God has appointed, and those who resist will incur judgment" (Romans 13:1-2). For many today it is like living in the twilight zone, giving loyalty and respect to institutions that they feel are corrupt, self-serving, and incapable of giving a straight answer when going to war. Ever since Jesus prayed for his people who were in the world but did not belong to the world, his people have had to struggle with what it is like to live in the twilight of this age and the dawn of the age to come.

For the most part, churches are not likely to win plaudits for living with this struggle. If anything, given the religious tenor of our times, faith communities are likely to be appreciated more for helping people escape or find a respite from this struggle.

Here are six ways of living in this twilight zone.

We are living in an in-between time that requires vigilance to watch our institutions precisely because embodying noble aims is a fragile business. Carl Shurz, a civil war general and former senator, enters into the field of sainthood when he wrote, "Our country right or wrong; if right kept right and if wrong to be set right."

More often than not the real saints are those who have been able to see both how wrong we can be and how right we might be. Winston Churchill wrote in the idiom of his day that. "Man's capacity for injustice makes democracy necessary and our capacity for justice makes it possible." People who faithfully live in the twilight zone of the letter to the Ephesians find themselves saying such things.

Those who live in the twilight zone between the realities of the age that is, and the consummation of the age to come have learned how to pick their battles. In the twilight zone, God is as likely to use our failures to build to his kingdom as our successes. We don't need to win every battle to win the war. Indeed, fighting every battle suggests that the ultimate triumph of the kingdom is more contingent on our efforts than on the hand of God. Living in the twilight zone demands something more of us than picking our fights. It requires us to discern which battle we believe, in God's plan, we are called to wage.

Saints have a prayer life, a communal life, and a biblical literacy that facilitates the discernment process.

Saints know that because they are saints they need not demonize others. They seek to keep the humanity of the other in focus. In the twilight zone, one never knows when the other will be given an opportunity to act like a saint and, given the right circumstance, might do so. It is easier to demonize than to keep one's eyes on this prize. Ephesians reminds us, "That, with the eyes of your heart enlightened, you may know what is the hope to which he has called you" (Ephesians 1:18).

The saints know that if their hope is to have their names written in the book of life, to enter the world to come they need not write anything in concrete in the world that is. The things they most value are always subject to development and growth. The ideals of liberty and justice that founded the United States have grown to eliminate officially sanctioned racism and sexism as well as include the rights of labor and religious minorities. If you live in this twilight zone, you can count on the refinement and development of your most cherished values beyond all human calculation. What is the hope to which he has called you, what are the riches of his glorious inheritance among the saints, and what is the immeasurable greatness of his power for us who believe?

The saints know that the one who has been made "head over all things for the church" (Ephesians 1:22) is the same one who came "not to judge the world, but to save the world" (John 12:47). The task of the church is less to judge than to connect with the world.

None of these will help us avoid the twilight zone. All of them will help us live through the experience of the time between the twilight and the dawn.

Luke 6:20-31

One of the themes of the *Twilight Zone* is that human beings cannot count on an ordinary way of calculating and calibrating their lives. Things do not add up in the way in which we expect. Reality twists and turns beyond human comprehension in ways that leave us vulnerable to having our world turned upside down. As much as I would like to believe that I live in safety beyond the vagaries of the twilight zone this pretty well describes my reality.

I buy a computer with the idea that it will save work time only to discover that the computer has a life of its own that overtakes me. Now I can do more things that have a way of quickly taking up the time that I thought I would gain through better organizing my time. Welcome to the twilight zone. Technology does not save work, it only makes new forms of work. I find myself gaining just enough mastery of the computer to increase the number of times that I am infantilized and reduced to tears by ever-advancing technology. Welcome to the twilight zone.

Part of learning in life is that I should count on having landed immigrant status in the twilight zone. Just about nothing I was told I could count on has stayed in place. I attended a workshop where the leader said organ music sounds to the current generation about like hard rock sounds to most middle-age people — total cacophony. Welcome to the twilight zone.

Something more than *Future Shock* is at work here. As I recall that work by Alvin Toffler, it was a reasoned explanation of the consequences of rapidly advancing technology. It feels like I am in a twilight zone of unforeseen consequences where I can count on very little. In the words of the gospel lesson for All Saints, things become even more unsettling. "Then he looked up at his disciples and said, 'Blessed are you who are poor, for yours is the kingdom of God. Blessed are you who are hungry now, for you will be filled. Blessed are you who weep now, for you will laugh. Blessed are you when people hate you, and when they exclude you, revile you, and defame you on account of the Son of Man. Rejoice on that day and leap for joy, for surely your reward is great in heaven; for that is what their ancestors did to the prophets' " (Luke 6:20-23). Here, again, is one more excursion into the twilight zone. As Frederick Buechner reminds us, this is living by a different set of calculations altogether when you say that those who give get more, you ought to go after the one missing sheep as against the 99 that you have, or the pay off for those who show up late is the same as for those who are the early hired. This confounding of the conventional shorts out my mind once again.

Whenever I have been part of a prolonged electrical blackout, the march of the electrical workers down the street to restore the energy flow looks to me like the saints marching. The saints are the ones who get the energy flowing. The energy flow here has less to do with calculation than with connection to God, each other, and myself. Out of the twilight zone comes a new light that can be cast on things — another example of the way the gospel has of confounding the conventional.

Application

When do you find yourself living in the twilight zone? Certainly, when it can be defined as that place in the shadows between the known and the unknown. However, as I reflect on that, I find myself realizing that I actually never leave the twilight zone. Things have a way of defying my plans, what I count on, and the folks I depend on can often disappoint me. What gets one into ministry is far from what keeps one there. New occasions do teach new duties and time does have the irritating way of eclipsing all my certainties. Clear logic and convincing arguments routinely fail to win the day or even make headway in my home or in my church. Welcome to the twilight zone. This is enough to cause anyone to want to change the channel.

For me, a saint is one who first and foremost knows that in this life, if the light does shine in the darkness, it is nevertheless at best a glimmer. When I was a child, the adults around me were fairly well convinced that Americans had all the light and other Anglo nations were in possession of it to the degree that they sought to follow the American model. It felt like entering the twilight zone when I discovered early on that America may not be the absolute light of the world and that it had a shadow side. It came as a shock to find out that we did not invent the television or the telephone and that Thomas Edison may have been as inventive in some of his financial arrangements as he was in anything else.

Saints know better and anticipate the shadow side of every glorious moment. Saints know that it is not our light but how the light has been refracted through our tragedies, miscues, and blunders that brings any hope into the world. Knowing that it is but a glimmer, saints welcome light from any source. They know enough that they should look to see how their faith commitments and mission appear in the light of others' experience.

On this day, I give thanks for all the saints who have helped me live faithfully in the twilight zone.

Alternative Applications

Luke 6:20-31; Daniel 7:1-3, 15-18. Which came first, the chicken or the egg? Of course this imponderable mystery has kept minds going for years. Does sainthood lead to belonging or does belonging lead to sainthood? Can we believe without belonging or can we belong without believing? I struggle with the reality that of the many of those whom I would call saints in my life I have not a clue as to what their religious background was. Coaches, teachers, some coworkers, who knew what their background was, but clearly in the foreground of their lives was a transparency that revealed a quality of life that invited one to thought and even reverence. Some were found in the church; many would not let themselves be found in church. Many of my saints were from well beyond the safe and familiar religious traditions that I have grown comfortable with. The holy comes at you from many different directions.

The visions of Daniel gave him a serious headache. "As for me, Daniel, my spirit was troubled within me, and the visions of my head terrified me" (Daniel 7:15). The blessings and woes contained in Luke's gospel are troubling if they express what nearness to God is and what distance from God is. There is much to ponder in my experience of sainthood and the scriptures. The route to sainthood has less to do with explaining it than receiving it wherever it shows up as a gift. Being in that number when the saints go marching in will have less to do with explaining it than accepting it.

Proper 26 / Pentecost 24 / Ordinary Time 31
Habakkuk 1:1-4; 2:1-4
2 Thessalonians 1:1-4, 11-12
Luke 19:1-10
Wayne Brouwer

Encouragement

Alan Loy McGinnis told of a woman who was honored by her company for outstanding performance during the just-ended fiscal year. Standing at the podium before hundreds of fellow-workers in a large banqueting hall, she clutched her trophy and wept as she told of the strange route that brought her to this moment of recognition.

A year earlier, this woman's marriage had unraveled, and she was down and out emotionally. She could not give her all to her job and too often she found herself coming up short against deadlines and assignments. She wanted to quit and several times wrote letters of resignation. But her supervisor, Susan, had always encouraged her to wait another day or another week and had pocketed her self-terminations without opening them. Between sobs, the winner breathed words of thanks to Susan and said to her, "You believed in me even when I couldn't believe in myself."

Some of the same is true in the combination of passages for today's homily. Through Habakkuk, God encourages those who give righteousness a good name during times of political and social unrest. Paul writes to encourage new believers who are weathering storms that deny them homes, families, and neighbors. Jesus nods toward Zacchaeus as a shining example of courage in a very misunderstanding world. Perhaps today we can bring some smiles of grace to the faces of discouraged and disheartened pilgrims who find the road to the kingdom by wandering through dark and lonely places.

Habakkuk 1:1-4; 2:1-4

Habakkuk lived in a time of social instability and political crisis. The threat of Assyrian invasion and domination had passed and in its wake came an almost giddy public release of euphoric immorality. For nearly a century, Habakkuk's predecessors had pointed north and warned God's people that Assyria was the tool of divine anger, coming soon to punish this wayward nation. There were bits of relief and breaks of release as other nations (particularly Syria) pushed back hard enough to make the menacing invaders stop and regroup before trying another onslaught. Eventually, even Judah's kinship neighbor, Israel, was felled by the Assyrian axmen, and Sennacharib swamped the south with his troops until the only island left was tiny Jerusalem.

When good king Hezekiah heard the taunts and threats of Sennacharib's boasts, he took the Assyrian general's pompous letter and laid it on the altar of burnt offering in the temple. Through Isaiah, word from heaven came that God would wage the battle and break the stranglehold of this arrogant crew. While the siege captives frittered nervously in disbelief, God miraculously sent the whole Assyrian army packing overnight in a fright that other historians would later describe as a plague. Suddenly, Judah stood free and independent again, splendidly isolated from looming conquest in its mountainous stronghold.

When the religious cries evaporated as the political crisis passed, the new era of peace and prosperity bred social pride and ethical debauchery. Yahweh's deliverance was either forgotten or bandied about as a historical legacy that proved God would always be on the side of this nation. Greed, corruption, and sexual indiscretions rapidly filled the vacuum of external threat. It was then that Habakkuk rose one day to argue with God.

"Why do you allow them to get away with their blatant sinfulness?" Habakkuk demanded. Whether or not he expected a direct and sentient response from Yahweh, we do not know. But this was an instance in which Yahweh took pains clearly and unmistakably to enter into dialogue with a prophetic spokesperson in the community.

"I won't let them get away with it," came the reply from heaven. "See, I'm sending the Babylonians to punish all who think they can live as if I do not matter."

But the cure was worse than the disease, for Habakkuk. "How can you use the Babylonians as a disciplining scourge against us?" he prayed incredulously. "They are even worse than us!"

The conversation continued for a time, with Yahweh more fully explaining the divine plan. Although the Babylonians were indeed a fierce and pagan nation, Yahweh would channel their international aggressions into a military "board of education" to swat some punishing correction into the puffed up little self-important strutter that Judah had become. Babylon itself would then face its own day of reckoning, and the full scales of international, political, and moral justice would be balanced.

Furthermore, according to the word of the Lord in the passage for today, "The righteous will live by his faith." As Yahweh explained to Habakkuk, this meant that those within the faith community of Judah who remembered who they were and *whose* they were would find their religious convictions and their moral faithfulness honored. Although the whole tiny nation would suffer greatly under Babylonian aggression, those who aligned themselves with the covenant that had given birth to the nation and still governed its expected lifestyle would find Yahweh a compassionate and forgiving God.

There are a number of themes that emerge from this brief prophecy, nestled in the times between Assyria's massive threat and Babylon's looming domination. First, there is testimony of absolute confidence in the one who observes the actions and lifestyles of people and nations and keeps sending report cards through cultural critics at every age. It is never wise to ignore those who speak with a prophetic voice of conscience, especially during times of peace and prosperity.

Second, the rise and fall of nations is part of a larger work of God in which unbridled immorality as well as unrestrained aggression will be stopped through international checks and balances. No corrupt regime ought to think it is above either United Nations assessments or divine judgment. There will be an auditing of the record in the end, and it may well come with a steep price.

Third, general godlessness or the failure of religious systems need never dissuade true believers from the rightness of their faith or its expressions. The heroes of history are those who had the fortitude to remain religiously grounded even when their cultures were doing whatever they could to erode places to stand and melt moorings into quicksand. We remember these folks in retrospect as saints, like Martin Niemoller or Mother Teresa or Groen van Prinsterer or Thomas More or Dietrich Bonhoeffer or William Stringfellow.

Fourth, the plan of God is long and comprehensive. It usually spans several generations, making our quick-fix religious solutions out-of-place and ecclesiastically irresponsible. God never promises immediate wealth and personal success if we just do three or four little exercises in holiness. The purposes of God are much broader and we are not asking the right questions if we stop at demanding what God can do for us. The real question, as John F. Kennedy put it to the American people in a slightly different form, is what can we do for the kingdom of God.

2 Thessalonians 1:1-4, 11-12

Paul was on his second mission journey when he stumbled into Thessalonica. He had just come through an eventful time in Philippi where a new Christian congregation had begun out of the most unusual circumstances, organized by the most unlikely people (see Acts 16). Now he was on his way to Corinth (see Acts 18), stopping in a few cities along the way.

Paul's time in Thessalonica didn't last very long — probably somewhere between three weeks and two months. After talking in the Jewish synagogue about Jesus as the promised Messiah, one segment of the congregation became highly perturbed, and Paul and Silas shifted their base of operations to the marketplace in town. Here the primary audience was Gentile, and a number of these people listened with rapt attention and responded with heartfelt conviction to the evangelists' call to repentance and belief. As these non-Jewish converts joined the synagogue believers to form a new Christian community, Paul's and Silas' opponents grew incensed. Not only had these travelers disrupted their synagogue stability by injecting a new twist on the old doctrines that divided the group into differing messianic parties, but now they had assisted in the creation of a religious organization that broke down the fundamental division between Jew and Gentile.

With what appears to be a great amount of rage, these antagonists drove Paul and Silas out of Thessalonica. The itinerant band split into several teams in order to bring the gospel message to a number of different towns but soon they regrouped in Corinth. From there, Paul sent two letters to the Thessalonians, wondering and hoping and praying that they were doing well and addressing at least one critical theological issue from two differing points of view.

These letters are among Paul's earliest pastoral-theological epistolary exhortations, written around the year 50 AD. In our New Testament, only Paul's letter to the Galatians precedes them.

The primary theological issue about which Paul needed to give some further clarity was the return of Jesus. First Thessalonians bubbles with enthusiasm about the way in which the church survived its first few months and became a stable witnessing community in a rather challenging environment. Paul was glad for the testimony brought by Timothy that the congregation was doing well in spite of the forced, quick exodus that prevented Paul and Silas from lingering to explain many ideas about Jesus or the plans of God more fully.

One question that surfaced rather abruptly among the Thessalonian Christians was an uncertainty as to what happened to those who died. Evidently, in the few short weeks since Paul and his team had been ejected from the city, at least one and possibly several new believers had died. Since Paul's preaching had focused on the resurrection as the primary proof endorsing Jesus' claim to be the Messiah, and because the urgency of Paul's evangelistic enterprise was based upon his conviction that Jesus was returning very soon — probably next week, but at the very outside next year — there was some confusion as to what happened to those who believed this good news, but then died before Jesus came back.

In his first letter, Paul gave warm and pastoral encouragement, assuring the grieving families that their loved ones who had died would also share with them the future new and glorious times with Jesus. This would happen because God would instigate a mass resurrection in which the dead would have a similar experience to Jesus' Easter morning reawakening.

Paul's message brought a great deal of comfort, but it also triggered an unforeseen side effect. In light of the dramatic expectation of Jesus' imminent return, many in the Thessalonian congregation set aside their normal social routines and began to meet together in extended worship settings, waiting for Jesus to burst through the door at any moment.

When Paul heard about this, he became more than a little distraught. The good news of salvation through Jesus was meant to energize life, not to make it irrelevant. Those who began to opt out of daily activities and responsibilities in some kind of eschatological frenzy were actually subverting the gospel testimony.

In haste, Paul penned this second letter, praising the group for their earnest and powerful witness but cautioning them quickly to re-engage their routines and obligations. Jesus was coming soon, Paul assured them, but there was likely to be a bit of a wait before that happened. In the intervening month, or perhaps even years, they should remain faithful to their families, friends, and fellows in the social arena who were counting on them for the normal care and support of life.

The verses for today's lectionary reading are marvelously beautiful in their positive affirmation of faithful trust, vibrant witness, and consistent godliness as displayed by this fledgling Christian community situated squarely on the crossroads of society. They were not unusually numerous, terrifically endowed, or powerfully positioned, but they understood the lifestyle implications of the gospel and lived them out in beauty and grace.

These verses cannot be preached so much as used to encourage and inspire. It is a bit like the fellow who met friends at the county fair midway, among the rides and the booths. The couple's young daughter was almost hiding behind a tower of cotton candy on a paper cone. "How can you eat all of that?" the man asked her with an impish twinkle. "You are much too small to get it all inside!"

After a brief hesitation to figure it out, the girl replied, "I guess I'm a lot bigger on the inside than I am on the outside!" That seems to have been Paul's understanding of the Thessalonian Christian, as well. In an alien environment, born out of persecution and conflict, this band of believers gave quick and sure evidence that the power and possibilities of God living within them was much bigger and stronger than anything projected upon them by the limiting perspectives of the world.

Luke 19:1-10

It is easy to jump quickly to conclusions in preaching on the story of Jesus and Zacchaeus. After all, this tale is as commonly known as any of the gospel stories and carries in our minds a great number of preconceptions. Zacchaeus must have been a bad person, most think, because he seems to have been sidelined by the crowds rushing to see Jesus. Moreover, Jesus singles him out for a special visit, likely indicating that he was in greater need of divine transformation than anyone else in town. Furthermore, when the two of them emerge from Zacchaeus' home later in the day, the short one makes promises of financial restoration (seemingly implying that he took fraudulent funds), and the tall one declares the arrival of salvation. All in all, our presumptions seem to add up to a quick perception that Zacchaeus was a bad man, and Jesus rescued him that day.

There are clear hints in the story, as Luke tells it, that point in other directions. First of all, the main character's name means "clean" or "innocent." This might be a foreshadowing of the outcomes of the narrative, but it could also simply be a hint that Zacchaeus was a good man, not a bad man.

Second, the historical developments of occupied Palestine give us every reason to believe that the designation "tax collector" was not a term of derision in the city or region. The Roman government had taken over direct taxation collection responsibilities by this time, and the task that produced Zacchaeus' occupation was more likely the oversight of customs booths for the trade caravans that entered the land at the Jericho portal. Since most occupations were inherited from parents, Zacchaeus probably grew up in a home where his father or grandfather had already developed the business.

Third, Zacchaeus' wealth was probably as much inherited as it was the result of good business activities. For that reason, it is not entirely certain that the man is making a confession of great wickedness when he talks about restoring any funds ill-gotten. He may be making a simple declaration of desire to be fully reliable in business and not blabbing about secret sins of the past.

Fourth, the word usually translated "short" in our Bibles, when referring to Zacchaeus, actually is better interpreted as "young." It is only because the story tells us that Zacchaeus went up a tree to see Jesus that we assume he was short. But it may well be that because of his younger age, he deferred to the older men who crowded around Jesus. In an inventive move, he was agile enough to quickly climb up a tree and get a position that no older men would dared to have taken.

Fifth, although Jesus says, at the conclusion of his visit to Zacchaeus' home, that salvation came today to this dwelling, it need not mean a radical transformation. After all, Jesus is himself the means of salvation. It is likely that Jesus only wanted the people to take note of this outsider among them and treat him with respect. After all, he says that "this man, too, is a son of Abraham," not implying that Zacchaeus had a sudden transformation, but that his neighbors need to respect him for what he truly is and not shove him to the side with their petty prejudices against rich folks.

Finally, Zacchaeus never admits having lived a life of theft and robbery. The present tense of his declaration that he gives half his income to the poor means that this was his already-taking-place-and-continuing practice of life. In other words, instead of ripping off those who came under his business interests, he was more likely to benefit them. He was a generous man, even before Jesus came to town.

All of this seems to imply that the story is told by Luke as an illustration for what Jesus wants to say about himself and what kind of authority he wields on behalf of his Father (see vv. 12-25). In effect, the tale of Zacchaeus, even standing by itself, is as much a call for people to be seen with grace and mercy rather than suspicion and judgment. Not a bad theme on which to preach.

Application
Although they contain rich images, if one wants to be faithful to the intent of the whole message, the passages from Habakkuk are hardest to preach. Both the epistle and gospel passages carry well the theme of encouragement. Dozens of illustrations would bring the message to a great conclusion, but the more personal they can be made, the more lasting impact they will have.

An Alternative Application
Habakkuk 1:1-4; 2:1-4. If you are up for a challenge, get into Habakkuk's times and dialogue and help your congregation wrestle with the problem of evil in a whole new way. Although the prophecy is short, it deals with the complexity of sin and divine punishment and the struggle to maintain godly behavior and perspectives in a twisted and compromised world.

A bright forecast

Primitive people, even more than we, were at the mercy of the weather. They were considerably less sheltered than we are. And they did not have the wide variety of resources that we do to compensate for a crop-killing frost or drought. Plus, for them, the weather had that extra element of mystery. It was beyond their knowledge and beyond their control. They did not know what tomorrow might bring, and they couldn't do anything to guarantee it.

Our relationship to the weather is somewhat different. We certainly still find ourselves overwhelmed by the forces of nature from time to time. We can't offer significant relief to whole regions devastated by heat. Our biggest cities can still be shut down by snow and ice, and we can't ward off the tornadoes or hurricanes that come our way.

On the other hand, we generally know when such things are coming our way. High-tech meteorology combines with high-tech communication to make the weather forecast perpetually accessible, and now we often know what tomorrow will bring — at least in terms of the weather.

When it comes to the rest of the future, though, we are in the very same situation as our ancestors thousands of years ago. Apart from the weather, we do not know what tomorrow may bring. And many of the people in our pews can bear witness to that. For as we come to the end of this calendar year, how many of us would raise our hands and say, "I had no idea back in the first part of January that by this time..."? Our lives can change in an instant. So can our world.

Apart from the weather, we lack a television channel, website, or government agency that is able to tell us what tomorrow may bring, we are often at odds about the forecast. The pessimist is quite certain of the gloom he sees (constantly) on the horizon. The optimist is equally sure that better days are still ahead. The worriers and the ambitious employ their imaginations in the service of their future paradigm. But no one knows.

There have always been a few in every generation who have believed that they could do something or other to affect or control the weather. There have been more than a few in every generation who have sought to control their own future. Both endeavors, however, inevitably prove futile.

Our three lections this morning are all about the future. The Lord speaks a hopeful word about it to the discouraged people of Haggai's day. Paul wrote to the Christians in Thessalonica, who were unsure about it. Jesus taught the Sadducees a thing or two they did not know about it. This week, we turn our attention to the forecast.

Haggai 1:15b—2:9

When this passage is read aloud in most of our churches, it will not likely sound familiar. This episode comes near the end of Old Testament history's time line, and most of our people are more familiar with the beginning and the middle. The stories of Adam and Abraham, Moses and Joshua, David and Solomon — these are all widely recognizable. But this episode comes from one of the post-exilic prophets and that may seem like foreign territory. Except for Daniel, Jonah, and a few cherished passages from Isaiah, the Old Testament prophets are just a confusing blur in the minds of so many.

It will be necessary for us, therefore, to set the stage for the hearing of this word. And that stage is the temple mount in Jerusalem.

Scene one must come about a decade into the reign of King Solomon, the son and successor of King David. When the throne passed from father to son, the united twelve tribes of Israel were strong and secure. They were, for the moment, the dominant power in the region. In time, Solomon gained the reputation of being one of the wisest men in the world. His reign was marked by peace, prosperity, and building.

After years of amassing the finest materials and constructing on the grandest scale, Solomon dedicated to God the temple that he had built there in Jerusalem. It was an epic event. The magnificent temple, combined with Solomon's fabulous offerings, made for a great spectacle in the eyes of the assembled people. Then God himself made his own awesome contribution to the spectacle and to the occasion.

Scene two comes some 400 years later. All the hallmarks of Solomon's era — the splendor, the wisdom, the peace, the security — are gone. Jerusalem is overrun by the unstoppable troops of the Babylonian army. The kings of Babylon have been calling the shots for Judah and Jerusalem for some years, and now they have exercised their force to put an end to all thought of rebellion. Jerusalem is decimated, and the temple — Solomon's masterpiece to the glory of God — lies in ruins.

Finally, scene three comes with our Old Testament lection. It is just forty-some years after scene two. That suggests there may be a few people in the cast who were present in both scenes.

The exiles who have returned from Babylon had begun the painful task of rebuilding the ruined temple. It is an easier thing, we know, to start fresh than to rebuild what has fallen down. The internal and external obstacles conspired to halt the work that those first folks had begun. After a few years of inactivity, the prophet Haggai appears on the scene: first, to challenge the people to resume the project and second, in our passage, to encourage them in the midst of the difficult and discouraging task.

What they started with were memories — burdensome memories. The glorious recollection of all that the former temple had been, plus the painful memories of its destruction. As they set out to rebuild, they recognized the inferiority of their effort. So the Lord asked them, "Who is left among you that saw this house in its former glory? How does it look to you now? Is it not in your sight as nothing?"

It is to that difficult situation and disheartened crowd that God speaks his powerful and reassuring word.

First, there is the magnificent promise of God's presence: "I am with you" and "my spirit abides among you." To those who know best, this is the real issue. For a glorious temple without his presence becomes a terrible and vulnerable thing. But even a simple place inhabited by his glory becomes a setting of inexpressible beauty. Indeed, we discover in Revelation that, when God is fully present, no temple is necessary at all (Revelation 21:22).

Second, when God promises to "shake the heavens" and the like, we are rightly reminded of the vast difference between what we can do and what he can do. The people would have been right to underestimate the project if its success and beauty depended entirely upon them; but it does not.

That truth leads, finally, to God's promise that "the latter splendor of this house shall be greater than the former." Is that because Zerubbabel has more resources than Solomon or that Joshua will be a better designer or builder? Not at all. Rather, it is by God's graciousness and good pleasure that the beauty of the future will eclipse even the best of the past.

Perhaps, then, that blessed prospect becomes scene four.

2 Thessalonians 2:1-5, 13-17

Most scholars agree that the Thessalonian epistles are probably the earliest of Paul's letters. In these two pieces, we discover that the return of Christ is a recurring theme. For his return was no doubt expected to be imminent by the first generation of believers, and so his seeming delay raised some practical and theological questions.

We and our people may not be immediately sympathetic to the Thessalonians' plight. After all, we have lived for generations with the problem that was completely new to them: namely, the long postponement of Christ's return. While those believers fully expected Christ's return any day, our level of expectation — and therefore, too, our level of disappointment — may be comparatively quite low.

The fact is that from the time Jesus first warned his disciples what would happen to him in Jerusalem, it was only a matter of months until it all took place. When he told them that he would rise again, or that he would go before them into Galilee, those things took place within a few days. When he instructed them to tarry in Jerusalem until he sent the Spirit, the time between instruction and fulfillment was only a few weeks. It was quite natural, therefore, for the earliest Christians to assume that his promised return would, likewise, come in very short order.

At the time of this writing, it had probably been some twenty years since Christ's ascension, and still he had not come back yet. That became the source of assorted theological and practical challenges, several of which we see Paul address in his two Thessalonian epistles.

Among the theological challenges, evidently, was the rumor that the anticipated "day of the Lord is already here." That teaching had the Thessalonians understandably concerned, for all that was anticipated to accompany that day had not transpired, at least in their experience.

Paul reassures the unsettled believers that they hadn't missed their flight. They should still wait patiently and hopefully. Then the apostle reminded them about what manner of opponent must first stride across the stage of history before Christ would return. Finally, having discussed the rebellion and apostasy that will necessarily precede Christ's coming, Paul affirms the Thessalonians in their faith, their calling, and their good future in Christ.

Luke 20:27-38

In order to set the context for this passage from Luke 20, we should observe that Luke 19 features the story of Palm Sunday. In other words, when we come to this particular dialogue between Jesus and the Sadducees, we are in the midst of that eventful, final week in Jerusalem. Accordingly, this particular discussion is just one of a handful of deliberate challenges that the Jewish leaders brought to Jesus. Immediately prior to this episode comes the touchy question about paying taxes to the Roman emperor. Prior to that was the question challenging Jesus' authority. Added to these, we find in the larger context several pointed teachings and parables by Jesus, which implicated those same Jewish leaders.

The other essential element for setting the stage is a little background information about the Sadducees. The Sadducees were one of the four main sects within Judaism at the time of Jesus (along with the Pharisees, the Zealots, and the Essenes). The Sadducees were theologically distinctive in their opposition to the oral tradition that was so important to the Pharisees, as well as their rejection of "resurrection, future rewards and punishments, angels and spirits, and providence" (John Bowdon, *A Source Book of the Bible for Teachers*, Robert C. Walton, editor [London: SCM Press Ltd., 1970], p. 227). Their characteristic emphases were on the five books of Moses and on the temple.

The basis for the Sadducees' question was the regulation in the Old Testament law that the brother of a man who died without having a son, was duty-bound to marry the widow and produce a son for his deceased sibling (Deuteronomy 25:5-10). It appears from the story of Onan (Genesis 38:1-10) that, even before the matter was codified in Deuteronomic law, the same expectation was already a part of the culture in the time of the patriarchs.

The Sadducees' endeavor, of course, was to make the idea of the resurrection seem like foolishness. It is standard fare in argumentation to try to make the opponent's position seem ridiculous. By their calculation, a resurrection of the dead would result in a most unsightly scandal in heaven: namely, a woman with seven different husbands waiting for her when she died. They no doubt expected that their clever proposal, based on scripture, would present Jesus with an embarrassing theological conundrum.

The advantage always goes to the questioner, of course, in a setting like this. It's an easy thing to play the part of the skeptic. He puts his opponent on the defensive, and he positions himself in such a place where he himself does not need to know much, but his opponent must be prepared to know everything. So the questioning skeptic is permitted to tear down someone else's construct, though without any obligation to offer something stable and viable in its place.

This was the simple and strategic role of the Sadducees in our story. But Jesus and his paradigm are undisturbed by their skepticism. The problem did not lie either in the regulations of the Old Testament law or in the future promise of the resurrection. Rather, the problem lay in the Sadducees themselves and their misunderstanding (see Matthew 22:29).

Jesus' answer makes a distinction between two ages: "this age" and "that age." What we are and what we do in this age are, not surprisingly, different from what we will be and what we will do in that age. Simple. So the conundrum that the Sadducees had proposed was an exclusively earthly problem. It would be no problem at all "in that age and in the resurrection."

In addition to making that simple, decisive distinction, Jesus adds a tantalizing caveat, "Those who are considered worthy of a place in that age." The tables are subtly turned. The Sadducees had, for a moment, sat as judges, passing down their uncharitable verdicts on Jesus and his foolish notion of a resurrection. In the turn of a phrase, they suddenly become the ones awaiting a verdict. What if there is such a resurrection? And what if it will not include everyone? At the outset, the Sadducees were certain that there was no future resurrection; but if there is a resurrection, then it becomes the Sadducees' future that is uncertain.

Application
The historical situations of our three selected passages are all quite different. Haggai preached to the Jews of sixth-century BC Palestine, just a generation removed from conquest and exile. Paul wrote to the first-century AD Christians of Macedonia, just twenty years removed from the earthly life and ministry of Jesus. Jesus himself conversed with the obstinate Sadducees of Jerusalem, who did not see clearly and thus opposed Jesus and the resurrection.

Likewise, the futures being contemplated in these several contexts are different. For Haggai's audience, both the splendors and the defeats of the past made it difficult for them to focus on the future, though God endeavored to point their faith to a glorious future, indeed. For Paul's congregation in Thessalonica, the future at issue was the return of Christ, with its uncertain (and debatable) timing. For Jesus and the Sadducees, the subject of a one-day resurrection was the disputed future.

For all of the differences, however, one great theme remains the same. Namely, the companion truths that the future is in God's hands and that he intends it to be very good.

The people of post-exilic Jerusalem were not the ones who could "shake the heavens and the earth and the sea and the dry land." But God could and he promised to do it. Similarly, the believers in ancient Macedonia were encouraged to trust God's timing for the day of the Lord, when he would make all things right. And the Sadducees had to be corrected, for they had underestimated the power of God and the full goodness of the future he has in store.

An Alternative Application
Haggai 1:15b—2:9. "Holy Prescription." We know what it is to read the instructions on a bottle of medicine. Perhaps it's the ordinary stuff of over-the-counter pain relief. In that instance, the diagnosis is left up to us. We identify the "indications" — headache, fever, congestion — and the bottle promises "temporary relief" or some such. Or, in the more rarefied business of prescription drugs, a doctor has made the diagnosis, and he has prescribed the cure. Whatever the case, the instructions on the bottle tell us what to take and when to take it.

In Jerusalem at the time of Haggai, see what the indications and symptoms were. The people and their country had been devastated. Their nation had been overrun and occupied by enemy forces, while their leaders, along with their best and brightest, had been carried off into exile. Their capital city had been laid waste and the temple of their God had been left in ruins. Indeed, if they didn't know better (thanks to the prophets), they might have been tempted to think that their God himself had been defeated by the gods of Babylon.

Now, a generation or so later, they were back in their homeland: somewhat free, somewhat prosperous, as they tried to establish new lives for themselves. In their midst stood a half-begun project — the rebuilding of the temple. But the sight of it bore duel witness to the rubble that preceded it and to the unmatchable glory of a day long gone by.

What do you take in that situation of feebleness, fear, and despair? God knew and he prescribed just what they needed. "Take courage, O Zerubbabel... take courage, O Joshua... take courage, all you people of the land."

We are sometimes inclined to think that courage is something that we feel or don't feel. Here it is not so passive. Rather, it is a conscious decision and deliberate action: take courage!

How? Well, we certainly know how to "take" discouragement. We focus on the troubles that surround us, the regrets of the past, the uncertainties of the future, and soon we are quite discouraged.

Conversely, we take courage by focusing elsewhere. We focus on the goodness, grace, love, and power of the one who is before us, beyond us, and all around us. "For I am with you, says the Lord of hosts... My spirit abides among you; do not fear."

Proper 28 / Pentecost 26 / Ordinary Time 33
Isaiah 65:17-25
2 Thessalonians 3:6-13
Luke 21:5-19
Craig MacCreary

What's new?

Life can be quite onerous depending on the answer given to this question. Many of us find ourselves perpetually overwhelmed by a steady stream of newness that is getting the best of us. Just when many of us have mastered one computer software, we find ourselves lusting after the newest operating system. I often feel that I spend a lifetime of unlearning the lessons I learned in seminary: It is now as legitimate to speak of thinking locally to act globally as the other way around; expectations are now that the preacher will insert personal illustrations lest they seem inauthentic, one will lead the sacraments in a personal tone of voice. There are days when there are just too many new heavens and earths to contend with. If this is what God is up to, then I must admit that I feel like my C-drive is beginning to fill up as I am being thrust into overdrive by the promise of a variety of new approaches to ministry. My prayer becomes, "O Lord, give it thou a rest for mine eyes grow weary and my congregation grows faint at all the fads. Let thou thy people depart in peace to process and reflect before thy preacher goes off to another workshop."

Of course, on the other end of the scale there are days when the congregation pleads for the pastor to get off his or her hobbyhorse and get with what is happening in the world. I now see congregations flinch when a pastor uses sexist language, for it is no longer the *lingua franca* of the day. Church school children do a duck and cover drill at the thought of having to walk where Jesus walked using a sixty-year-old flannel board. In what I thought was a brilliant move, I used the film *Good Will Hunting* with my confirmation class believing the popularity of Robin Williams would win the day, only to be asked, "Who is Robin Williams?" My prayer is also, "O Lord, do not let me shame myself in front of the confirmation class, spare me those flat seasons when my parishioners can mouth my sermons as I preach them. If thou cannot grant me a new heaven or earth at least spare me the hell of people avoiding me because I have become a 'Johnny One Note.' Save me from having my head in a book, from being stuck trying to balance the books, or trying to book the youth group for another fun event, when your new heaven and earth breaks out."

The problem with change is that we can have either too much of it or too little of it. We can either be overwhelmed by too much new heaven or earth or be left underwhelmed in our impact on life by the hellishness that comes from being out to lunch missing the great feast of newness that God is serving up. The text from Isaiah serves up the menu of what God is up to and gives some suggestions as to how we may partake of what God is attempting to do in our lives and in the world.

Well, why bother with the passage from 2 Thessalonians at all? We know where it is headed right from the start. Of course, the problem in our musty reading of this text might be that we are not open to the fresh implications in and between its lines. Or, do we favor the seeming reinforcement that this text offers to the middle-class lifestyles that many of us share and that not a few of us compulsively pursue as part of our redemption?

To paraphrase the old saying, "When all you have is a hammer then you are not likely to enjoy having your handiwork undone." The Luke texts suggest that many of us have been able to cobble together some pretty fancy work that would rival anything seen on PBS's *This Old House.* "When some were speaking about the temple, how it was adorned with beautiful stones and gifts dedicated to God, he said..." (Luke

21:5). The text offers a path to follow that will lead beyond survival to thriving in the midst of what God is bringing about.

Each of these texts suggests how much is at stake in answers we give to the question, "What's new?"

Isaiah 65:17-25

God is going to do a new thing. Well, the Hebrews must have thought it is about time. They are immersed in the rebuilding work following their exile in Babylon. Things have not gone quite as expected: the work is hard, the friction great, and their bad theology abundant. Bring on the newness.

Like us, I am sure they expected the newness to either conform to reasonable, manageable proportions or that it would be so sweeping that it would elevate them beyond the normal constraints and difficulties of human existence. Couples preparing for marriage often seem to be ready for a newness that will sweep away all obstacles in their lives. However, even in the heavenly city there are streets to be swept and no doubt garbage to be taken out and left at the curb of the golden streets. Or the young couple expects that they, much like Prince Charles and Camilla, will carry on life without much significant change to major parts of their former life. However, note that the text does not say that God will do away with all things, only make all things new. Neither does the text say that all things will be restored to the way they once were nor that people will live happily ever after. While infants do survive in the new order of things, there are still infants who need care and nurturing. While those who don't make it to 100 feel robbed, there will still be senior citizens whose needs must be addressed. While the order of one building and another inhabiting is overturned there is still much building to be done.

The new order of things will demand more than just sitting idly by. It will require actively participating in the new order by following a new set of blueprints, a new diet plan, and a new economic order of things. Of course, immediately we are presented with a bit of a chicken and the egg kind of issue. Is it the new blueprint, diet, and economic order that makes for the newness or is it the newness that makes it possible for this trinity? Of course, the really new thing is recognizing that it is both. Whichever end of the stick you pick up, it will lead you to the fulfillment of where God wants you to be.

Certainly, from whichever place we begin, there is going to be a lot of serious challenging change if these scenarios are enacted. Imagine if people did live to 100 on a routine basis. They would need to live with the consequences of much that they had planned for and worked for in ways they never had before. Visualize what it might mean to a family system's theory for people to regularly interact with their great, great, great, great, grandchildren. Certainly, our political life would take on quite a different coloration if politicians knew that they would be answerable to future generations in more than a metaphorical sense. Can you imagine a nation where the food supply is not controlled by huge corporate interests? "They shall not build and another inhabit; they shall not plant and another eat" (Isaiah 65:22). This vision would turn around the current energy crises if food was produced locally instead of needing to be shipped long distances. "They shall build houses and inhabit them; they shall plant vineyards and eat their fruit" (Isaiah 65:21). Here is a stunning vision of an alternative world that takes one's breath away.

2 Thessalonians 3:6-13

There are few texts in scripture that are more likely to send chills up and down my spine than this one. It is not so much because I find its rebuke of idleness addressed to me. Rather, it is the way that it has been interpreted and used over the years to reinforce a fairly prosaic moralistic stance toward life. "No work, no eat," do we really need this text to bring out this particular truth? If anything, this text tends to reinforce a pride in pulling one's own weight that belies the true interdependent human reality. The text becomes a little bit more comfortable if what is meant here is that I do my part that others may do their part just as their work makes it possible for me to do mine.

It is one thing to address this text to the well-educated, able-bodied, upwardly mobile with interesting jobs. It is quite another to address this text to those who haven't been able to find work in six months or who grind away at mind-numbing, soul-searing jobs.

If one examines the text closely, it is addressed to those who have been using their beliefs about the world to come or, in essence, to drop out of the world that is. Many Christians have advocated less than a spirited care of the environment because the issue of this life will soon be addressed by the second coming. Bill Moyers has commented on Glenn Scherer's *The Road to Environmental Apocalypse*. Read it and you will see how millions of Christian fundamentalists may believe that environmental destruction is not only to be disregarded but actually welcomed — even hastened — as a sign of the coming apocalypse.

Paul is saying here that whatever one's beliefs about the world to come, disengagement from the world that is likely to lead to an aridness of soul and dullness of mind is to be avoided. It is one thing to address this passage to a single working mom whose world weariness has come from the day in and day out struggle to keep human and to keep food on the table. It is quite another to address it to those whose disengagement from the world comes from their ability to live off their investments that free them from participating in the daily struggles that most of us must face. Something more is suggested here than the simple failure to work for a living. The King James Version, as it renders verse 6, highlights what Paul is after, "Now we command you, brethren, in the name of our Lord Jesus Christ that ye withdraw yourselves from every brother that walketh disorderly, and not after the tradition which he received of us." Often in scripture the phrase disorderly connotes those who have fallen out of military discipline: those who have gotten out of step or those who have fallen from the ranks. I am reminded of the price that George H.W. Bush paid for the political misstep of not knowing what the electronic price code bars were for on the items that he purchased. In the minds of many it demonstrated that he was not to be ranked among the people he sought to lead. Fairly or unfairly, the impression was given that somehow he was not one of us. Certainly this is to be avoided by Christians if they proclaim a gospel of redemption of the world as it is so that it can be what God intended it to be.

For Aristotle, the first task of persuasive rhetoric was to establish a fundamental rapport with the audience in which they recognized the speaker as basically one of them. It was for Aristotle the most important of the fundamental persuasive elements of speech: *ethnos*, *pathos*, and *logos*. How can we proclaim the redemption of the world if we are not seen as, like most others, taking the world that is very seriously? Certainly if we live in idleness we will not be understood to be taking the world very seriously. Work is to be redeemed not eliminated. Paul is adamant about this for there will be some serious missteps ahead if the church is seen as the people who are out of step with the way that most people must live their lives. The church will be seen as not only having nothing new to say to the world but nothing to say at all.

Luke 21:5-19

Having stood looking across the Kidron Valley toward the temple, I know the truth of Jesus' words. "When some were speaking about the temple, how it was adorned with beautiful stones and gifts dedicated to God, he said, 'As for these things that you see, the days will come when not one stone will be left upon another; all will be thrown down'" (Luke 21:5-6). All that one can see of the ruins of the temple is the retaining wall that Herod installed and that has become known world wide as the Wailing Wall. Occasionally, one can see the Israeli Arab conflict acted out in the clash of those who have come to the Wailing Wall and those who have come to visit the Dome of the Rock, the third holiest site in Islam that is only a few hundred yards away.

They asked Jesus, "Teacher, when will this be, and what will be the sign that this is about to take place?" In many ways, in the age that we live in, we have grown skeptical, not about the end time but that there could be anything ahead that will look like sustained good times. Energy crises, global warming, war, have all left us quite suspicious about anyone claiming that there could be an age of abundance ahead for us in any meaningful sense. Newness does not come easily for human beings in the first place. Fly by wire aircraft, which operated like an electronic organ console by making electronic connections instead of like a tracker organ where there is physical connection with the control surfaces, posed a serious problem for pilots who had been trained on older planes. Flying without an actual wheel in front of them that gave a physical sense of the plane was well outside of the comfort zone of most pilots. The pilots were only pacified when a fake wheel was installed that they could hold onto during the flight. Newness does not come easily. Well into WWII, the British still trained their artillery crews to hold the horses as the guns fired even though they no longer used the animals to move the guns. Newness does not come easily. We come to terms and find ourselves not expecting anything more than nations rising up against nation and the general run of plagues and famines that make up the nightly news.

Many will come claiming that they know when these events will have taken a turn from which there is no return as the heavens either close up on our future or when will they open up a new future for us.

What is new here is that it seems the option to just retreat into our shell will be foreclosed. "But before all this occurs, they will arrest you and persecute you; they will hand you over to synagogues and prisons, and you will be brought before kings and governors because of my name. This will give you an opportunity to testify" (Luke 21:12-13). Along with the opportunity to testify, there will be family divisions and public opposition. Yet Jesus says that the community will get through these things even though we cannot imagine beforehand how. As a matter of fact, we will not only survive but will find ourselves thriving as we gain our souls.

There is much to be gained as we handle family divisions, face public opposition, and find ourselves giving public account of our faith. We gain soul power and a depth of soul that will not perish. It is certainly new to see a time of internal division, external opposition, and a general accounting as the place where we need to be. I don't see this presented in much of the church renewal literature as the way we ought to go. However, our attempts to either paper over differences or cut ourselves off from each other, along with our unwillingness to endure real hatred for the sake of deeper relationships, may be preventing us from going anywhere.

Application

Let us be clear about what the Hebrew text says here. It is God who will be making a new heaven and a new earth. If God is doing this in our age, it is certainly rearranging our understanding of what heaven and earth is about. At this point, many of us find ourselves saying, "Check, please!" We are hard-pressed to see how a new heaven or a new earth can be carved out of the mess that we are in. Yet, look around and there are signs that this just may be what is happening. Certainly, something new is brewing when a group of evangelical leaders unite to take global warming seriously.

My home conference of the United Church of Christ devoted its latest annual meeting to the themes of evangelism and prayer. Michael Ignatieff, deputy leader of the Liberal party of Canada, recently wrote an apology in the *New York Times* for having backed the Iraq War. What struck me was not so much his new position as the model he chose to emulate in his thinking. Daring leaders can be trusted as long as they give some inkling of knowing what it is to fail. They must be men of sorrow acquainted with grief, as the prophet Isaiah says, "Something is going on here that reflects a new heaven and earth."

Of course, this is going to cause some problems for some people as they discover that this new heaven and new earth may burst the bounds of old churches, theologies, and understandings. This newness sounds familiar, "And no one puts new wine into old wineskins; otherwise, the wine will burst the skins, and the wine is lost, and so are the skins; but one puts new wine into fresh wineskins" (Mark 2:22). Indeed, it may be that "the old, old story" is what makes all things new. Perhaps in the church we get all bollixed up over change because we fall short of offering a new heaven and a new earth. To many people it seems that the church is about the same pettiness and narrowness of vision and self-serving pursuit that they see in the rest of the world.

Yet, what always haunts and can often help is that it has always been such people that surrounded Jesus.

An Alternative Application

2 Thessalonians 3:6-13. Part of the Hippocratic Oath is the pledge, "to do no harm." It might not be a bad thing for a similar pledge to be part of ordination and confirmation vows, as well as membership commitments. For all our high-minded theology, visionary statements, and impassioned mission we find ourselves all too often falling into hurtful patterns in the life of the church. I know of no pastor who does not find him or herself engaged from time to time in a ministry to those who are seeking transformed lives but are church-phobic. They fear that they will find the same abusive patterns in church that they see in the outside world.

Our fear to offend or embarrass ourselves often overtakes us when we are given an opportunity to testify and are afraid to enter into the openness to what God can do with those opportunities that, according to Jesus, will be given us to testify.

Unlike Paul, all too often we have been a burden for we have not done the work of making our congregations free of sexual abuse. We have done harm because we have not done the work of examining our life to see to what degree it partakes of a sexual understanding that have left the weakest and most vulnerable among us exposed to hurt. Like Paul, who knew he needed to work to earn his keep and keep his credibility, we have to do our homework in order to maintain our credibility as a source of vitality in our society.

I wonder to what degree our slavishness to expediency, a survival mentality, and the desire to draw lines between each other rather than draw circles that include each other prevents us from being a joy and our people a delight.

Perhaps the new thing that God is doing among us is the call to do no harm. If we begin there, we will end up where "the wolf and the lamb shall feed together, the lion shall eat straw like the ox; but the serpent — its food shall be dust! They shall not hurt or destroy on all my holy mountain, says the Lord" (Isaiah 65:25).

Christ the King (Proper 29)
Jeremiah 23:1-6
Colossians 1:11-20
Luke 23:33-43
David Kalas

A week to preach up

I was still just a boy when I felt my call to the ministry. At the time, my father gave me a couple of books he thought would be helpful to me as I explored and pursued my call. In one of those books, I came across a quote that penetrated my heart and mind. It has remained with me for over thirty years since I first read the book.

The quote was a bit of counsel from John Berridge, an eighteenth-century British preacher, who said: "Avoid all controversy in preaching, talking, or writing; preach nothing down but the devil, and nothing up but Jesus Christ." (From "John Berridge," *Preacher and Prayer*, by E.M. Bounds [Grand Rapids: Zondervan, 1946], p. 65.)

Some colleagues, I know, would think it cowardice to avoid all controversy in preaching. They would say that such a policy would be disobedient to their call. That said, however, we should also readily concede that some preachers may relish controversial preaching, but not by reason of their calling so much as by reason of their temperament. These are opinionated and bellicose people, who take pleasure in tweaking, disturbing, and provoking others — and since they are not talented enough to write a syndicated column, they hold a pulpit hostage, instead.

Furthermore, in some instances, controversial preaching may be its own sort of cowardice. Most of our pulpits, after all, furnish us with more protection than risk. It would be a far more courageous thing to say some things one-on-one, in dialogue, or in honest debate, than to hide behind the sacred, public monologue of the pulpit.

Whatever we think of the merits and demerits of controversy in preaching, I believe that Berridge's conclusion is inarguably wise. "Preach... nothing up but Jesus Christ."

It is tempting to "preach up" all sorts of things: causes and movements, issues and candidates, needs and opportunities — all sorts of things that you and I may believe in. But in doing so, we may reduce the overall value of the pulpit. For as people perceive that only some of what comes from the pulpit is of eternal value, while the rest is rather ordinary and temporal, then the whole enterprise is diminished. And if I preach such an assortment of things that I believe in — one Sunday, I preach about the Savior I believe in and the next Sunday I preach about some cause that I believe in — then I have given equal weight to Christ and to some cause. But could any cause deserve equal billing with him?

This week's lections remind me of Berridge's sage counsel. For our selected passages invite us to preach Christ up this Sunday.

Jeremiah 23:1-6

Shepherds are the theme du jour.

Shepherds and sheep are common, familiar, and cherished images in the pages of the Old and New Testament. We are, perhaps, best acquainted with — and most fond of — the use of the image in which the Lord himself is the shepherd (Psalm 23; Luke 15:1-7; John 10:1-18). In this particular passage from the Old Testament prophet Jeremiah, however, someone else plays the part of the shepherd. Surely our understanding of a good shepherd will be informed by seeing the Lord in that role. But in this passage, the sheep represent God's people collectively, and the shepherds represent their human leaders. It is a use of the sheep-and-shepherd imagery similarly used by the prophet Ezekiel (ch. 34).

The prophetic word begins as a sober one: "woe." The underlying Hebrew word, *hoy*, should not be read strictly as a scolding exclamation. In 1 Kings 13:30 and Jeremiah 22:18, it is clearly used as a lament, an expression of grief. In Isaiah 55:1, it is a more positive attention-getting exclamation. In many of its appearances in the Old Testament prophecies, it seems to convey a weary quality — like the mother of bickering youngsters who sighs, "Can't we just have two minutes of peace?"

The "woe" is addressed to the shepherds of God's people. We detect God's displeasure and grief with the situation. Consequently, the grief will soon belong to the shepherds.

Judgment is not the only response of God's displeasure. He will not only displace the current, inadequate shepherds; he will replace them with shepherds who will properly lead the people.

Thus we have juxtaposed pictures of the bad and good shepherds. We are told what the former are doing, as well as what the latter will do. And then, beyond that, there is a still better picture: "a righteous branch" for David, who "shall reign as king and deal wisely, and shall execute justice and righteousness in the land. In his days, Judah will be saved and Israel will live in safety."

In the good future promised by God, "they shall be fruitful and multiply," which recalls the beauty and perfection of Eden. Meanwhile, the reference to David recalls Israel's greatest (human) shepherd.

The anticipated "righteous branch" from David, of course, is a messianic image, which we understand to be fulfilled in Jesus Christ. Within the original context of the prophet's speech, it suggests a third era. The present is the era of the bad shepherds, "who destroy and scatter." In the future era, God "will raise up shepherds over them" who will properly tend his flock. But those shepherds — plural — are succeeded and eclipsed by one particular leader. His reign, as described here, surely has the hallmarks of a messianic era.

So it is that, in the end, we return again to the most cherished sheep-and-shepherd image: namely, when the Lord, himself, is the shepherd.

Finally, it is worth noting the combination of "justice and righteousness." It's a combination that we see over two dozen times in the Old Testament, from God's purpose for Abraham (Genesis 18:19) to high praise for Solomon (1 Kings 10:9); from attributes associated with God (Psalm 33:5; 97:2) to an ethical emphasis in Proverbs (21:3) and the prophets (Jeremiah 22:3; Amos 5:24). Loosely speaking, we might characterize righteousness as the chief desire of God in an individual or society, and justice is the necessary antidote where individual or societal righteousness fails.

Colossians 1:11-20

As with all of the New Testament epistles, the modern reader is like someone overhearing just half of a telephone conversation. We can infer some things about who is on the other end and what their situation is, but we have to depend entirely upon the half to which we are privy.

Here, in the case of Paul's letter to the Colossians, we depend upon these four chapters from Paul's end to glean some information about the people on the other end. The scholarly consensus about the church and the situation to which Paul wrote is that the Colossian Christians were in the midst of a doctrinal crisis. Specifically, the false teaching to which they had been exposed and evidently by which they had been influenced — suggested a low Christology. Paul undertook to write to the Christians in Colossae about no less a theme than the person and work of Christ.

On this Christ the King Sunday, we are rightly directed to this marvelous opening passage from Paul's letter to the Colossians. We are reminded, along with those first-century believers, about all that Jesus is and does.

While Paul's statement about Christ in this selected lection seems more extemporaneous than systematic, we might take what he says and organize it into five categories. Or, more precisely, five relationships.

First, there is Christ's relationship to God the Father. It might be worth considering, individually, which of these five relationships we preach most often or most seldom. It may be that many of us should preach this part of the truth about Jesus Christ more, for surely the pluralism of our day has caused an erosion in American Christology. Therefore, we do well to explicate and affirm that "he is the image of the invisible God" and that "in him all the fullness of God was pleased to dwell."

Second, there is Christ's relationship to us. This is where the gospel's rubber meets the road. Jesus is the one "in whom we have redemption" and "the forgiveness of sins." Of course, this part of the good news has been somewhat discounted by our society's discontinuance of the word "sin." The whole concept has been subtly dismissed as judgmental and archaic, and so we have gradually eliminated it from the American lexicon. Of course, calling cancer by some other name is not the same thing as curing cancer. Our many euphemisms and redefinitions of sin have not eliminated the problem. It has just made the diagnosis more difficult. But the cure remains available in the same place as always — in him — and that is what you and I are called to proclaim.

Third, there is Christ's relationship to creation. This may be an underemphasized truth in our day, for contemporary American Christianity — unlike the ancient church — has not had the need (or perceived the need) to affirm vigorously the divinity and pre-existence of Christ. But his status as "firstborn of all creation," in whom and for whom "all things in heaven and on earth were created" and in whom "all things hold together," is a recurring assertion and theme through the pages of the New Testament.

Fourth, there is Christ's relationship to the church. This is a recurring theme and image (Ephesians 1:22-23, 5:23-30; Colossians 1:24) and, of course, Paul offers a fuller picture of the church as Christ's body in 1 Corinthians 12:12ff. The matter is not much elaborated here, but Paul's brief reference invites our explication of the lovely truth that Jesus is "the head of the body, the church."

Finally, there is Christ's relationship to, shall we say, the re-creation. Just as the New Testament reveals Christ's central role in the original creation of the world and the universe, it also looks forward to God's perfect recreation and restoration of all things. Once again, Christ is central to that work, for he is "the firstborn from the dead," which anticipates the resurrection. "Through him God was pleased to reconcile to himself all things," which is an essential part of God's loving redemption of all creation.

The Christians in Colossae had a problem with their Christology, and so the apostle Paul wrote to remind them that Jesus Christ is unique and supreme. In our day, when there are so many cultural efforts to marginalize or domesticate Jesus, we would do well to remind our congregations, too, of all that he — and only he — is.

Luke 23:33-43

"Did you turn to the wrong page, preacher?" some church member might ask this Sunday. "Doesn't that passage belong in the spring?"

The scene at the cross may surprise the people in our pews this week. After all, we're looking ahead to the Christmas season, with all the festivities that it entails. Why, at this juncture in the holiday seasons, would we preach the scene at the cross?

Why? "Because it's Christ the King Sunday," we reply. Yet, still the quizzical look on the congregant's face remains. Even with the liturgical holiday identified, the passage does not seem, at the surface, a natural match. What does the cross have to do with the king?

Give me a passage from Easter Sunday, with the stone rolled triumphantly away and the guards mortified. Give me a parable of Jesus in which he anticipates his glorious and victorious return. Even give me, a few weeks early, the story of the wise men looking for the one born to be king, but naked and helpless on a cross? A victim at best, and a criminal at worst? What does the cross have to do with the king?

Ask that question of the thief on the right.

"Jesus, remember me when you come into your kingdom," he said.

These are not the words of one who has sidled up next to Jesus amidst the ticker-tape parade on Palm Sunday. This request does not come on the heels of the transfiguration or the booming affirmation from heaven at Jesus' baptism. The request does not come from Lazarus after he has been raised or a leper after he has been cleansed.

Rather, this is the gasping request of one dying man to another. And as such, it represents a most improbable faith. The writer of Hebrews famously defines faith as "the conviction of things not seen" (Hebrews 11:1). Surely the dying thief exemplified that faith, for the kingship and kingdom of Jesus must have been entirely out of sight at that moment.

That Jesus would one day rule over a kingdom might have seemed likely in any of the other aforementioned scenarios. But here, in this moment of apparent defeat, who could have believed it?

Notice that everyone else in this passage got it wrong. "If he is the Messiah," the Jewish leaders scoffed, "let him save himself." Likewise, the soldiers challenged, "If you are the king of the Jews, save yourself!" And the other criminal, too, bought into the same, errant paradigm, "Are you not the Messiah? Save yourself."

Such is the fallen human presumption about power, authority, and status. If Jesus really were the Messiah, the king, then surely he would exercise his power to save himself. But they had completely misunderstood. For while they sought proof of who he was in a display of power that was self-serving, they overlooked the proof of who he was in a display of love that was self-sacrificing.

Somehow that one remarkable criminal perceived the truth. Though all reasonable signs seemed to point in the other direction, he recognized that a king hung on the cross next to him. And not a king whose reign was past and ending. Rather, amazingly, he perceived that Jesus' kingdom was still ahead.

On this Christ the King Sunday, we affirm the faith of that anonymous, paradise-bound criminal. And we celebrate the king, whom we recognize even on a cross.

Application

Here is a frustrated artist who can't seem to make a living by using his skill for noble purposes. Instead, he works at an amusement park, drawing quick, ten-minute caricatures of people and their friends. The onlookers marvel; the recipients have a good laugh. He turns out dozens a day. His work is rolled up and taken home along with gaudy carnival prizes.

Here is another artist whose skill is recognized. He is at the right place at the right time, and he is commissioned to paint the portraits of corporate CEOs, wealthy benefactors, and even a United States president or two. His work is framed and it hangs in the dignified settings of conference rooms, libraries, universities, and even the White House.

You and I are not relegated to the first artist's plight, and we must not choose his path. For we need not devote our craft to silly and temporary things. The sermon does not belong in the company of carnival trinkets. Instead, we are called upon to devote ourselves this Sunday to the noblest subject of all.

Consider the one who sits for us to paint his portrait this week — every week. He is no less than "the image of the invisible God," "the head of the body," and "the firstborn of all creation" in Paul's letter to the Colossians. He is the promised shepherd and ruler in Jeremiah. He is the dying Savior and the anticipated king of Matthew's lection.

Every week, it is our privilege to portray him to our congregations — especially this week. God grant that our skill and effort do justice to the task at hand!

An Alternative Application

Luke 23:33-43. "Strange Bedfellows." Sift through the cacophony that day on Golgotha. Strain out the moaning of those being executed and the weeping of those who loved them. Remove the sounds of donkeys, camels, and such along the nearby road. Eliminate the routine conversation of passersby and soldiers. Excerpt out the marvelous words of Jesus and of the thief who said, "Remember me."

What's left?

Taunting — mocking — and most of the mocking seems to be directed at one particular person. He is rightly placed on the middle cross, for he seems to be the great center of attention.

But see *whose* attention. Take note of *who* mocks Jesus.

"The leaders scoffed at him" (v. 35). "The soldiers also mocked him" (v. 36). "One of the criminals who were hanged there kept deriding him" (v. 39).

What a strange group picture. Is there any other time or place where those particular individuals — the Jewish leaders, the Roman soldiers, and a condemned criminal — would be allied? We can think of a dozen circumstances in which there would be animosity among those parties. In what other situation would they be cheering for the same thing?

Jesus makes strange bedfellows. He brings unity among his followers, even when they are unlikely companions for one another (such as Simon the Zealot and Matthew the tax collector). And he evokes a certain unity, too, among those who oppose him.

That is as it should be, for it bears witness to the significance of Christ. To be blasé about him is to be uninformed or intellectually dishonest. As C.S. Lewis wrote, "Either this man was, and is, the Son of God or else a madman or something worse. You can shut him up for a fool, you can spit at him and kill him as a demon; or you can fall at his feet and call him Lord and God. But let us not come with any patronizing nonsense about his being a great human teacher. He has not left that open to us. He did not intend to." (From C.S. Lewis, *The Best of C.S. Lewis* [New York: Iverson Brother Associates, 1969], p. 440.)

That all sorts of different people come together to follow and worship him testifies to who he is. And, likewise, the fact that all sorts of different people come together to oppose him also bears inadvertent witness to who he is.

Thanksgiving Day
Deuteronomy 26:1-11
Philippians 4:4-9
John 6:25-35
Wayne Brouwer

The secret of a perfect Thanksgiving

Mehmed II was the great Ottoman conqueror who captured Constantinople in 1453. Because of his uncertain parentage, unhappy childhood, and turbulent adolescence while his royal status was challenged, Mehmed became known for his great secretiveness. Once when asked what he was planning to do, he replied, "If a hair of my beard knew, I would pluck it out."

Most of us live lives more open than that, but we have all felt the pull of secrets. Secrets can be a source of power when knowledge is shared by only a few. Secrets can form a bond among friends who know intimate details that others are not privy to. Secrets are sometimes necessary in international negotiations in order to ensure that outcomes will not be sabotaged by information received and acted upon too quickly by others.

In fact, Jesus seemed somewhat secretive at times. On a number of occasions, particularly as recorded in the gospel of Mark, we are told that when Jesus performed a miracle or cast out a demon, he would instruct those who witnessed it not to tell anyone else. We might be mystified about that, thinking everybody should immediately hear the wonders of Jesus' divine skills. But at the time, Jesus appeared to have been concerned that some people might too quickly misinterpret his power and try, by force, to make him a human king, when his actual destiny was so much greater. Sometimes secrets are a good thing.

The secret of a perfect thanksgiving is both open and hidden. On the one hand, as Moses tells the Israelites in Deuteronomy, thanksgiving is best lived out in the community. At the same time, as Paul reminds the Philippian congregation, thankful hearts are honed in the secret places of remembered history. Finally, there is the teaching of Jesus, who turns the world of his hearers upside down, until the things they think they need are hidden away and until that which they don't know they need emerges from its secret place.

Deuteronomy 26:1-11

The idea of first fruit offerings is a pervasive scriptural concept. Abel appears to have brought the first fruits of his flocks, while Cain did not do the same from his garden (Genesis 4), indicating the level of investment each had in their acts of worship. "First fruits" was declared by God at Sinai to be one of the major religious and social holidays of the Israelite year (Leviticus 23:9-14). Its location on the calendar showed its heightened significance, for it took place on Abib 16 (the first month of the year), during the weeklong Feast of Unleavened Bread (Abib 15-21) that amplified the people's yearly celebration of the high and holy event of Passover (Abib 14). Since the Passover was one of the three pilgrim feasts that brought the entire population together at the tabernacle and later the temple, the Feast of First Fruits was indeed a national celebration.

On the Feast of First Fruits, each household was to gather into a sheaf the first cutting of grain in the barley harvest. This was to be taken to the altar of burnt offerings in the courtyard of the tabernacle or temple, waved before the Lord with ritual prayers of thanks, and then burned so that Yahweh could enjoy the first feast from the crop. The implications were several. First, the land and its produce belonged to God and were only granted by way of stewardship to the people. Second, the highest devotion of the people was to worship Yahweh of the Sinai Covenant and no other alliances or allegiances were to come in between. Third, this first fruit offering was also a matter of trust: Those who brought it believed that God would provide the complete harvest and that they need not worry about it.

Moses broadens the impact of the Feast of First Fruits here in Deuteronomy 26. For one thing, he calls on the Israelites to go beyond the barley harvest and think about all aspects of their agricultural existence when making offerings of thanks to God. Grains did not grow well in all parts of Palestine and many homes would focus their energies on vineyard crops, olive groves, or cattle care. Moses' instructions take all of those into account and encourage every branch of agricultural production to practice its own type of first fruit celebration.

Second, Moses removes the limits of the specific festival red-lettered into the yearly liturgical calendar of the people by making first fruit offerings a year-round expression of piety and devotion. Since the barley harvest occurred very early in the year, the institutional Feast of First Fruits was situated perfectly to mark the beginning of that season. But agricultural cycles produced various crops throughout the year, and animal husbandry knew of animals born on numerous occasions during the changing months, and Moses' instructions about first fruit offerings that are not limited to the feast of that name encourages year-round thank-offerings.

Third, Moses ties these ongoing first fruit offerings to a social consciousness. He instructs the people that when they bring their first fruit offerings they must make a public testimony reciting their history as slaves, the deliverance brought by Yahweh, their current state of landowner wealth, and the plight of those who are not as fortunate. In so ordering, Moses perpetuates among the people a historical rootedness that undergirds thankfulness and an eye for benevolence. They are never to take their possessions or opportunities for granted or become self-important with false notions of entitlement. Nor were they to become insulated or isolated in their riches so that they began to live in ghettoed suburbs or gated communities where they could escape the bothersome annoyance of seeing poor people. In fact, as the verses that follow today's lesson indicate, a portion of the first fruit offerings were to be shared with the poor in the towns where those who were bringing the gifts themselves resided. First fruit offerings were an active investment in social care.

The implications for Thanksgiving Day are huge. First, true thankfulness is an acknowledgment that life itself, along with the treasures that have accreted to each person along the way, is a gift. When life is taken for granted, it is desacralized and robbed of any significance. If thankfulness is taken out of the picture, atheistic evolutionism wins, and the result is the not-very-pretty carnage of the survival of the fittest, all of whom deserve exactly what they get.

Second, Thanksgiving cannot be limited to a single day, nor is it the primary provenance of a particular type of agricultural community. As Moses indicated, the first fruit offerings need to be made from all forms of livelihood. Barley is not the only crop of blessing, nor are farmers the only people dependent on the graciousness of God. Since Moses did not write the official Feast of First Fruits out of the national calendar, he was not saying that it was a trite and meaningless celebration. Instead, Moses was affirming the good of a single day on which there was a national thankful focus, and then using that celebration to build recurring acts of gratitude into the general life of the population.

Third, in Moses' instructions is a reminder of the meta-narratives that drive life and nurture its meaning. Busy lives and time-crunching planners atomize and fragment our lives into smaller and smaller chunks of efficiency. Our increased productiveness does not necessarily broaden or deepen our sense of meaning and self, however. So it is that festivals like first fruits or Thanksgiving give us opportunities to step away from the minutiae and re-engage the big testimonies of our lives or our cultures or our faith. Almost none of the people hearing Moses' words for the first time in Deuteronomy 26 could recall the hardships of slavery in Egypt. That entire generation had died during the forty years of wilderness wanderings. Along with that, none of those present had firsthand knowledge of the lives of the patriarchs who were "wandering Arameans." When they owned these histories, they were bound together again in a camaraderie of identity and purpose. So, too, in today's Thanksgiving celebrations. From our many little tales we are gathered again to enter the big sweep of redemptive history so that we remember again who we are and whose we are.

Fourth, Moses reminds us that Thanksgiving is a very social holiday. It is not about turkey and football, nor primarily about gathering with one's relatives and friends, although these things can be very important. True thankfulness sees the marginalized of society and seeks to do something about the injustices that make some scramble for crumbs while others don't know what to do with their waste. Thanksgiving may begin for many in the church, but it does not continue as thankfulness if it ends there.

Philippians 4:4-9

Paul would never forget his first time at Philippi. He was coming off the high of endorsement and influential success that had happened at the Jerusalem Council (Acts 15). There his church-planting work with Barnabas in Antioch had been affirmed, and the intense struggles of their first mission journey had been vindicated over against some in the church who wanted Gentiles to become Jews before they became Christians. Paul was on the road again to bring this news of hope and liberation to others. He had already stopped at the congregations of the first mission journey in central Asia Minor and was heading out into new territory.

At the same time, Paul was likely still smarting under the pain of separation from his old mentor and friend, Barnabas. During their first mission journey they had taken young John Mark along as an aid. Mark was Barnabas' cousin, and someone who had come under the older man's care since Mary, Mark's mother, had lost her husband. So Mark joined the team with a spirit of adventure but lost heart when the trip was longer and harder than expected. Halfway through, he left them to return home to Jerusalem. Now when Paul and Barnabas wanted to take the positive results of the Jerusalem Council back to their friends in Asia Minor, Barnabas thought Mark ought to be given a chance to redeem himself. Paul thought such a move was madness, and in a huff of angry words, these two great leaders split.

One more thing was likely in Paul's mind when he arrived at Philippi on the first occasion. Recently he had received the services of Dr. Luke, over in Troas, and had gained a friend and an ally in the process. At the same time, Paul had experienced a clear and unmistakable vision calling him and the others to venture into new European territory, well beyond the limits of typical Jewish settlement. When Paul stumbled into Philippi, he was entering with new friends and sensing the excitement of a divinely initiated missional challenge.

It began to unfold quickly. In a city with almost no Jews (ten Jewish males were required, at minimum, in any city in order to form a synagogue; there was no synagogue in Philippi, so Paul and Silas found a few Jewish believers down by the river at a place for ritual purifications), the first to believe their message of Jesus as Messiah was an independently wealthy business woman named Lydia (Acts 16). Her gracious hospitality provided them with a base of operations from which to roam Philippi's streets, preaching about Jesus. In short order, they got into trouble, however, when a demon-possessed slave girl rattled them with her accusations and then lost her unusual fortune-telling voice as Paul restored her spiritual wholeness. Angered by his tampering into their financial affairs, the girl's owners threw Paul and Silas into prison. The oddness of the events continued to spiral as an earthquake destroyed the facility, the crusty old pensioned Roman soldier who owned the place nearly committed suicide, and after a midnight revival meeting, the place was turned into a church.

With such a strange history, and in a church organized by this incredibly variegated initial group of believers, it would not be hard to imagine a tough survival rate for its membership. Unlike the Corinthian congregation, the church in Philippi seemed to thrive and became one of Paul's favorites among his key congregations. This letter, written by Paul from prison in Rome around 59-60 AD (see Acts 28), bubbles with delight and resonates with goodwill.

While there seems to have been a few relational issues to challenge the stability of the team in Philippi (see Philippians 4:2-3), for the most part, Paul exudes joy and graciousness when thinking about these folks. He himself is facing uncertainty in this appeal process to Caesar and that comes through in the verses that follow today's reading. All in all, the message of Philippians 4:4-9 is one of enthusiasm, encouragement, strength, and delight.

Paul's words are not so much to be preached as they are to be chanted, cheered, and championed. They are not a teaching but a testimony. They have not the weight of instruction so much as they carry themselves with illumination and insight. They need to be sung in choral enthusiasm as "To God Be the Glory, Great Things He Has Done," or blasted through the speakers in a stirring rendition of "Shout to the Lord." This is thanksgiving that stirs the passions and challenges the emotions to come alive with dancing.

John 6:25-35

Jesus is the greatest spokesperson of all times for understanding the blessings of God. No one experienced more of the richness of divine wealth or power than he or understood more fully the intent of God toward human development and fulfillment. As the incarnation of deity into the human race, Jesus could have configured his own existence in such a way that material possessions or social standing were his at a mere whim or grasp. Yet he makes very clear that these are not the beginning, ending, or meaning of human existence.

Furthermore, in his very life, Jesus made clear that our personal desires are not always fulfilled and that there is a deeper purpose for our existence than the accumulation of wealth or power. When tempted by the devil in the wilderness at the start of his ministry, Jesus resisted efforts to be drawn into the game of "If I want it, I can have it." When urged by the crowds to rule as king in Galilee, he set aside these honors to chart a course to the cross. Even when wrestling in the Garden of Gethsemane with his Father for a way to step back from pain and difficulty, Jesus admitted that his desires ought not rule the day.

Jesus' lifestyle is itself a negation of the secret of the popular book, *The Secret*. His teaching here makes it very clear that our priorities ought to shape our desires and that our desires are best focused when they look beyond ourselves to the things of the kingdom of God.

As the people come out to see him and to seek from him some kind of blessing, he challenges their very assumptions about the cravings inside. If one surveys the idea of "blessing" in the Bible, several core concepts come to mind. To bless is to take note of someone with love and pleasure, wish that person well, and then to do what one can to participate in bringing about that person's welfare and good fortunes. Thus "blessing," in scripture, is always at heart a relational idea. It is based upon the commitments of people to people (such as parents who bless their children), God to people (as when the priests would pronounce the blessing of God over the people — see Numbers 6:22-27), and even people to God (notice the language of Psalm 103 in the King James Bible — "Bless the Lord, O my soul!"). Any material benefits that might flow out of such relationships of tenderness and commitment are secondary to the essence of the blessing itself.

For that reason, mere desire for food can actually take the focus off the issues of real need in life. So if one desires to be blessed in this life, the wrong place to begin is visualizing material possessions or career advancement opportunities. These, in fact, may serve to cloud our horizons and keep us from seeing the real values of our existence. This is always the danger on Thanksgiving Day, where the mythical abundance of food, and people who are "stuffed" with too much turkey, can make the day less religious than it ought to be. Thankfulness is not always engendered by full bellies.

Years ago Madeleine L'Engle was "Writer in Residence" at St. John's Cathedral in New York City. She and the bishop often talked about creativity, and after one conversation they concluded that it had usually come in both their lives through times of difficulty and pain. As he left her office, the bishop turned to make his farewell and said, "I don't know quite how to say this, Madeleine, but have a bad day!" They both laughed but she knew what he meant; sometimes for the creative grace of God to be deeply experienced, it would flow out of difficult circumstances.

In this manner, Jesus' words about eating the divine manna are prophetic of his own coming bad day. For those who would receive the blessings of heaven must first remember the cost that fell on Jesus.

Application

The message today might start out with sharing "secret recipes" for Thanksgiving meal dishes. How might one set the perfect Thanksgiving table? What would Martha or Oprah say is the secret to a perfect holiday celebration? Then it might be possible to transition into the scripture themes noted above that give picture-perfect thankfulness a different twist.

An Alternative Application

Deuteronomy 26:1-11. The Deuteronomy passage is marvelous. Call out the themes from that section of the study and a great thanksgiving message leaps to life.

About the Authors

Wayne Brouwer teaches Religion, Theology, and Ministry Studies at both Hope College and Western Theological Seminary in Holland, Michigan. He holds degrees from Dordt College (A.B.), Calvin Theological Seminary (M.Div., Th.M.), and McMaster University (M.A., Ph.D.), and spent three decades as a pastor and international missionary teacher. Along with hundreds of published articles, Wayne Brouwer has authored thirteen books, including *Covenant Documents: Reading the Bible Again for the First Time* (Cognella), *The Literary Development of John 13-17: A Chiastic Reading* (SBL), and *Being a Believer in an Unbelieving World* (Hendrickson).

Timothy B. Cargal currently serves as Associate for Preparation for Ministry with the General Assembly of the Presbyterian Church (USA). For some twenty years he combined pastoral ministry with teaching biblical studies in universities and seminaries. He is the author of two books, including *Hearing a Film, Seeing a Sermon: Preaching and Popular Movies* (Westminster John Knox Press), and has contributed to several other books, study bibles, dictionaries, and journals in the areas of New Testament studies and preaching. He holds a Ph.D. in Religious Studies from Vanderbilt University.

David Kalas is the pastor of First United Methodist Church in Green Bay, Wisconsin. Before moving to Green Bay, he pastored churches in Whitewater, Wisconsin; Appleton, Wisconsin; and Hurt, Virginia. He also led youth ministries in Cleveland, Ohio, and Richmond, Virginia. David earned his undergraduate degree from the University of Virginia in Charlottesville and his Master of Divinity degree from Union Theological Seminary in Richmond, Virginia. He has also done coursework at Pittsburgh Theological Seminary and Asbury Theological Seminary.

In addition to the present volume, David has also contributed to other preaching resources published by CSS, is a regular contributor to *Emphasis: A Lectionary Preaching Journal* (CSS Publishing Company, Inc.), and has also written curriculum materials for the United Methodist Publishing House. David and his wife, Karen, have been married nearly 30 years and have three daughters, Angela, Lydia, and Susanna.

The late **R. Craig MacCreary** was pastor of South Congregational Church, United Church of Christ in Newport, New Hampshire. He held pastorates in Pennsylvania, West Virginia, and Massachusetts. He earned degrees from Elon University (B.A.), Lancaster Theological Seminary (M. Div.), and Hartford Seminary (D. Min.). His work appeared in *Colleague*, *Pulpit Digest*, and *The United Church News*. He was a guest on National Public Radio and was a contributor to *Candles in the Dark: Preaching and Poetry in Times of Crises*, edited by James Randolph.

Mark Molldrem has served as a pastor in the Evangelical Lutheran Church in America for 37 years. He has had parishes in Cobb/Edmund, Wisconsin; Beaver Dam, Wisconsin; Mondovi/Modena, Wisconsin; and Saginaw, Michigan. Currently he is Senior Pastor at First Lutheran Church in Beaver Dam, Wisconsin. Molldrem has written previously for CSS. He has authored numerous articles in various national magazines and journals. He received his Master of Divinity and also his Doctor of Ministry degrees from Luther Theological Seminary, St. Paul, Minnesota. He is very involved in his community, supporting People Against a Violent Environment (domestic violence) and developing community leadership through the Chamber of Commerce. Throughout the years, he has enjoyed art glass, martial arts, landscaping, preaching and teaching in the Lutheran Church in Liberia (West Africa), playing with his grandchildren, and vacationing with his wife, Shirley, with whom he has raised two children.

www.ingramcontent.com/pod-product-compliance
Lightning Source LLC
Chambersburg PA
CBHW080512110426
42742CB00017B/3083